Index to America: Life and Customs— Eighteenth Century

Useful Reference Series No. 108

OTHER FAXON TITLES BY NORMA OLIN IRELAND

Books in print

Index to Fairy Tales, 1949–1972, Including Folklore, Legends and Myths in Collections
Index to Full Length Plays, 1944 to 1964
Index to Inspiration: A Thesaurus of Subjects for Speakers and Writers
An Index to Monologs and Dialogs
An Index to Monologs and Dialogs, Supplement
Index to Scientists of the World from Ancient to Modern Times: Biographies and Portraits
An Index to Skits and Stunts
Index to Women of the World from Ancient to Modern Times: Biographies and Portraits
The Pamphlet File in School, College, and Public Libraries
The Picture File in School, College, and Public Libraries

Books forthcoming

Index to America: Life and Customs—Seventeenth Century
Index to America: Life and Customs—Nineteenth Century
Index to America: Life and Customs—Twentieth Century

Index to America: Life and Customs— Eighteenth Century

Compiled by

Norma Olin Ireland

F. W. FAXON COMPANY, INC./WESTWOOD, MASSACHUSETTS

ISBN 0-87305-108-4
Library of Congress Catalog Card Number 76-7196

MANUFACTURED IN THE UNITED STATES OF AMERICA

DEDICATION

To my sister, *Lucretia Olin Rowe,* who has lived a "life of love and service" in countless ways:

(1) She has completed 50 years of teaching, including 20 years as a missionary.

(2) She is an ordained minister, as well as a missionary. She received a gold medal from the King of Belgium for valuable work given to the Congolese people.

(3) She is a lecturer, linguist, and writer. She has authored textbooks used in advanced schools in the Congo and has translated sections of the Bible into the Lonkundo dialect of the Bantu language.

(4) She is a worthy descendant of early American pioneers who settled in New England, fought in the Revolutionary War, and migrated to Ohio. One early ancestor was Henry Adams (gr.-gr.grandfather of John Adams), and she is descended through the maternal line (Samuel[2], Susanna[3]). Nine of her forebears fought in the Revolution.

(5) She has lived 80 years (two-fifths of America's 200 years) and has served her God and country well. She is recognized in *Who's Who of American Women* as an educator of note.

(6) Last but not least, she has been a devoted and loyal wife, an understanding mother, and to me a loving sister, always. To "Lukie" dear, I dedicate this book.

N.O.I.

PREFACE

This book is the second volume of a four-volume series—*Index to America: Life and Customs.* It covers the 18th century and is published first because of its timeliness for the Bicentennial year of 1976. Other volumes to follow are:

Vol. 1—17th century,
Vol. III—19th century,
Vol. IV—20th century.

Purpose and Scope

The purpose of this *Index* is to coordinate in one work many of the chief publications about the 18th century and its life and customs, concentrating on recent books, but also including some older, readable volumes of historic value.

We have indexed a representative selection of 116 books which can be found in major libraries, both in the adult and juvenile departments. Some books, although not catalogued as strictly juvenile, are certainly suitable for young people and are thus indicated in the key to easy-to-remember symbols for the books indexed, beginning on page 1. At first we thought to limit our index to 50 titles, but with new books coming out all the time for the Bicentennial, we soon extended our list. However, since the purpose of the *Index* is to cover all phases of the 18th century and quite a few of these new publications are on the Revolutionary War alone, we were selective, not wanting to make the book top-heavy with this particular subject.

We are delighted that so many good, out-of-print books have been reissued during the past several years in attractive reprints, albeit with some high prices. Therefore, since these classic authorities are on library shelves again and also available for personal collections, we have been able to include them. Some paperbacks have also been indexed because of their increasing popularity in libraries and bookstores.

The percentage of books indexed, according to date of publication, is as follows:

1970–1975	36%,
1960's	33%,
1950's	16%,
1940's	11%,
1930's and earlier	4%.

We have tried to choose books representative of all areas and periods of the 1700's while emphasizing, of course, life and customs. We could not cover every colony/state and city of this period and have preferred general books and local accounts, rather than state histories. At first we thought to exclude history and wars, but that, naturally, proved impossible and unreasonable because certainly the life and times of people are influenced by political events. The Revolutionary War played such a major role in the history of 18th-century America that we have, therefore, included its highlights, major events, and personalities. Although we don't usually index biographies, we did make exceptions in the case of Abigail Adams, Samuel Adams, Thomas Jefferson, and Paul Revere, whose lives covered such a large spectrum of subjects in very readable form. Many others could have been included but were not, including George Washington; in his case we already had so much material on him that we feared an overbalance.

Encyclopedias have been omitted, except for a few which have good summary material on art, music, etc., not found elsewhere. Students of this period, however, must remember to consult such classic sets as *Chronicles of America, Pageant of America, Dictionary of American History,* and other works in multiple volumes. Readers will also want to seek out books on certain specific subjects impossible to index in detail, such as Antiques, Architecture, Costume, Gardens, etc.

Arrangement and Subjects

The *Index* is arranged alphabetically by subject in one alphabet. Many biographical listings have been included because personalities certainly mirror the life and times of a century. For example, all the signers of the Declaration of Independence have been indexed. Dates of lives have not been given, however, because the *Index* is not intended as a biographical dictionary .

There is, necessarily, some overlapping of centuries in a few of the "colonial-life" books indexed. We have tried to separate, however, to the best of our ability, watching for specific dates when given. The *Index* gives dates only when they are relevant to the subject and clarify its meaning.

An appendix, "Women of the 18th Century (as found in this *Index*)," has been attached. There are 154 women included in this appendix, and we have been generous in our inclusion of subjects about women, in both main entries and cross-references. Too many history books have long neglected the women of the 18th century, but their importance is clearly evident in most of the books we have included in this *Index*. There is still gross neglect in some books, however: for instance, in one book we indexed, 300 notable Americans were listed, including but one woman who flourished during the 18th century!

Over *1,960* different subjects have been included in the *Index,* not counting subheadings or cross-references. Our subject headings are mostly specific, for convenient use, but some general subjects are included, with liberal cross-references. There is no one source for our headings; rather, they developed as the *Index* grew, as we used many books using similar subjects in their own indexes.

It was difficult, however, to decide which subjects should be main headings and which should be subheadings under *locality,* as both were equally important in those days of growth and development. In general, we have followed library practice and placed topics of historical or descriptive nature as subheadings under locality; topics of arts, sciences, and specific subjects under subject, with locality subdivisions. There has been some duplication, or conflict of interest, but we have tried to be consistent in our decisions. In using locality main headings, the reader should remember to check all subject main references that would be of interest to that city, such as Education, Music, etc.; and *"See also"* references for additional information have been included.

Acknowledgements and Personal Note

Again we thank the staff members of the Fallbrook branch of the San Diego County Library for their cooperative help, especially Mrs. Betty W. Simmons, assistant, for her willing interlibrary-loan service, and the

late Mrs. Geraldine Bauer, Librarian, as always, for securing books requested from all over the state.

This compilation has been a great personal pleasure because of our special interest in early America. Perhaps our interest has been "whetted" by our genealogical hobby. In searching for information, it has been fascinating to read firsthand stories of the pioneers as found in various local histories. Here we found the *real* life and customs of the period: family life, amusements, victories, and vicissitudes. Pioneer land records tell of legal struggles, wills list prized possessions, and letters tell of daily duties, childbearing, etc. We are personally fortunate to have old family letters and diaries of those early days. But for years we had searched and finally given up on our *Austin* family forebears because one letter said, "When we came to this country in the 1800's," and we thought they meant *America*; later we were to find a quitclaim deed of the 1700's which proved that they came from Connecticut, and by "this country" meant New York, enroute to Ohio!

Because our ancestors were a miniscule part of America's 18th century, living and loving and fighting for their country, we are doubly proud to give you this *Index,* with the hope that it may bring alive many forgotten events and personalities and help to locate easily facts on the 18th century's "life and customs," to be studied and quoted for speech or writing. This is our "Thank you" to this great land of ours in 1976, two hundred years after its independence was first declared.

LIST OF COLLECTIONS ANALYZED IN THIS WORK AND KEY TO SYMBOLS USED

*ADAMS — ALBUM
Adams, James Truslow, ed. *Album of American history, colonial period.* Chicago, Consolidated Book Pubs., 1944. 411p.

ADAMS — PROVINCIAL
Adams, James Truslow. *Provincial society, 1690-1763.* Reprint of 1927 ed. Chicago, Quadrangle Books, 1971. 374p.

*ADELMAN — FAMOUS
Adelman, Joseph. *Famous women.* New York, Ellis M. Lonow Co., 1926. 328p.

ALDEN — PIONEER
Alden, John R. *Pioneer America.* New York, Alfred A. Knopf, Inc., 1966. 309p.

AMER. HER. — REV.
The American Heritage *Book of the Revolution.* New York, Simon & Schuster, Inc., 1958. 384p.

AMER. READER
The American reader. From Columbus to today. Being a compilation or collection of the personal narratives, relations and journals concerning the society, economy, life and times of our great and many-tongued nation, by those who were there. Chicago, Rand McNally & Co., 1958. 703p.

ANGLE — BY
Angle, Paul M. *By these words. Great documents of American liberty, selected and placed in their contemporary settings.* Chicago, Rand McNally & Co., 1954. 427p.

AXTELL — 18TH
Axtell, James L., comp. *America perceived: a view from abroad in the 18th century.* West Haven, Conn., Pendulum Press, Inc., 1974. 239p.

*BAKELESS — SIGNERS
Bakeless, John. *Signers of the Declaration.* Boston, Houghton Mifflin Co., 1969. 300p.

* *suitable for young people*

*BALDWIN — IDEAS
Baldwin, Leland D. *Ideas in action. Documentary and interpretive readings in American history.* Vol. 1 (to 1877). New York, American Book Co., 1968. 553p. paper.

BARTLETT — NEW
Bartlett, Richard A. *The new country. A social history of the American frontier 1776-1890.* New York, Oxford University Press, 1974. 487p.

BEACH — SAMUEL
Beach, Stewart. *Samuel Adams. The fateful years, 1764-1776.* New York, Dodd, Mead & Co., 1965. 329p.

BELOTE — COMPLEAT
Belote, Julianne. *The compleat American housewife.* Concord, Calif., Nitty Gritty Productions, 1974. 183p. paper.

BENSON — WOMEN 18TH
Benson, Mary S. *Women in eighteenth-century America: A study of opinion and social usage.* Port Washington, N.Y., Kennikat Press, 1935, 1966. 343p.

BOORSTIN — AMERICANS
Boorstin, Daniel J. *The American. The colonial experience.* New York, Random House, 1958. 434p.

BRIDENBAUGH — REVOLT
Bridenbaugh, Carl. *Cities in revolt. Urban life in America, 1743-1776.* Reprint of 1955 ed. New York, Capricorn Books, 1964. 434p.

BRIDENBAUGH — WILD.
Bridenbaugh, Carl. *Cities in the wilderness. The first century of urban life in America, 1625-1742.* New York, Oxford University Press, 1938, 1966. 500p.

BRODIE — JEFFERSON
Brodie, Fawn. *Thomas Jefferson. An intimate history.* New York, Bantam Books, Inc., 1974, 1975. 811p. paper.

BROOKS — DAMES
Brooks, Geraldine. *Dames and daughters of colonial days.* New York, Thomas Y. Crowell and Co., Pub., 1900. Reprint. New York, Arno Press, 1974. 284p.

BURNER — AMERICA
Burner, David, Robert D. Marcus, and Jorj Tilson. *America through the looking glass. A historical reader in popular culture.* Vol. 1. Englewood Cliffs, N.J., Prentice-Hall, Inc., 1974. 350p.

BURT — PHILA.
Burt, Struthers. *Philadelphia, holy experiment.* Garden City, N.Y., Doubleday, Doran, 1945. 396p.

* *suitable for young people*

BUTTERFIELD — AMER.
Butterfield, Roger. *The American past. A history of the United States from Concord to Hiroshima, 1775-1945.* New York, Simon & Schuster, Inc., 1947. 476p.

CABLE — AMERICAN
Cable, Mary, and the Editors of *American Heritage. American manners and morals. A picture history of how we behaved and misbehaved.* New York, American Heritage Publishing Co., 1969. 399p.

CARMAN — HISTORY
Carman, Harry J., Harold C. Syrett, and Bernard W. Wishy. *A history of the American people.* Vol. 1. (to 1877). New York, Alfred A. Knopf, Inc., 1961. 860p.

COLBOURN — COLONIAL
Colbourn, H. Revor, ed. *The colonial experience. Readings in early American history.* Boston, Houghton Mifflin Co., 1966. 419p.

COLLINS — STORY
Collins, Alan C. *The story of America in pictures.* Rev. ed. Garden City, N.Y., Doubleday & Co., Inc., 1953. 480p.

COOK — WHAT
Cook, Fred J. *What manner of men. Forgotten heroes of the American Revolution.* New York, William Morrow & Co., Inc., 1959. 335p.

CRÈVECOEUR — SKETCHES
Crèvecoeur, Michel de. *Sketches of eighteenth century America.* New Haven, Conn., Yale University Press, 1925. 342p.

DANNETT — YANKEE
Dannett, Sylvia G. L. *The Yankee doodler.* New York, A. S. Barnes & Co., Inc., 1973. 320p.

DAVIE — PROFILE
Davie, Emily, comp. *Profile of America. An autobiography of the U.S.A.* New York, Thomas Y. Crowell Co., 1954. 415p.

*DAVIS — HEROES
Davis, Burke. *Heroes of the American Revolution.* New York, Random House, Inc., 1971. 146p.

DEXTER — COLONIAL
Dexter, Elizabeth Anthony. *Colonial women of affairs. A study of women in business and the professions in America before 1776.* Boston, Houghton Mifflin Co., 1924. 204p.

DOLAN — YANKEE
Dolan, J. R. *The Yankee peddlers of early America.* New York, Clarkson N. Potter, Inc., 1964. 270p.

* *suitable for young people*

DOW — EVERY
Dow, George Francis. *Every day life in the Massachusetts Bay Colony.* New York, Benjamin Blom, Inc., Pubs., 1935, 1967. 290p.

DOWNEY — OUR
Downey, Fairfax. *Our lusty forefathers. Being diverse chronicles of the fervors, frolics, fights, festivities, and failings of our American ancestors.* New York, Charles Scribner's Sons, 1947. 359p.

DREPPARD — PIONEER
Dreppard, Carl W. *Pioneer America, Its first three centuries.* Garden City, N.Y., Doubleday & Co., Inc., 1949. 311p.

DULLES — HISTORY
Dulles, Foster Rhea. *A history of recreation: America learns to play.* 2nd ed. New York, Appleton-Century-Crofts, 1965. 446p.

*EARLE — CHILD
Earle, Alice Morse. *Child life in colonial days.* New York, Macmillan Co., 1899, 1915. 418p. *See also* GLUBOK — HOME.

*EARLE — COLONIAL
Earle, Alice Morse. *Colonial dames and good wives.* Reprint. New York, Frederick Ungar Publishing Co., Inc., 1962. 315p.

*EARLE — CUSTOMS
Earle, Alice Morse. *Customs and fashions in old New England.* Reprint of 1894 ed. Rutland, Vt., C. E. Tuttle Co., Inc., 1973. 387p. paper.

*EARLE — HOME
Earle, Alice Morse. *Home life in colonial days.* Reprint of 1898 ed. Stockbridge, Mass., Berkshire Traveller Press, 1974, 70p. paper. *See also* GLUBOK — HOME

EARLY AMER. LIFE — YRBK. 1970
Early American Life. *1970 Yearbook* Annapolis, Md., Early American Society, 1971. 163p. paper.

ELLET — EMINENT
Ellet, Elizabeth. *Eminent and heroic women of the United States.* Reprint of 1873 ed. New York, Arno Press, 1974. 763p.

EVANS — WEATHER.
Evans, Elizabeth. *Weathering the storm. Women of the American Revolution.* New York, Charles Scribner's Sons, 1975. 372p.

* *suitable for young people*

FORBES — PAUL
Forbes, Esther. *Paul Revere and the world he lived in.* Boston, Houghton Mifflin Co., 1942. 498p.

*GLUBOK — HOME
Glubok, Shirley, ed. *Home and child life in colonial days.* Abridged from Alice Morse Earle's *Home life in colonial days,* and *Child life in colonial days.* New York, Macmillan Publishing Co., Inc., 1969. 357p.

GOULD — EARLY
Gould, Mary Earle. *The early American house. Household life in America 1620–1850.* Rutland, Vt., C .E. Tuttle Co., Inc., 1949, 1965. 152p.

GOWANS — IMAGES
Gowans, Alan. *Images of American living; four centuries of architecture and furniture as cultural expression.* Philadelphia, J. B. Lippincott Co., 1964. 498p.

GREENE — REVOL.
Greene, Evarts Boutell. *The Revolutionary generation 1763–1790.* New York, Macmillan Publishing Co., Inc., 1958. 487p.

*HALE — THROUGH
Hale, Jeanne, editor-in-chief. *Through golden windows. Stories of early America.* Ed. by Nora Beust, Phyllis Fenner, Bernice E. Leary, Mary Katherine Reely, Dora V. Smith. Eau Claire, Wisc., E. M. Hale & Co., 1958. 336p.

HANDLIN — THIS
Handlin, Oscar. *This was America.* Cambridge, Mass., Harvard University Press, 1949. 602p.

HOFSTADTER — AMER.
Hofstadter, Richard. *America at 1750; a social portrait.* New York, Alfred A. Knopf, Inc., 1971. 293p.

HOLLIDAY — WOMAN'S
Holliday, Carl. *Woman's life in colonial days.* Williamstown, Mass., Corner House Pubs., 1926, 1960. 319p.

HOWARD — OUR
Howard, John Tasker. *Our American music. Three hundred years of it.* New York, Thomas Y. Crowell Co., 1946. 841p.

*INGRAHAM — ALBUM
Ingraham, Leonard W. *An album of the American Revolution.* New York, Franklin Watts, Inc., 1971. 96p.

KRAUS — U.S. (1)
Kraus, Michael. *The United States to 1865.* Vol. 1. Ann Arbor, Mich., The University of Michigan Press, 1959. 529p.

* *suitable for young people*

LANDMARKS LIBERTY
Landmarks of liberty. Maplewood, N.J., Hammond Inc., 1970. 93p.

*LANGDON — EVERY.
Langdon, William Chauncy. *Everyday things in American life 1607-1776.* Vol. 1. New York, Charles Scribner's Sons, 1937. 353p.

LAWLOR — BICEN.
Lawlor, Robert. *The Bicentennial book.* New York, Dell Publishing Co., Inc., 1975. 246p. paper.

*LIFE — NEW
The *Life* history of the United States. *The new world.* Vol. 1 (before 1775). New York, Time-Life Books, 1963, 1975. 176p.

*LIFE — MAKING
The *Life* history of the United States. *The making of a nation.* Vol. 2 (1775–1789). New York, Time-Life Books, 1963, 1975. 160p.

*LIFE — GROWING
The *Life* history of the United States. *The growing years.* Vol. 3 (1789-1829). New York, Time-Life Books, 1963, 1974. 176p.

*LIFE — 100 EVENTS
Life. Special Report. *The 100 events that shaped America.* New York, Time, Inc., 1975. 116p. paper.

LINTON — BICENTENNIAL
Linton, Calvin D., ed. *The Bicentennial almanac. 200 years of America, 1776–1976.* New York, Thomas Nelson, Inc., 1975. 448p.

LOCKE — BIRTH
Locke, Raymond F., comp. and ed. *The birth of America.* Los Angeles, Mankind Pub. Co., 1971. 252p. paper.

LOSSING — BIOG.
Lossing, Benson J. *Biographical sketches of the signers of the Declaration of American Independence. . . .* Philadelphia, Davis, Porter & Co., 1866. Reprint. Philadelphia, Benchmark Pub. Co., 1970. 384p.

*McDOWELL — REV.
McDowell, Bart. *The Revolutionary war. America's fight for freedom.* Washington, D.C., National Geographic Society, 1967. 199p.

MAIN — SOCIAL
Main, Jackson Turner. *The social structure of Revolutionary America.* Princeton, N.J., Princeton University Press, 1965. 330p.

** suitable for young people*

MALONE — STORY
Malone, Dumas. *The story of the Declaration of Independence.* New York, Oxford University Press, 1954. 282p.

MIERS — AMERICAN
Miers, Earl Schenck. *The American story. The Age of exploration to the Age of the atom.* Great Neck, N.Y., Channel Press, 1956. 352p.

MILLER — COLONIAL
Miller, John C. *The colonial image. Origins of American culture.* New York, George Braziller, Inc., 1962. 500p.

MILLER — FIRST
Miller, John C. *The first frontier: life in colonial America.* New York, Delacorte Press, 1966. 288p.

MILLER — ORIGINS
Miller, John C. *Origins of the American Revolution.* Boston, Little, Brown & Co., 1943. 519p.

MORISON — OXFORD (1)
Morison, Samuel Eliot. *The Oxford history of the American people.* Vol. 1 (prehistory to 1789). New York, New American Library, 1965, 1972. 422p. paper.

MORRIS — AMERICAN
Morris, Richard B., ed. *The American Revolution 1764–1783. A Bicentennial collection.* Columbia, S.C., University of South Carolina Press, 1970. 361p.

MORRIS — ENCY.
Morris, Richard B. *Encyclopedia of American history.* New York, Harper & Brothers, 1953. 776p.

MORRIS — VOICES
Morris, Richard B., and James Woodress. *Voices from America's past.* Vol. 1. New York, E. P. Dutton & Co., Inc., 1961, 1963. 256p.

NATIONAL — HISTORY.
National Geographic Society. *America's historylands.* Washington, D.C., National Geographic Society, 1962. 576p.

NYE — UNEMBAR.
Nye, Russel B. *The unembarrassed muse: the popular arts in America.* New York, Dial Press, 1970. 497p.

*PETTENGILL — YANKEE
Pettengill, Samuel B. *The Yankee pioneers. A saga of courage.* Rutland, Vt., C. E. Tuttle Co., 1971. 175p

QUAIFE — HISTORY
Quaife, Milo M., Melvin F. Weig, and Roy E. Appleman. *The history of the United States flag. From the Revolution to the present, including a guide to its use and display.* 2nd ed. New York, Harper & Row Pubs., Inc., 1961. 190p.

* *suitable for young people*

ROSS — TASTE
Ross, Ishbel. *Taste in America.* New York, Thomas Y. Crowell Co., 1967. 343p.

*RUBLOWSKY — MUSIC
Rublowsky, John. *Music in America.* New York, Macmillan Publishing Co., Inc., 1967. 185p.

*SANDERLIN — 1776
Sanderlin, George. *1776: Journals of American independence.* New York, Harper & Row Pubs., Inc., 1968. 262p.

SCHEMMER — ALMANAC
Schemmer, Benjamin, and the Editors of *Armed Forces Journal. Almanac of liberty. A chronology of American military anniversaries from 1775 to the present.* New York, Macmillan Publishing Co., Inc., 1974. 262p.

*SCOTT — SETTLERS
Scott, John Anthony. *Settlers on the Eastern shore 1607–1750.* The Living History Library. New York, Alfred A. Knopf, Inc., 1967. 227p.

SCOTT — TRUMPET
Scott, John Anthony. *Trumpet of a prophecy. Revolutionary America, 1763–1783.* New York, Alfred A. Knopf, Inc., 1969. 307p.

SIRKIS — REFLECT.
Sirkis, Nancy. *Reflections of 1776; the Colonies revisited.* New York, Viking Press, Inc., 1974. 217p.

*SLOANE — SPIRITS
Sloane, Eric. *The spirits of '76.* New York, Walker & Co., 1973. 64p.

*SMITH — COLONIAL
Smith, Helen Evertson. *Colonial days and ways. As gathered from family papers.* New York, Frederick Ungar Publishing Co., Inc., 1966. 376p.

*SOMERVILLE — WOMEN
Somerville, Mollie, comp. *Women and the American Revolution.* Washington, D.C., The National Society of the Daughters of the American Revolution, 1974. 67p. paper.

SPEARE — LIFE
Speare, Elizabeth George. *Life in colonial America.* New York, Random House, Inc., 1963. 171p.

SPRUILL — WOMEN'S
Spruill, Julia Cherry. *Women's life and work in the Southern colonies.* New York, W. W. Norton & Co., Inc., 1938, 1972. 426p.

* *suitable for young people*

*STEARNS — STORY
Stearns, Monroe. *The story of New England.* New York, Random House, Inc., 1967. 179p.

STEMBER — NORTH
Stember, Sol. *The war in the North.* The Bicentennial Guide to the American Revolution, vol. 1. New York, Saturday Review Press/E. P. Dutton & Co., Inc., 1974. 391p.

STEMBER — MIDDLE
Stember, Sol. *The Middle Colonies.* The Bicentennial Guide to the American Revolution, vol. 2. New York, Saturday Review Press/E. P. Dutton & Co., Inc., 1974. 173p.

STEMBER — SOUTH
Stember, Sol. *The war in the South.* The Bicentennial Guide to the American Revolution, vol. 3. New York, Saturday Review Press/E. P. Dutton & Co., Inc., 1975. 217p.

STORIES. *See* HALE

SWEET — RELIGION
Sweet, William Warren. *Religion in the development of American culture, 1765–1840.* Gloucester, Mass., Peter Smith Publisher, Inc., 1963. 338p.

SWEET — STORY
Sweet, William Warren. *The story of religion in America.* New York, Harper & Bros., 1950. 492p.

TRAIN — STORY
Train, Arthur, Jr. *The story of everyday things.* New York, Harper & Bros., 1941. 428p.

TREASURY AMER.
A Treasury of American Heritage. *A selection from the first five years of The Magazine of history.* New York, Simon & Schuster, Inc., 1954, 1960. 398p.

*TUNIS — COLONIAL
Tunis, Edwin. *Colonial craftsmen and the beginnings of American industry.* Cleveland, World Publishing Co., 1965. 159p.

*TUNIS — FRONTIER
Tunis, Edwin. *Frontier living.* Cleveland, World Publishing Co., 1961. 166p.

*TUNIS — LIVING
Tunis, Edwin. *Colonial living.* Cleveland, World Publishing Co., 1957. 157p.

*TUNIS — TAVERN
Tunis, Edwin. *Tavern at the ferry.* New York, Thomas Y. Crowell Co., 1973. 109p.

* *suitable for young people*

*TUNIS — YOUNG
Tunis, Edwin. *The young United States 1783 to 1830. A time of change and growth; a time of learning democracy; a time of new ways of living, thinking and doing.* Cleveland, World Publishing Co., 1969. 159p.

*200 YEARS
200 years. A Bicentennial illustrated history of the United States. Vol. 1. Washington, D.C., U.S. News and World Report, Inc., 1973. 351p.

WERTENBAKER — GOLDEN
Wertenbaker, Thomas J. *The golden age of colonial culture.* 2nd rev. ed. New York, New York University Press, 1949. 171p.

WHEELER — VOICES
Wheeler, Richard. *Voices of 1776.* New York, Thomas Y. Crowell Co., 1972, 1973. 480p.

WHITNEY — ABIGAIL
Whitney, Janet. *Abigail Adams.* Boston, Little, Brown & Co., 1947. 357p.

WILSON — AMERICAN
Wilson, Mitchell. *American science and invention. A Pictorial history.* New York, Bonanza Books, 1906. 437p.

WILSON — EARLY
Wilson, Everett Broomall. *Early America at work; a pictorial guide to our vanishing occupations.* Cranberry, N.J., A. S. Barnes & Co., 1963. 188p.

WOODWARD — WAY
Woodward, W. E. *The way our people lived.* New York, E. P. Dutton & Co., Inc., 1944. 402p.

WRIGHT — CULTURAL
Wright, Louis Booker. *The cultural life of the American colonies, 1607-1763.* New York, Harper & Brothers, 1957. 292p.

WRIGHT — FRONTIER
Wright, Louis Booker. *Everyday life on the American frontier.* New York, G. P. Putnam's Sons, 1968. 256p.

WRIGHT — NEW
Wright, Louis Booker, and Elaine W. Fowler. *Everyday life in the New Nation, 1787–1860.* New York, G. P. Putnam's Sons, 1972. 256p.

* *suitable for young people*

INDEX TO AMERICA

LIFE AND CUSTOMS — 18TH CENTURY

A

ACADEMIES
Greene — *Revol.* p.120-122, 166, 289-290, 375, 377-378, 414-415
Sweet — *Story* p.144-145
Tunis — *Young* p.130
- *Salaries*
Main — *Social* p.93-94
- *Women and girls*
Benson — *Women 18th* p. 136-152

ACCESSORIES
See also names of accessories
- *Women*
Speare — *Life* p.16-17
Spruill — *Women's* p.124-125
Train — *Story* p.162-163
Tunis — *Living* p. 147

ACCIDENTS
Pettengill — *Yankee* p.156-157

ACROBATS
Dulles — *History* p. 42

ACTORS AND ACTRESSES
See also **Road shows; Theater; Variety shows;** names of players and companies
Dannett — *Yankee* p.249-263
Dexter — *Colonial* p.153-166
- *South*
Spruill — *Women's* p.259-262

ADAMS, ABIGAIL SMITH
Adelman — *Famous* p.86-87
Amer. Her. — *Rev.* p.150, 152, 211, 271
Belote — *Compleat* p.19
Benson — *Women 18th* p.57-58, 142, 147, 171, 219, 246-247, 250, 255-256, 277, 302, 305
Brodie — *Jefferson.* See index p.785
Brooks — *Colonial* p.169-214
Butterfield — *Amer.* p.24
Earle — *Child* p.93-94, 171
Ellet — *Eminent* p.298-303
Evans — *Weather.* p.1, 5-6, 19-20, 22, 29-30
Greene — *Revol.* p.120, 139, 232, 243, 249, 325, 327, 396, 419
Holliday — *Woman's.* See index p.315
Life — *Growing* p.14
Malone — *Story* p.3, 83, 115, 252
Ross — *Taste* p.245
Whitney — *Abigail.* See index p.351
, in France
Whitney — *Abigail* p.186-196
, in London
Whitney — *Abigail* p.197-218
, in New York
Whitney — *Abigail* p.229-245
- *Letters to*
Whitney — *Abigail.* See index p.351
- *Women's rights*
Belote — *Compleat* p.19
- *Writings*
Treasury Amer. p.124-127

ADAMS, JOHN
Alden — *Pioneer.* See index p.i
Amer. Her. — *Rev.* See index p.380
Bakeless — *Signers* p.45-58
Beach — *Samuel.* See index p.323
Benson — *Women 18th* p.160-161, 176, 242, 247-248, 250-251, 256-259

ADAMS, JOHN (*continued*)
Bridenbaugh — *Revolt. See* index p.1
Brodie — *Jefferson. See* index p.785-786
Burt — *Phila. See* index p.381
Butterfield — *Amer.* p.17, 20-21, 24-25
Collins — *Story* p.464
Davis — *Heroes* p.18-29
Forbes — *Paul. See* index p.487
Glubock — *Home* p.39, 89-90, 129, 166-168
Greene — *Revol. See* index p.457
Handlin — *This* p.75
Life — *Growing. See* index p.172
Life — *Making. See* index p.156
Life — *New. See* index p.172
Locke — *Birth* p.149-178
McDowell — *Rev. See* index p.196
Malone — *Story* p.112-115; *See also* index p.280
Miers — *American* p.101-102
Miller — *Origins. See* index p.507
Morison — *Oxford (1). See* index p.409
Ross — *Taste* p.245
Sanderlin — *1776. See* index p.255
200 Years. See index p.345
Whitney — *Abigail. See* index p.352

- Administration
Life — *Growing* p.33-41
- and Declaration of Rights
Sanderlin — *1776* p.126-127
- and Independence Resolution
Sanderlin — *1776* p.207-210
- and Independence vote
Sanderlin — *1776* p.215-216
- Biography
Lossing — *Biog.* p.27-32
Morris — *Ency.* p.629
200 Years p.316-317
- Cabinet
Carman — *History* p.786
Life — *Growing* p.39
- Dignity
Wright — *New* p.61
- Dinners
Belote — *Compleat* p.166
- Letters and diaries
Dannett — *Yankee* p.101-103, 160
Morris — *Voices* p.98-100
- on government
Morris — *American* p.298-305
- on women
Benson — *Women* p.160
Evans — *Weather.* p.1, 5-6
- Presidency
Kraus — *U.S. (1)* p.289-291, 294-297
Morris — *Voices* p.181-190
- Writings
Treasury Amer. p.124-127

ADAMS, JOHN QUINCY
Brodie — *Jefferson. See* index p.786
Butterfield — *Amer.* p.24
Earle — *Child* p.147, 169-170
Greene — *Revol.* p.150, 323, 327, 329, 368-369, 380-382
Whitney — *Abigail. See* index p.352

- Biography
Morris — *Ency.* p.629-630

ADAMS, LOUISA JOHNSON
Glublok — *Home* p.123-124, 202

ADAMS, SAMUEL
Amer. Her. — *Rev.* p.59, 61-62, 66-68, 70-72, 91, 93, 101
Bakeless — *Signers* p.17-33
Beach — *Samuel* p.11-33; *See also* index of book
Bridenbaugh — *Revolt* p.115, 220-222, 285, 361-362, 392, 395
Collins — *Story* p.128
Forbes — *Paul. See* index p.487
Greene — *Revol. See* index
Life — *Making* p.7-8, 34-35, 46
Malone — *Story* p.109-111; *See* also index p.280
Miers — *American* p.76-77, 79
Miller — *Origins. See* index p.507
Morison — *Oxford (1). See* index p.409
Morris — *Voices* p.79-84, 103-104
Sanderlin — *1776. See* index p.255
Stearns — *Story* p.76-80, 82-83, 91
200 Years p.19, 22, 24-26, 29, 34-35, 67, 70-73, 176, 290-291

Whitney — *Abigail* p.28-29, 34-37, 50, 53, 55-56, 58, 61, 65, 75-77, 80-81, 86-87
- *and Committees of Correspondence*
Ingraham — *Album* p.25
- *Biography*
Lossing — *Biog.* p.33-36
Morris — *Ency.* p.630

ADAMS FAMILY
, Historical records
Treasury Amer. p.124-127

ADMIRALTY COURTS
Miller — *Origins* p.85-86, 119-120, 180, 266, 270, 281

ADVERTISING
Greene — *Revol. See* index p.457
, by merchants
Dexter — *Colonial* p.19-38
Spruill — *Women's* p.279-292
, Marital
Spruill — *Women's* p.178-184
- *Newspapers*
Speare — *Life* p.130-131

AGE OF REASON
See also **Rationalism**
Tunis — *Young* p.33-34

AGING
See also **Longevity**
Axtell — *18th* p.211-212

AGRARIANISM
See also **Shays' Rebellion**
Greene — *Revol.* p.278, 337-340, 353-354
Kraus — *U.S. (1)* p.131-132
Wright — *Cultural* p.1-22

AGRICULTURAL MACHINERY. See Farm implements

AGRICULTURE
See also **Farmers and farming**
Greene — *Revol. See* index p.457
Handlin — *This* p.25-27
Life — *New. See* index p.172
Morris — *Ency.* p.476-479
Tunis — *Living* p.104-105
- *Agronomy*
Sloane — *Spirits* p.44-47
- *Appalachian plateau*
Bartlett — *New* p.175-188
- *Associations*
Greene — *Revol.* p.335
- *Connecticut*
Langdon — *Every.* p.275
- *Middle Colonies*
Train — *Story* p.195
- *New England*
Train — *Story* p.165
- *North*
Morris — *Ency.* p.478
- *Republic*
Train — *Story* p.239-242
- *Revolution*
Amer. Her. — *Rev.* p.51-52, 75, 81
, Scientific
Morris — *Ency.* p.478
- *South*
Morris — *Ency.* p.477-478
Train — *Story* p.214-215
- *Views of Crèvecoeur*
Crèvecoeur — *Sketches* p.6-7, 12, 41, 54, 65, 79, 116-117, 231, 235-236, 242

ALAMANCE, NORTH CAROLINA
, Battle of
Greene — *Revol.* p.167-168
Morris — *Ency.* p.79-80

ALBANY, NEW YORK
Axtell — *18th* p.126-140
Cable — *American* p.41
Glubok — *Home* p.57-58, 124, 188-189, 295, 316-317
Handlin — *This* p.33-34
Speare — *Life* p.60-62
- *Canoes of traders*
Axtell — *18th* p.136-138
- *Description*
Axtell — *18th* p.130-131
- *Dutch in*
Axtell — *18th* p.128-129, 133-136
Locke — *Birth* p.50
- *Food*
Axtell — *18th* p.135-136
- *Trade and traders*
Axtell — *18th* p.131-132, 136-140

ALBANY PLAN OF UNION
Carman — *History* p.152-153
Colbourn — *Colonial* p.215-227
Life — *Making* p.37-38, 108
Life — *New* p.133, 146, 155
Sanderlin — *1776* p.7-10
Treasury Amer. p.89-95

ALCOHOLISM
Cable — *American* p.74
Downey — *Our* p.3-9

ALIEN AND SEDITION ACTS
Alden — *Pioneer* p.139-140
Kraus — *U.S. (1)* p.292-294
Life — *Growing* p.36-37
Miers — *American* p.103-107
Morris — *Ency.* p.129-130
Morris — *Voices* p.187-190
Wright — *New* p.46-47

ALLEGHENY MOUNTAINS
, as frontier
Langdon — *Every.* p.113-114

ALLEN, ETHAN
Burner — *America* p.113-117
Evans — *Weather.* p.57-60, 66
Hale — *Through* p.116-127
Life — *Making* p.11-12, 24-25, 109
McDowell — *Rev.* p.45, 47, 57-59, 61
Morris — *Voices* p.90-93
Scott — *Trumpet* p.160-169
Stearns — *Story* p.69-70, 86
200 Years p.49-52

ALMANACS
See also names of almanacs
Adams — *Album* p.339
Burt — *Phila.* p.173
Dannett — *Yankee* p.217-226
Earle — *Customs* p.273-275
Greene — *Revol.* p.133-134, 139, 430
Speare — *Life* p.168
Wright — *Frontier* p.72
- Poetry
Nye — *Unembar.* p.92-93

ALMSHOUSES
See also **Poor relief**
Bridenbaugh — *Wild.* p.234, 385, 393-397
- Boston
Bridenbaugh — *Revolt* p.125, 319
- Charlestown
Bridenbaugh — *Revolt* p.125, 322
- New York
Bridenbaugh — *Revolt* p.124-125, 324
- Newport, R.I.
Bridenbaugh — *Revolt* p.125, 324
- Philadelphia
Bridenbaugh — *Revolt* p.125-126, 218, 321

ALMY, MARY GOULD
Benson — *Women 18th* p.170
Evans — *Weather.* p.245-270

ALPHABETS
, Script, Ephrata
Langdon — *Every.* p.78-81

ALSTON, WASHINGTON
Morris — *Ency.* p.600

AMERICA
See also **Americans; "Nation, New"**; names of colonies, states, and related names
Howard — *Our* p.126-127
- Parodies
Howard — *Our* p.127
- Strengths and weaknesses
Ingraham — *Album* p.44
- Use of names
Alden — *Pioneer* p.48, 60-61
- Views of Peter Kalm
Scott — *Settlers* p.167-186

AMERICAN ACADEMY OF ARTS AND SCIENCES
Greene — *Revol.* p.294, 379, 383-384

AMERICAN COMPANY
Wright — *Cultural* p.184-185

AMERICAN PEACE COMMISSIONERS
- John Jay's defense
Morris — *American* p.275-278

AMERICAN PHILOSOPHICAL SOCIETY
Adams — *Provincial* p.263-264
Burt — *Phila.* p.158-159, 241
Carman — *History* p.106
Greene — *Revol.* p.91, 115-116, 124, 134, 143, 294, 383
Morris — *Ency.* p.529
Tunis — *Young* p.56
Wertenbaker — *Golden* p.68-69
Wright — *Cultural* p.231, 236-237

AMERICAN REVOLUTION. *See* **Revolutionary War**

AMERICAN SOCIETY FOR PROMOTING USEFUL KNOWLEDGE
Miller — *Origins* p.373

AMERICANISM. *See* **Nationalism; Patriotism**

"AMERICANISMS"
Adams — *Provincial* p.288-290

AMERICANS
Miller — *Colonial* p.479-498
- Character
Axtell — *18th* p.238
Handlin — *This* p.93-103
Morris — *American* p.195-204
- Definition
Axtell — *18th* p.211-239
Davie — *Profile* p.75
Sanderlin — *1776* p.6-7
200 Years p.304
- Emergence of
Carman — *History* p.117
- Hope of
Baldwin — *Ideas* p.188-189
, Reluctant
Axtell — *18th* p.151-176
- 1789
Kraus — *U.S. (1)* p.269-270
, Unrejected
Burt — *Phila.* p.66

AMES, FISHER
Morris — *Voices* p.175-176

AMES ALMANAC
Greene — *Revol.* p.48, 64, 86-87, 133-134, 136, 145-146, 181

AMUSEMENTS
See also **Sports and games;** names of amusements
Adams — *Album* p.325-328
Adams — *Provincial* p.76
Bridenbaugh — *Revolt* p.157, 162-169, 361-371
Bridenbaugh — *Wild.* p. 274-280, 434-442
Dreppard — *Pioneer* p.97-99, 101
Earle — *Colonial* p.206-239
Ross — *Taste* p.79-80
Tunis — *Living* p.149-151
Tunis — *Young* p.119-126
- Army
Greene — *Revol.* p.5, 255, 285
- Attitudes
Greene — *Revol.* p.114, 326-327
- Backwoods
Spruill — *Women's* p.109-112
- Boston
Axtell — *18th* p.145
- Cavaliers
Amer. Reader p.55-57
- Colleges and universities
Greene — *Revol.* p.127
- Frontier
Greene — *Revol.* p.406
- International influences
Greene — *Revol.* p.13
- New York
Smith — *Colonial* p.316-327
- Organizations
Greene — *Revol.* p.327-328
- Philadelphia
Speare — *Life* p.66-67
- Plantations
Greene — *Revol.* p.21-22
- Revolution
Dulles — *History* p.65-66
Greene — *Revol.* p.285-286
- South
Train — *Story* p.221-224

ANABAPTISTS
Life — *Growing* p.25
- Philadelphia
Axtell — *18th* p.180

ANARCHY
Morris — *American* p.208-212

ANATOMY
Burt — *Phila.* p.240

ANDIRONS
Glubok — *Home* p.32
Gould — *Early* p.63-65

ANDRÉ, JOHN
Burt — *Phila.* p.289-293
Life — *Making* p.65, 72-73
Morris — *Voices* p.118-121
Scott — *Trumpet* p.209, 212, 230, 232
Stember — *North. See* index p.169
Wheeler — *Voices* p.245, 259, 266, 297, 382, 385-394
, and Arnold
Amer. *Reader* p.117-119
- Death
Scott — *Trumpet* p.250-256
- Song
Scott — *Trumpet* p.253-256

ANGLICANS
See also **Episcopalians**
Alden — *Pioneer* p.43, 50, 54-55, 57, 66, 82, 290
Bridenbaugh — *Revolt* p.139, 152-154, 355-358
Carman — *History* p.92-93, 149
Colbourn — *Colonial* p.73-80
Greene — *Revol. See* index p.461
Hofstadter — *Amer. See* index p.iii
Kraus — *U.S. (1)* p.136, 207, 241
Life — *Making* p.34, 40
Life — *New* p.123-124
Miller — *Origins* p.187-197, 215
Morison — *Oxford (1)* p.208-209, 239, 244, 246, 312, 361, 381-382
Sweet — *Religion* p.14-26
- Bishops
Sweet — *Story* p.173-175
- Missions
Sweet — *Story* p.165-167
- Philadelphia
Axtell — *18th* p.177-178
- Virginia
Cable — *American* p.44-45

"ANIMAL DRIVERS"
Wilson — *Early* p.127-130

ANIMALS
See also **Livestock;** names of animals
- Exhibits
Dulles — *History* p.39-41
- Husbandry
Crèvecoeur — *Sketches* p.40, 42-43, 46-49, 102, 111, 113, 129, 235
Dolan — *Yankee* p.137
, Pack
Pettengill — *Yankee* p.63-67
, Stray
Pettengill — *Yankee* p.105-107
, Wild
Pettengill — *Yankee* p.112-120

ANNAPOLIS, MARYLAND
See also under special subjects
Greene — *Revol.* p.130, 146-147, 153, 215, 236, 297, 424
Wertenbaker — *Golden. See* index p.159
- Society
Spruill — *Women's* p.91-93

ANNAPOLIS CONVENTION (1786)
Alden — *Pioneer* p.114
Morris — *Ency.* p.115

ANTES, JOHN
Howard — *Our* p.29

ANTHONY, SUSANNA
Benson — *Women 18th* p.119, 261

ANTIFEDERALIST PARTY
Alden — *Pioneer* p.122-125
Carman — *History* p.260-265
Life — *Making* p.113, 130, 133-136
Whitney — *Abigail* p.252-253, 278

ANTIQUES
See also **Peddlers;** names of objects
- Origin
Dolan — *Yankee* p.113-190
, Scientific, etc.
Dreppard — *Pioneer* p.91-92, 94

ANTISLAVERY MOVEMENT
Morris — *Ency.* p.513-514
Sweet — *Story* p.168, 171
- *1st tract, by Judge Samuel Sewall*
Earle — *Customs* p.89-90

APOTHECARIES
Bridenbaugh — *Wild.* p.243-245, 403-406
Langdon — *Every.* p.325-326
Tunis — *Colonial* p.44-46
- *Utensils*
Langdon — *Every.* p.99

APPAREL. See Clothing and dress; names of apparel

APPLE-PARING BEES
Gould — *Early* p.137

APPLES
Gould — *Early* p.135-138
Earle — *Home* p.146-147

APPRENTICES
Adams — *Album* p.285
Bridenbaugh — *Revolt* p.86, 124, 176, 285, 322
Bridenbaugh — *Wild.* p.199-200, 288-289, 357, 443
Dolan — *Yankee* p.116-117
Forbes — *Paul* p.8-11, 28, 280-381
Tunis — *Colonial* p.14-15
- *Girls, Southern*
Spruill — *Women's* p.188-189
- *Laws*
Benson — *Women 18th* p.179, 224-225

ARCHITECTURE
See also **Houses; Mansions;** names of buildings
Adams — *Album* p.312-318, 346
Bridenbaugh — *Revolt* p.19, 142-143, 229
Gould — *Early* p.42
Greene — *Revol.* p.7, 21-22, 122, 146-147, 276-277, 396-397, 447
Kraus — *U.S. (1)* p.172-173
Langdon — *Every.* p.129-130
Life — *New* p.72-73, 112-113, 128, 140-141
Morris — *Ency.* p.597-599
Tunis — *Young* p.97-98
Wright — *Cultural* p.199-203
, Adam style
Gowans — *Images* p.164-172
, and architects
Gowans — *Images. See* index p.194
, and firms
Gowans — *Images. See* index p.104
- *Annapolis*
Wertenbaker — *Golden* p.98-100
- *Boston*
Wertenbaker — *Golden* p.29-32
- *Charleston*
Wertenbaker — *Golden* p.127-128, 130-133
- *Charlestown*
Bridenbaugh — *Wild.* p.150, 150n, 309
, Classical
Gowans — *Images* p.115, 214-222, 239
, Dutch
Langdon — *Every.* p.45
Sirkis — *Reflect.* p.83, 85
Wertenbaker — *Golden* p.49-52
, Federal. See **Architecture, Adam style; Architecture, Regency**
, Georgian
Dreppard — *Pioneer* p.15, 17-24
Gowan — *Images* p.151-163
Langdon — *Every.* p.125-146
Sirkis — *Reflect.* p.24-25, 28-29
Train — *Story* p.151-155, 179, 181-183, 205-206, 225-227, 230
Tunis — *Living* p.127-128
Wertenbaker — *Golden* p.30-31, 50-51
, German
Train — *Story* p.181
- *Jefferson, Thomas*
See also **Monticello**
Train — *Story* p.227-229
Treasury Amer. p.135-147
- *Maryland*
Wertenbaker — *Golden* p.103-104

ARCHITECTURE (*continued*)
- *Mercantile society*
  Gowans — *Images* p.199-209
- *Middle class*
  Gowans — *Images* p.209-210, 214-222
- *New Hampshire*
  Gowans — *Images* p.196
- *New York*
  Bridenbaugh — *Wild.* p.308
  Wertenbaker — *Golden* p.41-42, 49-52
- *Newport, R.I.*
  Bridenbaugh — *Wild.* 310-311, 460-461
- *North Carolina*
  Gowans — *Images* p.188-196
- *Philadelphia*
  Bridenbaugh — *Wild.* p.306-307, 456
  Gowans — *Images* p.188-199
  Train — *Story* p.182-183
  Wertenbaker — *Golden* p.74-75

, Regency
  Ross — *Taste* p.10
- *South*
  Ross — *Taste* p.8-9
  Train — *Story* p.205-206
  Adams — *Album* p.316-317
- *Styles*
  Gowans — *Images. See* index p.496
  Sirkis — *Reflect.* p.148
- *Williamsburg, Va.*
  Wertenbaker — *Golden* p.114-115

ARISTOCRACY
Adams — *Provincial* p.59-84
Alden — *Pioneer* p.48-52, 57, 103-105
Bridenbaugh — *Revolt. See* index p.i, ii
Bridenbaugh — *Wild.* p.251-257, 414-416
Dulles — *History* p.44-66
Greene — *Revol. See* index p.458
Hofstadter — *Amer.* p.132-134, 138-139, 158, 162-167
Life — *Growing* p.136-137
Miller — *Origins* p.55-60
- *Maryland*
  Wertenbaker — *Golden* p.9-10

ARITHMETIC
See also **Mathematics**

, Teaching of
  Glubok — *Home* p.148-155

ARMINIANISM
Hofstadter — *Amer.* p.187, 210, 219, 226-229, 233-234, 236, 252, 289

ARMY
See also **Continental army; Militia**; names of wars, special subjects
- *Commanders (1775-1799)*
  Schemmer — *Almanac* p.232

ARNETT, HANNAH WHITE
Somerville — *Women* p.36-39

ARNOLD, BENEDICT
Adams — *Album* p.395
Amer. Her. — *Rev. See* index p.380
Collins — *Story* p.120-121
Dannett — *Yankee* p.168-169, 225
Ingraham — *Album* p.79
Life — *Making* p.11-13, 25-26, 57-59, 65, 70-72, 85
Locke — *Birth* p.217-252
McDowell — *Rev. See* index p.196
Morris — *Ency.* p.103-104
Morris — *Voices* p.118-121
Stember — *North. See* index p.375
200 Years p.49, 52, 54-55, 57-62, 64, 120, 123-126, 129-130, 144, 147
Wheeler — *Voices. See* index p.473

ARNOLD, MARGARET SHIPPEN
Amer. Her. — *Rev.* p.267, 269-270
Ellet — *Eminent* p.430-437
McDowell — *Rev.* p.145-146, 158

ART
See also **Artisans; Artists; Crafts and craftsmanship; Painters and paintings; Portraits and portrait painting; Sculpture;** other special subjects and types of art
Greene — *Revol.* p.395-397, 417, 446-447
Life — *New* p.127-128
- Annapolis
Wertenbaker — *Golden* p.95-98
- Associations
Greene — *Revol.* p.148-149
- Boston
Wertenbaker — *Golden* p.32-34
- Charleston
Wertenbaker — *Golden* p.135-136
, Children's
Earle — *Child* p.321-341
, Collecting
Bridenbaugh — *Revolt* p.198, 403-404
- Dealers
Bridenbaugh — *Revolt* p.198, 337, 407-408
- Design
Burner — *America* p.129-133
- Home furnishings. See **Home furnishings**
- Philadelphia
Wertenbaker — *Golden* p.82-83
, Popular
Nye — *Unembar.* p.1-2
- Virginia
Wertenbaker — *Golden* p.117

ARTICLES OF CONFEDERATION
Alden — *Pioneer* p.97-98, 104, 114-115, 118, 121, 123
Amer. Her. — *Rev.* p.217, 270-271, 367
Angle — *By* p.65-78
Beach — *Samuel* p.303-304, 306
Carman — *History* p.213-214, 237, 245-246, 250-253, 260
Colbourn — *Colonial* p.388-392
Greene — *Revol.* p.348, 364-365
Kraus — *U.S. (1)* p.245-249, 256-257
Life — *Making* p.38, 105, 110, 131
Lossing — *Biog.* p.310-328
Morison — *Oxford (1)* p.362-367
Morris — *American* p.223-231
Morris — *Ency.* p.98
Morris — *Voices* p.143-146, 158, 162
Tunis — *Young* p.13-14
200 Years p.161-177
Wright — *New* p.12
- Defects
Alden — *Pioneer* p.112-113
- Maryland's opposition
Morris — *American* p.231-235

"ARTICLES OF PEACE" (preliminary)
Morris — *American* p.12-16, 279-284

ARTILLERY. *See* **Guns**

ARTISANS
See also **Crafts and craftsmanship;** special subjects
Bridenbaugh — *Revolt.* p.76, 134, 161, 272-274, 284-285, 287
Bridenbaugh — *Wild.* p.190-192, 345-348
Earle — *Colonial* p.276-315
Main — *Social. See* index p.305
- Association
Forbes — *Paul* p.380-382
- Philadelphia
Tunis — *Young* p.55-56

ARTISTS
See also **Painters and paintings; Portraits and portrait painting**
Adams — *Album* p.345
Burner — *America* p.61
, Traveling
Dolan — *Yankee* p.133-137
- Women, Southern
Spruill — *Women's* p.259

ASSOCIATIONS
See also names of subjects, professions; etc.
, Scientific
Greene — *Revol.* p.142-144, 294, 384
, Social
Greene — *Revol.* p.93-94, 327-328

ASSOCIATIONS (*continued*)
, Student
Greene — *Revol.* p.127

ASTELL, MARY
Benson — *Women 18th* p.28-33

ASTOR, JOHN JACOB
- Biography
Morris — *Ency.* p.632

ASTRONOMY
Boorstin — *Americans* p.243-251
Bridenbaugh — *Revolt* p.202-203, 412-415
Greene — *Revol.* p.124, 142, 144, 386
Morris — *Ency.* p.528-529

ATROCITIES
See also names of massacres
Scott — *Trumpet* p.243-245, 247
200 Years. See index p.345

ATTICS
Earle — *Home* p.10-11
Gould — *Early* p.22, 29-30

ATTUCKS, CRISPUS
Scott — *Trumpet* p.59-60, 62

AUCKLAND, HARRIET
Ellet — *Eminent* p.97-101

AUCTIONS
Bridenbaugh — *Revolt* p.78-79, 180, 226, 276-277
Bridenbaugh — *Wild.* p.192, 307, 345-348
- Augusta, Ga.
Stember — *South* p.35-38

AUTHORS
See also names of authors; types of authors
Earle — *Customs* p.275-278
Tunis — *Young* p.126-127
- North Carolina
Wright — *Cultural* p.169
- Virginia
Wright — *Cultural* p.166-168
- Women
Benson — *Women 18th* p.118-119, 170-171, 177, 192, 215-216, 256, 279, 307
Dexter — *Colonial* p.133-142
Earle — *Customs* p.268-269

AUTUMN
- Duties
Speare — *Life* p.73

"AWAKENING, GREAT." ***See* "Great Awakening"**

AWARENESS
- Spirit of
Sloane — *Spirits* p.57-60

B

BABIES
Glubock — *Home* p.94-99
, Mortality, Southern
Spruill — *Women's* p.47-49, 52-54
- Sickness, remedies for
Earle — *Child* p.7-10

BACHE, SARAH FRANKLIN
Adelman — *Famous* p.87
Benson — *Women 18th* p.133, 164, 252, 295
Ellet — *Eminent* p.262-278
Somerville — *Women* p.48-51

BACKBOARDS
Glubok — *Home* p.126-127

BACKWOODS. *See* under special subjects

BAILEY, "MAD ANNE" HENNIS
Cook — *What* p.235-238

BAKER, RACHEL WARDER
Tunis — *Tavern* p.14, 19-23, 48

BAKER, SAMUEL
Tunis — *Tavern* p.5-6, 12, 14, 16-23, 31-32, 45-47, 59, 64

BAKERS AND "BAKE HOUSES"
Gould — *Early* p.91-92
Tunis — *Colonial* p.43-44

ALLAD OPERAS
Dannett — *Yankee* p.264
Howard — *Our* p.31-32
Morris — *Ency.* p.612

ALLADS
See also **Broadsides**
Dannett — *Yankee* p.121-191
Nye — *Unembar.* p.306-307
Scott — *Settlers* p.187-208
Scott — *Trumpet* p.253-256, 285-286
, Scotch-Irish
Rublowsky — *Music* p.73-80

ALLISTICS
See also **Guns**
, of Benjamin Thompson
Wilson — *American* p.26

ALLOONS
Earle — *Customs* p.245-256
Speare — *Life* p.164

ALLS AND BALLROOMS. *See* **Dances and dancing**

ALTIMORE, MARYLAND
See also special subjects
Adams — *Album* p.295
Greene — *Revol.* p.42, 48, 60, 68, 208, 236, 277, 297, 349, 389

ANGS, ISAAC
Scott — *Trumpet* p.133, 135-137, 140

ANISTER, JOHN
Wertenbaker — *Golden* p.123-124

ANK OF NORTH AMERICA
Greene — *Revol.* p.273, 354

ANK OF THE UNITED STATES
Alden — *Pioneer* p.133-134
Morris — *Ency.* p.123, 504
200 Years p.231-234

ANKS AND BANKING
See also **Currency; Money;** names of banks
Greene — *Revol.* p.39-40, 189, 250, 273, 354-356
Morison — *Oxford (1)* p.236, 305-306, 370
Morris — *Ency.* p.504
Tunis — *Young* p.73
- Founding
Stearns — *Story* p.64
, National
Morris — *American* p.261-266
, of Alexander Hamilton
Butterfield — *Amer.* p.18

BANNOCKS
Gould — *Early* p.74, 91

BAPTISM
Glubock — *Home* p.95-96

BAPTISTS
See also **Dunkers (Dunkards);** etc.
Bridenbaugh — *Revolt* p.152, 174, 354, 357, 378
Bridenbaugh — *Wild.* p.59, 261-263
Greene — *Revol. See* index p.459
Hofstadter — *Amer.* p.183-184, 187-188, 201, 206, 208-209, 211, 268, 284
Sweet — *Religion* p.33-36, 56-58, 203-204
Sweet — *Story* p.149-152, 182-183, 204, 215-218, 224-225
Wright — *New* p.206-209

BARBARY PIRATES
Morris — *Voices* p.176-180

BARBERS
See also **Wigs and wigmakers**
Tunis — *Colonial* p.41-43
- Boston
Bridenbaugh — *Wild.* p.345-346

BARKER, JOHN
Morris — *Voices* p.85-86

BARKER, PENELOPE PAGETT
McDowell — *Rev.* p.24, 30
Somerville — *Women* p.18-23

BARLOW, JOEL
Morris — *Voices* p.176-180, 187

BARNS
Gould — *Early* p.34
Tunis — *Living* p.109-110
- *Views of Crèvecoeur*
Crèvecoeur — *Sketches* p.26, 141-143, 146, 182, 201, 203

BARTERING
See also **Trade and traders**
Gould — *Early* p.105, 130-131

BARTLETT, JOSIAH
Bakeless — *Signers* p.223-225
Malone — *Story* p.98-99
- *Biography*
Lossing — *Biog.* p.13-16

BARTRAM, JOHN
Burt — *Phila.* p.233-234
Wright — *Cultural* p.229-230

BASINS
Earle — *Home* p.106

BASKETS
Dolan — *Yankee* p.182-183
Earle — *Child* p.390, 392

BASTARDS. *See* **Illegitimacy**

BATHS AND BATHING
Earle — *Customs* p.308-309

"BATTLE OF THE KEGS" (Philadelphia, 1778)
Wheeler — *Voices* p.291-293

BATTLE STREAMERS
Schemmer — *Almanac* p.218, 220, 225, 228

BAY PSALM BOOK
Howard — *Our* p.15-16
Morris — *Ency.* p.611
Rublowsky — *Music* p.15, 17

BAYBERRY
Earle — *Home* p.39-40
Glubok — *Home* p.21, 201
- *Candle wax*
Earle — *Colonial* p.303-306
Earle — *Home* p.39-40

BAYLOR MASSACRE
Stember — *North* p.177-180, 191

BEARBAITING
- *Massachusetts*
Dow — *Every* p.114

BEAUTY
See also **Cosmetics**
- *Aids*
Belote — *Compleat* p.152-155
Earle — *Customs* p.307-308, 310-311
- *Aids, Southern*
Spruill — *Women's* p.127-128
- *Longing for*
Speare — *Life* p.81-82

BEDS AND BEDROOMS
Gould — *Early* p.24, 27-29
Sirkis — *Reflect.* p.25, 28
Tunis — *Living* p.131

BEECHER, LYMAN
Sweet — *Story* p.223-224

BEEKMAN, CORNELIA
Ellet — *Eminent* p.418-429

BEER
Gould — *Early* p.83, 105-106

"BEES." *See* types of bees, e.g. **Apple-pairing; Chopping; Husking; Piling; Quilts and quilting; Sewing; Spelling; Stone,** etc.

BEES, HONEY
Earle — *Home* p.111
Pettengill — *Yankee* p.94-96

BEISSEL, JOHANN CONRAD
Langdon — *Every.* p.75, 82, 86, 88
Rublowsky — *Music* p.27-31
Wright — *Cultural* p.194

BELKNAP, JEREMY
, on women
Benson — *Women 18th* p.60, 137, 143, 145, 147-148, 155, 157

"BELL HOUSE"
Langdon — *Every.* p.90-93, 99-100

BELLOWS
Gould — *Early* p.80

BELLS
See also **Liberty Bell**
, of Paul Revere
Forbes — *Paul* p.370-372, 446, 467
- Village
Speare — *Life* p.45

BEMIS HEIGHTS, NEW YORK
, Battle of
Scott — *Trumpet* p.196-197
200 Years p.129-130

BENEVOLENT ENTERPRISES. *See* **Almshouses; Charities; Friendly societies; Granaries; Missions; Poor relief, etc.**

BENNINGTON, VERMONT
, Battle of
Amer. Her. — *Rev.* p.241-243, 250
Stember — *North* p.4, 55, 59, 66, 83-90

BENTLEY, JOHN
Howard — *Our* p.7, 102-103

BERNARD, FRANCIS
See also **Stamp Act — Riot**
Beach — *Samuel. See* index p.323
Morris — *American* p.73-75

BEST SELLERS
Morris — *Ency.* p.560, 562, 565

BETHLEHEM, PENNSYLVANIA
See also **"Bell House"; Moravians**
Greene — *Revol.* p.30, 96, 104, 166
Langdon — *Every.* p.87-109

BETTY LAMPS
Earle — *Home* p.43-44

BEVERAGES
See also **Caudle; Flip;** etc.
Adams — *Provincial* p.75
Earle — *Customs* p.172-183
Earle — *Home* p.163
Glubok — *Home* p.50, 82-83, 90-93
Gould — *Early* p.82-83, 105-107
- Glossary
Belote — *Compleat* p.130-131
- Health
Belote — *Compleat* p.113-131
- Peddlers
Dolan — *Yankee* p.257-259
- South
Spruill — *Women's* p.67
- Taverns
Dolan — *Yankee* p.105

BEVERLEY, ROBERT
- on Indian customs and manners
Miller — *Colonial* p.248-256
- on Virginia
Miller — *Colonial* p.293-309

BEVERLY, MASSACHUSETTS
Greene — *Revol.* p.264, 267-268

BIBLE
- on women
Benson — *Woman 18th* p.14-15, 25, 58, 108, 120, 124, 184
, Reading of
Glubok — *Home* p.297-298

"BICENTENNIAL"
Sloane — *Spirits* p.7-11, 55

BILL OF RIGHTS
Alden — *Pioneer* p.121-124, 128
Angle — *By* p.116-118
Baldwin — *Ideas* p.201-203
Morison — *Oxford (1)* p.354-358
Morris — *Ency.* p.121
- Maryland
200 Years p.297

BILL OF RIGHTS (*continued*)
- *Massachusetts*
  Morris — *American* p.308-312
- *Ratification*
  200 Years p.7, 173, 176
- *Virginia*
  Morris — *American* p.305-308
  200 Years p.297

BILLIARDS
Dulles — *History* p.36

BILLINGS, WILLIAM
Howard — *Our* p.49-57

BINGHAM, ANN WILLING
Burt — *Phila.* p.257-258, 301

BINGHAM, CALEB
Glubok — *Home* p.125, 151-152

BIRCH BARK
- *Uses*
  Earle — *Home* p.6, 83, 310
  Glubok — *Home* p.44-45, 121, 214, 332

BIRTH RATE
See also **Population**
Miller — *Origins* p.275, 433-434

BLACKJACKS
Earle — *Home* p.95-96

BLACKS. *See* Antislavery movement; Negroes; Slaves and slavery

BLACKSMITHS
Gould — *Early* p.68
Main — *Social* p.17, 19-20, 22, 29, 46, 52, 76, 80, 134, 182, 274-275
Speare — *Life* p.123
Tunis — *Colonial* p.18-21, 58-61
- *Women*
  Dexter — *Colonial* p.53

BLAIR, SAMUEL
Hofstadter — *Amer.* p.220-221, 234, 265-266, 286

BLASPHEMY. *See* Profanity

BLEACHING
Earle — *Home* p.175, 234, 261

BLEEKER, ANN ELIZA
Benson — *Women* p.216, 303-304, 307-308

BLOCKHOUSES
Tunis — *Living* p.102
Tunis — *Young* p.147
, and garrisons
  Adams — *Album* p.270

BOARDING SCHOOLS
Bridenbaugh — *Wild.* p.282, 449-450
Dexter — *Colonial* p.89-95
- *South*
  Spruill — *Women's* p.197-201

BOAT RACING
200 Years p.306

BOATMEN
See also **Ferries**; etc.
Wilson — *Early* p.141-143

BOATS. *See* types of boats

BONDSERVANTS. *See* Servants — Indentured

***BONHOMME RICHARD* (ship)**
, and "Serapis"
  Morris — *Ency.* p.102
  200 Years p.131

BOOKBINDERS
Tunis — *Colonial* p.98-101

BOOKPLATES
Earle — *Customs* p.286

BOOKS AND READING
See also **"Best sellers"; Children's books and reading; Libraries; Textbooks**; etc.
Adams — *Album* p.287
Adams — *Provincial* p.304
Boorstin — *Americans* p.319-324
Earle — *Colonial* p.191-195
Earle — *Customs* p.263-288
Glubok — *Home. See* index p.348

Greene — *Revol. See* index p.459
Nye — *Unembar.* p.23
Speare — *Life* p.167-168
- *Boston*
  Boorstin — *Americans* p.296-301
  Wertenbaker — *Golden* p.26-27
- *Burning*
  Earle — *Customs* p.288
- *Collectors*
  Wright — *Cultural* p.145-146
- *Cost*
  Main — *Social* p.254
- *Etiquette*
  Glubok — *Home* p.53-54, 107-108
- *in education*
  Main — *Social* p.253-254
- *Newport, R.I.*
  Bridenbaugh — *Wild.* p.459-460
- *Ownership*
  Main — *Social* p.256-260
- *Philadelphia*
  Boorstin — *Americans* p.306-312

, Religious
  Earle — *Child* p.249, 260-263
  Glubok — *Home* p.303-311
- *South*
  Spruill — *Women's* p.210-231
- *Women*
  Benson — *Women 18th* p.21, 36, 49, 54, 71, 73, 83-84, 112-115, 150, 160-165, 305, 307-308, 311-312
  Spruill — *Women's* p.210-231

BOOKSHOPS AND BOOKSELLERS
Bridenbaugh — *Revolt* p.179-184, 380-388, 398
Bridenbaugh — *Wild.* p.293, 295, 452, 456-457, 461
Earle — *Customs* p.263-265
Greene — *Revol.* p.135-136, 392
Wright — *Cultural* p.152-153
- *Advertisements*
  Earle — *Child* p.267
- *Annapolis*
  Wertenbaker — *Golden* p.91
- *Boston*
  Bridenbaugh — *Wild.* p.291
  Wertenbaker — *Golden* p.26-27
  Wright — *Cultural* p.152-153
- *New York*
  Wertenbaker — *Golden* p.46-47
  Wright — *Cultural* p.153
- *Philadelphia*
  Wertenbaker — *Golden* p.71
- *Williamsburg, Va.*
  Wertenbaker — *Golden* p.112-113
- *Women*
  Dexter — *Colonial* p.30

BOONE, DANIEL
Amer. Reader p.147-150
Hale — *Through* p.158-165
Wright — *Frontier* p.49-54, 75

, and Cumberland Gap
  Collins — *Story* p.139
- *Biography*
  Morris — *Ency.* p.637

BOSTON, MASSACHUSETTS
Adams — *Album* p.256
Alden — *Pioneer. See* index p.i
Amer. Her. — *Rev.* p.62, 98, 104, 111-112
Axtell — *18th* p.140-149
Beach — *Samuel. See* index p.323-324
Bridenbaugh — *Revolt* p.17, 41, 47-48, 60, 76, 78, 248
Forbes — *Paul. See* index p.488
Glubok — *Home. See* index p.348
Greene — *Revol. See* index p.459
Handlin — *This* p.68-71, 73-74
Life — *Making* p.7, 9, 11-13, 25
McDowell — *Rev.* p.20-22, 24-25, 27, 29, 34, 73, 138-139
Main — *Social. See* index p.306
Miller — *Origins. See* index p.508
Morison — *Oxford (1). See* index p.410
Morris — *Voices* p.29-32, 73, 104
National — *History.* p.185-188
Ross — *Taste* p.7-8
Sanderlin — *1776* p.45-49, 53-54, 85-88, 116, 145, 147, 251
Scott — *Trumpet. See* index p.301

BOSTON, MASSACHUSETTS (*cont.*)
Speare — *Life* p.49-51
Stember — *North* p.289-297
Tunis — *Young. See* index p.152
200 Years p.16, 20-21, 29-30, 34-35, 44-47, 49, 291
Wertenbaker — *Golden. See* index p.160
Wheeler — *Voices* p.36-39, 48-49, 51-52, 117, 125-130
- Bicentennial
Lawlor — *Bicen.* p.3-28
- Blockade
Amer. Her. — *Rev.* p.106-112
Sanderlin — *1776* p.85-88
- Bread riots
Bridenbaugh — *Wild.* p.196-197
, British in
Amer. Her. — *Rev.* p.112, 118, 193, 203
Collins — *Story* p.108
Ingraham — *Album* p.37
McDowell — *Rev.* p.76-77
Scott — *Trumpet* p.37-62
- Censorship
Bridenbaugh — *Wild.* p.130-131
, Continental army in
Scott — *Trumpet* p.90-92
- Culture
Wertenbaker — *Golden* p.38-39
- Government
Bridenbaugh — *Revolt* p.6-7, 116, 221-222
- North End
Forbes — *Paul* p.22, 29, 49, 114, 167-168, 189, 320
- North Square
Forbes — *Paul* p.8, 164-167, 235, 439
- Social life
Axtell — *18th* p.143-144
Earle — *Colonial* p.109-134
Forbes — *Paul* p.351-356
- Streets
Forbes — *Paul. See* index p.497 (Streets)
, Victory in
Ingraham — *Album* p.51
, Views of Dr. Alexander Hamilton
Miller — *Colonial* p.413-415
- Women
Axtell — *18th. See* index
Benson — *Women 18th* p.280, 292-294, 298-299

BOSTON EVENING POST
Dexter — *Colonial* p.6-7, 19-20, 38

BOSTON FIRE SOCIETY
Bridenbaugh — *Wild.* p.211-212, 367-368

BOSTON MASSACRE
Adams — *Album* p.362-353
Amer. Her. — *Rev.* p.64-65, 93
Beach — *Samuel* p.184-196, 213-214
Bridenbaugh — *Revolt* p.308
Carman — *History* p.169-170
Colbourn — *Colonial* p.336-339
Collins — *Story* p.97
Dannett — *Yankee* p.25
Forbes — *Paul* p.125, 145-161, 170, 172-173, 229-231, 457-458
Ingraham — *Album* p.22
Kraus — *U.S. (1)* p.195-196
Life — *New* p.153, 159, 161
McDowell — *Rev.* p.18-19, 25, 27
Malone — *Story* p.22-25
Miller — *Origins* p.295-298, 395, 440
Morris — *American* p.104-110
Morris — *Ency.* p.79
Morris — *Voices* p.73-76
Sanderlin — *1776* p.64-71, 150
Scott — *Trumpet* p.58-60, 62
Sirkis — *Reflect.* p.31
Stember — *North* p.291-295
200 Years p.23-25, 32, 290

BOSTON NEWS-LETTER
Adams — *Provincial* p.129-130
Dexter — *Colonial* p.177

BOSTON PORT ACT
Amer. Her. — *Rev.* p.68-69, 98, 113
Bridenbaugh — *Revolt* p.234, 320, 401
Dannett — *Yankee* p.28
Ingraham — *Album* p.29
Miller — *Origins* p.334, 358-369, 386, 397
Morison — *Oxford (1)* p.275-278
Sanderlin — *1776* p.85-86, 90

BOSTON TEA PARTY
Adams — *Album* p.365
Amer. Her. — *Rev.* p.24, 47, 68, 94, 154
Beach — *Samuel* p.251-252, 257
Bridenbaugh — *Revolt* p.308
Carman — *History* p.178-179
Collins — *Story* p.98
Dannett — *Yankee* p.25
Forbes — *Paul* p.188-193, 432-433
Ingraham — *Album* p.26-28
Kraus — *U.S. (1)* p.201-203
Life — *New* p.154, 159, 165
McDowell — *Rev.* p.23, 29
Malone — *Story* p.29-34
Miller — *Origins* p.267, 329, 343, 346-349, 355-358, 364
Morris — *American* p.123-124
Morris — *Ency.* p.81
Morris — *Voices* p.76-80
Sanderlin — *1776* p.74-79, 251
Scott — *Trumpet* p.66-70
Stearns — *Story* p.81
200 Years p.26-27, 29, 291

BOTANICAL GARDENS
Wright — *Cultural* p.229-230
, First
Bridenbaugh — *Wild.* p.294

BOTANY AND BOTANISTS
Boorstin — *Americans* p.162-163
Bridenbaugh — *Revolt* p.204-205, 415
Greene — *Revol.* p.143, 145, 385
Morris — *Ency.* p.528-530
- Women
Benson — *Women* p.163, 307, 312
Earle — *Colonial* p.85-87

BOTTLES
Earle — *Home* p.82, 95

BOUCHER, JONATHAN
, on anarchy
Morris — *American* p.208-212

BOUNTIES
Colbourn — *Colonial* p.263-264

BOUNTY COATS
Earle — *Home* p.248

BOWDITCH, NATHANIEL
- Navigation science
Wilson — *American* p.44-45

BOWDOIN, JAMES
Beach — *Samuel* p.115, 198, 200, 219-220, 232, 255, 307

BOWLS
Gould — *Early* p.36-37, 85-87

BOWNE, ELIZA SOUTHGATE
Benson — *Women 18th* p.178, 184-186, 268

BOXES
Gould — *Early* p.36

BOYCOTTS
See also **Boston Tea Party; "Buy American" campaign**
Life — *New* p.50-1153, 155
Miller — *Origins. See* index p.508

BOYLE, JOHN
Forbes — *Paul* p.73, 75, 78, 98, 199-200, 207, 223, 265, 292-293, 319-320, 324

BOYLSTON, ZABDIEL
Bridenbaugh — *Wild.* p.242-243, 243n, 402-403

BOYS
Glubok — *Home. See* index p.348-349
- Games
Tunis — *Living* p.149

BRADDOCK, EDWARD
Adams — *Album* p.348
Burt — *Phila.* p.169-170
Collins — *Story* p.90
Morris — *Voices* p.54-57
- Provisions, inventory
Earle — *Home* p.336-337

BRAINERD, DAVID AND JOHN
Glubok — *Home* p.206-207
Sweet — *Story* p.161-162

BRANDYWINE CREEK, PENNSYLVANIA
, Battle of
See also **Germantown, Penn., Battle of**
Amer. Her. — *Rev.* p.211-213, 225
Ingraham — *Album* p.62
Morison — *Oxford (1)* p.238
Morris — *Ency.* p.95
Stember — *Middle* p.88-110

BRATTON, MARTHA
Ellet — *Eminent* p.169-179

BRAXTON, CARTER
Bakeless — *Signers* p.101-103
Malone — *Story* p.216-217
- Biography
Lossing — *Biog.* p.197-200

BRAY, THOMAS
Wright — *Cultural* p.146-147

BRAZIERS
Tunis — *Colonial* p.141-143

BREADS AND BISCUITS
See also **Bannocks; Cakes and desserts; Hoe cakes;** etc.
Belote — *Compleat* p.37-53
Glubok — *Home* p.35-36
Gould — *Early* p.74-75, 91

BREAKFASTS
Earle — *Home* p.148
Gould — *Early* p.82
- South
Spruill — *Women's* p.72, 72n

BRECK, SAMUEL
Morris — *Voices* p.140-142

BRECKINRIDGE, JOHN
Butterfield — *Amer.* p.28

BREED'S HILL, MASSACHUSETTS. ***See* Bunker Hill, Battle of**

BRENT, MARGARET AND MARY
Brooks — *Dames* p.59-73
Dexter — *Colonial* p.98-100

BREWERIES. ***See* Distilleries and breweries**

BRICKS
Gould — *Early* p.44, 50

BRIDGES
See also **Covered bridges**
Bridenbaugh — *Wild.* p.161-162, 319-321
Earle — *Home* p.348-349
Tunis — *Living* p.121
Tunis — *Young* p.37, 77

BRIER CREEK, GEORGIA
Stember — *South* p.31-33

BRISSOT, JEAN PIERCE
Handlin — *This* p.67-87

BRITISH
See also **England and English; Great Britain**
Greene — *Revol. See* index p.460
Scott — *Trumpet* p.3-18
, Abuses of
Malone — *Story* p.9-31
- Army
Burt — *Phila.* p.287-288
Forbes — *Paul. See* index p.488
Scott — *Trumpet. See* index p.301-302
Wheeler — *Voices. See* index p.473
, Deserters
Forbes — *Paul* p.224-225
- Fleet
Scott — *Trumpet. See* index p.302
- Imports
Earle — *Colonial* p.248-249
, Plundering of
Scott — *Trumpet* p.156-157, 192, 207, 209, 211, 233, 242, 247
- Policy
Carman — *History* p.142-144
Morris — *American* p.50-56
Scott — *Trumpet* p.19-36

BROADSIDES
See also **Ballads**
Adams — *Album* p.329

Bridenbaugh — *Revolt* p.179, 190-191, 382, 398
Dannett — *Yankee* p.192-216
Nye — *Unembar.* p.89-92, 306-307

BROOKLYN HEIGHTS
, Battle of
Morris — *Voices* p.106-108
Stember — *North* p.218, 226-324
Wheeler — *Voices* p.151-169

BROOMS
Dolan — *Yankee* p.181-182
Earle — *Colonial* p.298-301
Earle — *Home* p.301-305
Glubok — *Home* p.211-212
Gould — *Early* p.36, 80, 126-127

BROWN, ANDREW
Benson — *Women* p.137-140, 142, 145, 154-155, 163, 215

BROWN, WILLIAM
Howard — *Our* p.102-103

BRUYN, BLANDINA
Ellet — *Eminent* p.541-546

BUCHANAN, SARAH
Ellet — *Eminent* p.710-725

BUDD, RACHEL
Crèvecoeur — *Sketches* p.207-220

BUILDERS AND BUILDING
See also **Architecture**
Bridenbaugh — *Revolt* p.13-25, 99, 224-232, 292, 298, 321
Bridenbaugh — *Wild.* p.140, 146-149, 305-311
Morris — *Ency.* p.599
Tunis — *Colonial* p.85-87
Tunis — *Living* p.127-128
- Materials
See also types of materials
Gould — *Early* p.42
Langdon — *Every.* p.132-133

BULFINCH, CHARLES
Stearns — *Story* p.101-102
- Biography
Morris — *Ency.* p.640

BUNDLING
Adams — *Provincial* p.160
Benson — *Women 18th* p. 229, 275-277
Cable — *American* p.36-37, 86-87
Downey — *Our* p.161-170
Dulles — *History* p.28-29
Earle — *Customs* p.62-63
Ross — *Taste* p.281

BUNKER HILL
, Battle of
Amer. Her. — *Rev.* p.107-109, 116-118
Amer. Reader p.93-94
Beach — *Samuel* p.288-289
Collins — *Story* p.104
Greene — *Revol.* p.232, 240
Ingraham — *Album* p.38-39
McDowell — *Rev.* p.41, 50, 52-54, 62-67, 120, 151
Miller — *Origins* p.410-411, 417, 428
Morison — *Oxford (1)* p.289-290, 302, 327
Morris — *Ency.* p.87-88
National — *History.* p.194-195
Sanderlin — *1776* p.164-169
Stearns — *Story* p.88
Stember — *North* p.281, 284, 292, 297-301
200 Years p.43-47
Wheeler — *Voices* p.31, 54-73, 80, 85, 119, 122, 299
Whitney — *Abigail* p.104-108

BURGOMASTERS
Wilson — *Early* p.22
, Dutch
Speare — *Life* p.57-59

BURGOYNE, SIR JOHN
Amer. Her. — *Rev. See* index p.381
Amer. Reader p.109-110
Dannett — *Yankee* p.147-148, 151-153
Life — *Making* p.9, 17, 57-59, 67, 70-71, 109
McDowell — *Rev.* p.47, 52, 110, 112, 114, 116-117, 119-123
Morison — *Oxford (1). See* index p.410

BURGOYNE, SIR JOHN (*continued*)
Morris — *Voices* p.93, 111-114
Scott — *Trumpet. See* index p.302
Stember — *North* p.48-114; *See also* index p.377
200 Years p.64, 120-126, 128-130, 133, 139-140
Wheeler — *Voices. See* index p.473
- *Song*
Scott — *Trumpet* p.202-203

BURIALS. *See* Cemeteries; Death; Funerals

BURKE, EDMUND
Carman — *History* p.121, 158, 179, 185-186, 214-215
Miller — *Origins. See* index p.508
Morris — *American* p.152-160, 219-222

BURR, AARON
- *Biography*
Morris — *Ency.* p.640
- *Relations with Hamilton*
Locke — *Birth* p.101-132

BURR, ESTHER EDWARDS
Benson — *Women 18th* p.51-52, 114, 117-118, 125n, 142

BURR, THEODOSIA
Benson — *Women 18th* p.182-183

BURWELL, REBECCA
Brodie — *Jefferson* p.12, 63-69, 74

BUSHNELL, DAVID
Morris — *Ency.* p.535

BUSINESS
See also **Artisans; Commerce; Trade and traders;** types of businesses, etc.
Greene — *Revol.* p.35-66
Wilson — *Early* p.52-88
- *Cycles*
Morris — *Ency.* p.508
- *Ethics*
Bridenbaugh — *Revolt* p.89
- *Leaders, Northern*
Adams — *Provincial* p.235-236
- *Literature*
Bridenbaugh — *Revolt* p.52, 89
- *Services*
Bridenbaugh — *Revolt* p.286

BUSINESS DEPRESSIONS
Forbes — *Paul* p.94-95
Morris — *Ency.* p.508
Wright — *New* p.41

BUSKS
Earle — *Home* p.320
Glubok — *Home* p.127, 217

BUTCHERING
Wright — *Frontier* p.67-68

BUTTER
Belote — *Compleat* p.12-13
Earle — *Home* p.149
Gould — *Early* p.37-38, 104-105, 143-144

BUTTONS
Dreppard — *Pioneer* p.293-294, 297
Tunis — *Living* p.141

"BUY AMERICAN" CAMPAIGN
Miller — *Origins* p.271-272

BYRD, ELIZABETH HILL CARTER
Spruill — *Women's* p.170-171

BYRD, WILLIAM, II
Burner — *America* p.46-52
Speare — *Life* p.17-18
Wright — *Cultural. See* index p.277
- *"History of the dividing line"*
Miller — *Colonial* p.310-349
- *"Marriage"*
Miller — *Colonial* p.141-153
- *on Indian trade*
Wright — *Frontier* p.25-26
- *on life in North Carolina (1728)*
Wright — *Frontier* p.41-45
- *on life in South*
Morris — *Voices* p.61-65

- on women
Benson — *Women* p.25n, 284-286, 289
- "Riding through Virginia"
Miller — *Colonial* p.159-166

C

CABINET
- Origins
Morris — *Ency.* p.124

CABINETMAKERS
See also **Furniture**
Adams — *Provincial* p.143
Dolan — *Yankee* p.123-125
Speare — *Life* p.124-125
Tunis — *Colonial* p.88-92
Wertenbaker — *Golden* p.76-77, 102, 118-119, 133-134, 157
Wright — *Cultural* p.204-206
- Williamsburg, Va.
Wertenbaker — *Golden* p.118-119

CAGES (punishment)
Earle — *Home* p.385

CAKES AND DESSERTS
Belote — *Compleat* p.101-111
Gould — *Early* p.74
- Tarts
Gould — *Early* p.94

CALASHES (carriages)
Train — *Story* p.167

CALASHES (hoods)
Earle — *Home* p.289
Train — *Story* p.162

CALDWELL, HANNAH
Ellet — *Eminent* p.349-358

CALDWELL, RACHEL
Ellet — *Eminent* p.387-395

CALIFORNIA
- "Golden Gate" discovery
Collins — *Story* p.85

CALLENDER, HANNAH
Benson — *Women 18th* p.265, 268n, 294-295

CALLENDER, JAMES THOMSON
Brodie — *Jefferson* p.416-424

CALVINISM
Hofstadter — *Amer.* p.187, 212, 226-227, 236-237, 242-243, 252, 256
Sweet — *Religion* p.190-192

CAMBRIDGE, MASSACHUSETTS
Handlin — *This* p.71-73, 76
McDowell — *Rev.* .p.37, 52-54
Stember — *North* p.113, 297, 303-305
Wheeler — *Voices* p.36, 71, 74, 80-82, 85, 118-120, 120a

CAMDEN, SOUTH CAROLINA
Stember — *South* p.39, 42, 71, 74, 79-89, 84, 86-91

CAMP MEETINGS
Dolan — *Yankee* p.220-222

CAMPBELL, JANE
Ellet — *Eminent* p.408-417

CANADA AND CANADIANS
See also names of cities, etc.
Miller — *Origins* p.70, 72, 141, 375, 456-459, 482
200 Years p.48-64, 121-122, 129
- American invasion
Amer. Her. — *Rev.* p.122-126, 129-131, 142, 203
Collins — *Story* p.107
Stember — *North* p.4, 20, 25-27, 29-47
, British in
Amer. Her. — *Rev.* p.234-254
Wheeler — *Voices* p.44-47
, Campaign in
Morison — *Oxford (1)* p.216-220, 282-283, 286-288, 324-327, 349-350
Wheeler — *Voices* p.85-108
- French
Alden — *Pioneer* p.31, 44-46, 64-66, 68, 77, 85
, Patriot invasion of
Alden — *Pioneer* p.84-85
- Views of Crèvecoeur
Crèvecoeur — *Sketches* p.172, 174-175

CANALS
Greene — *Revol.* p.342-344
Morris — *Ency.* p.420
Tunis — *Young* p.143

CANDLES AND CANDLEMAKING
See also **Bayberry**
Bridenbaugh — *Revolt* p.73-74, 264, 270-271
Dow — *Every* p.96-97
Earle — *Colonial* p.303-308
Earle — *Customs* p.125-127
Earle — *Home* p.39-40
Glubok — *Home* p.17-22
Gould — *Early* p.121-124, 143
Scott — *Settlers* p.172-181
Speare — *Life* p.76
Tunis — *Living* p.134-135

CANDLEWOOD
Glubok — *Home* p.16-17

CANNON. ***See*** **Guns**

CANOES
Glubok — *Home* p.331-332
- Swedish use
Earle — *Home* p.326-327

CANTEENS
, Horn
Earle — *Home* p.321

CAPITAL. ***See*** **Finance**

CAPITOLS
- Classical architecture
Gowan — *Images* p.116-119
- Social centers, Southern
Spruill — *Women's* p.90-93, 95-101
- Washington, D.C.
Landmarks Liberty p.12-13

CAPRON, HENRI
Howard — *Our* p.103-104

CAPSTANS
Rublowsky — *Music* p.76

CARD PLAYING
Cable — *American* p.66-67
Earle — *Customs* p.239-240
Speare — *Life* p.157
- South
Spruill — *Women's* p.92-94, 98, 105, 108

CAREY, MATHEW
Tunis — *Young* p.56

CARLETON, SIR GUY
Stember — *North* p.4, 22, 26, 29-30, 32, 38-41, 45, 47, 50, 52, 60, 176
Wheeler — *Voices* p.85, 95, 97-98, 103, 107-108, 131-141, 177-178, 181-184, 240

CARLISLE COMMISSION
Morris — *American* p.272-274

CAROLINAS
See also **North Carolina; South Carolina**
Axtell — *18th* p.13-19
Miller — *Origins* p.14, 53, 56
- Commerce
Axtell — *18th* p.15
- Crops and plants
Axtell — *18th* p.15, 19
- Frontier
Morris — *Ency.* p.63-64
- Government
Axtell — *18th* p.16
- Men and women
Axtell — *18th* p.18-19
- Population
Axtell — *18th* p.15
- Trees
Axtell — *18th* p.17

CARPENTERS
Main — *Social* p.29, 77, 79, 81, 275

CARPENTERS' COMPANY (carpentry)
Train — *Story* p.183

CARPETS
Earle — *Customs* p.120-121

CARR, BENJAMIN
Howard — *Our* p.96-101

CARRIAGE MAKERS
Wilson — *Early* p.137-138

CARRIAGES
See also **Coaches;** types of carriages
Dolan — *Yankee* p.58-60; 82-83
Earle — *Customs* p.192-193
Earle — *Home* p.353-354
Tunis — *Living* p.120
- South
Spruill — *Women's* p.89-90

CARROLL, CHARLES
Bakeless — *Signers* p.233-240
Greene — *Revol. See* index p.460
Malone — *Story* p.190-193
- Biography
Lossing — *Biog.* p.157-161

CARTER, ROBERT ("King")
Adams — *Provincial* p.83
Glubok — *Home* p.279-280
Train — *Story* p.215-216
Wright — *Cultural* p.11-15, 76, 111-112

CARTERS AND DRAYMEN
Bridenbaugh — *Wild.* p.197-198, 256, 316, 354

CARTOONS AND CARICATURES
Dannett — *Yankee* p.17-71
Malone — *Story* p.5, 17, 31-32, 36-37, 39
Tunis — *Young* p.11

CARVING TERMS
Belote — *Compleat* p.163
Glubok — *Home* p.54-55

CASTINE, MAINE
Stember — *North* p.257-264

CASTLE WILLIAM AND MARY, NEW HAMPSHIRE
- Raid
Stember — *North* p.278-279

CATECHISMS
Glubok — *Home* p.145, 309

CATHOLICISM
See also **Roman Catholic Episcopate**
Bridenbaugh — *Revolt* p.155-156
Greene — *Revol. See* index p.480
Life — *New* p.68, 123
Miller — *Origins* p.48, 190-191, 264, 373-374, 457
Sweet — *Religion* p.45-50, 75-80
Sweet — *Story* p.184-185, 202-203, 222
- New England
Forbes — *Paul* p.5, 327, 397, 424
- Philadelphia
Axtell — *18th* p.180

CATS (trivets)
Gould — *Early* p.77

CAT'S CRADLE
Glubok — *Home* p.185-186

CATTLE
See also **Cowherds**
Belote — *Compleat* p.10-11
Crèvecoeur — *Sketches. See* index p.334
- Calf keepers
Earle — *Home* p.400
- Earmarks
Earle — *Home* p.400

CAUDLE (drink)
Gould — *Early* p.106

CELLARS
Earle — *Home* p.10
Gould — *Early* p.21-22

CEMETERIES
See also **Tombstones**
- Connecticut
Dolan — *Yankee* p.39
- Norfolk, Va.
Handlin — *This* p.91

CEREAL FARMING
See also **Corn; Rice;** etc.
Life — *New* p.101, 115-116

CHAIRS
Train — *Story* p.232-233
- *Chippendale*
Gowans — *Images* p.155, 180
- *Queen Anne*
Gowans — *Images* p.179
- *Rocking*
Train — *Story* p.187-188
- *Windsor*
Tunis — *Living* p.131

CHAMBERS OF COMMERCE
Bridenbaugh — *Revolt* p.287-288
, *First*
Adams — *Album* p.303

CHAMPLAIN, LAKE
Morris — *Voices* p.90-93, 105, 118
Stember — *North. See* index p.377
Wheeler — *Voices. See* index p.476

CHANDLERS
Tunis — *Colonial* p.37-38, 116-119

CHANTERS AND CHANTEYS
Rublowsky — *Music* p.73-75

CHAPERONAGE
See also **"Dragons"**
Earle — *Colonial* p.200-201

CHARCOAL
Gould — *Early* p.139-140
Tunis — *Living* p.113-114

CHARITIES
See also **Almshouses; Friendly societies; Granaries; Missions and missionaries; Poor relief,** etc.
Bridenbaugh — *Revolt* p.102-103, 122-128, 132, 218, 235, 305, 320, 322-325
Bridenbaugh — *Wild.* p.393-396
Sweet — *Story* p.168-171
- *Associations*
Greene — *Revol.* p.321-322

CHARLESTON, SOUTH CAROLINA
See also special subjects
Axtell — *18th* p.83-88
Greene — *Revol. See* index p.461
Life — *Making* p.13, 81-82, 94-95, 103, 136
Life — *New* p.71, 123, 126, 128, 160
Main — *Social.* See index p.308
Miller — *Origins* p.54, 131, 134, 349-351, 416
National — *History.* p.158-165
Stember — *South. See* index p.210
Wertenbaker — *Golden. See* index p.161
Wheeler — *Voices. See* index p.474
- *Aristocracy*
Wertenbaker — *Golden* p.129-130
- *Culture*
Wertenbaker — *Golden* p.128-130, 136-137, 149-150
- *Defense*
Scott — *Trumpet* p.104-114
- *Expedition*
200 Years p.73-75
- *Fall*
Morison — *Oxford (1)* p.338-339
- *Foreign trade*
Wertenbaker — *Golden* p.128-129
- *Merchants*
Wertenbaker — *Golden* p.128-129
- *Museum*
Wertenbaker — *Golden* p.145-146
- *Negroes*
Main — *Social* p.69, 126
- *Planters*
Wright — *Cultural* p.16-19
, *Revolutionary*
Amer. Her. — *Rev. See* index p.381
- *Siege*
200 Years p.139, 157
- *Society*
Main — *Social* p.59-60, 63-64

- *Standard of living*
Main — *Social* p.118, 121

CHARLESTON LIBRARY SOCIETY
Wright — *Cultural* p.149-150

CHARLESTOWN, MASSACHUSETTS
Bridenbaugh — *Revolt* p.9-11, 218-219
Wheeler — *Voices* p.54-55, 57, 60-63, 67, 71-73, 79, 122, 127

CHARTER OF FREE PEOPLE
See also **Declaration of Independence**
Malone — *Story* p.67-92

CHASE, SAMUEL
Bakeless — *Signers* p.244-247
Butterfield — *Amer.* p.28
Life — *Growing* p.36
Malone — *Story* p.196-198
Miller — *Origins. See* index p.508-509
- *Biography*
Lossing — *Biog.* p.146-150

CHEESE AND CHEESE MAKING
Gould — *Early* p.128-131
- *Presses*
Gould — *Early* p.37

CHEMISTRY
Greene — *Revol.* p.142, 385-386
Morris — *Ency.* p.530

CHEROKEE INDIANS
Greene — *Revol.* p.169, 172, 399
Morison — *Oxford (1)* p.236, 265, 336, 361, 374

CHERRY VALLEY, NEW YORK
- *Massacre*
Evans — *Weather.* p.271-282
Morris — *Ency.* p.100, 417
Stember — *North* p.72-83
Wheeler — *Voices* p.321-322

CHESAPEAKE BAY
Scott — *Trumpet* p.29, 207, 263-266
Wheeler — *Voices* p.248, 436-437, 441-443, 446
- *Provinces*
Greene — *Revol. See* index p.461
- *Wild fowl*
Glubok — *Home* p.69-70

CHILDBEARING
See also **Babies**
Evans — *Weather.* p.20-22

CHILDREN AND CHILDHOOD
See also **Babies; Boys; Girls;** special subjects, e.g. **Children's books and reading**
Adams — *Album* p.335-338
Adams — *Provincial* p.92-93
Glubok — *Home* p.104-113, 349
Miller — *First* p.209-212, 219-220
- *Clothing and dress*
Earle — *Child* p.44-61
Speare — *Life* p.104-105
- *Courtesy*
Earle — *Child* p.219-226
- *Diligence*
Earle — *Child* p.305-320
- *Discipline*
Earle — *Child* p.195-208
Glubok — *Home* p.135-137
Holliday — *Woman's* p.128-129
, *Dutch*
Speare — *Life* p.60
- *Education*
Glubok — *Home* p.350
Greene — *Revol.* p.118-122
- *Etiquette*
Earle — *Child* p.219-226
Earle — *Home* p.102-103
- *Games*
Earle — *Child* p.343-351, 358, 360
Glubok — *Home* p.187
Tunis — *Frontier* p.34-35
- *Guardianship*
Benson — *Women 18th* p.239-240
- *Labor*
Wilson — *Early* p.98-102
- *Life*
Earle — *Customs* p.17, 19-31
Speare — *Life* p.100-102, 113

CHILDREN AND CHILDHOOD (*cont.*)
- *Precocity*
  Earle — *Child* p.179-186
- *Punishment*
  See also types of punishment
  Earle — *Customs* p.33-35
- *Religion*
  Earle — *Child* p.246
- *South*
  Spruill — *Women. See* index p.401
- *Virginia*
  Speare — *Life* p.19-20

CHILDREN'S BOOKS AND READING
Adams — *Album* p.337-338
Earle — *Child* p.265-303
Earle — *Customs* p.26-28
Glubok — *Home* p.170-183
Greene — *Revol.* p.392-393
Nye — *Unembar.* p.60

CHILDREN'S TOYS. *See* Toys

CHIMNEYS
Gould — *Early* p.40-41, 44-46
, Catted
  Glubok — *Home* p.8, 27-28
- *Cleaning*
  Bridenbaugh — *Wild.* p.207-208, 365-366
  Wilson — *Early* p.27

CHINA
- *Trade*
  Greene — *Revol.* p.350-351, 416
  Tunis — *Young* p.90-91
  Wright — *New* p.162-164

CHINAWARE AND PORCELAIN
See also **Pottery and potters**
Adams — *Album* p.320
Earle — *Home* p.100-101
Tunis — *Living* p.135-136
- *Sale*
  Dexter — *Colonial* p.26-28

CHITTENDEN, THOMAS
Stearns — *Story* p.102

CHOCTAW INDIANS
Morison — *Oxford (1)* p.192, 237, 374

CHOPPING BEES
Earle — *Home* p.403-404

CHRIST CHURCH (Philadelphia)
Adams — *Album* p.396
Burt — *Phila.* p.174-175

CHRISTMAS
Bridenbaugh — *Wild.* p.296
Gould — *Early* p.142
Holiday — *Woman's* p.204-205
Speare — *Life* p.159-160
Tunis — *Young* p.120-121
- *Dinner menu*
  Belote — *Compleat* p.162
- *Revolutionary*
  McDowell — *Rev.* p.102, 195
  Tunis — *Tavern* p.89-97
- *Yule log*
  Gould — *Early* p.65

CHRONOLOGY (dates)
See also **1700's**
Bakeless — *Signers* p.xi-xiv
Life — *Growing* p.168
Life — *Making* p.152-153
Life — *New* p.169
Morris — *Ency.* p.57-130, 409-614
Schemmer — *Almanac* p.1-33, 185-215
Sirkis — *Reflect.* p.23-24

CHURCH, BENJAMIN
Forbes — *Paul. See* index p.489

CHURCH AND STATE
Carman — *History* p.222-223
Morris — *Ency.* p.550
Sweet — *Story* p.189-193

CHURCH OF ENGLAND. *See* Anglicans

CHURCHES
See also **Meetinghouses; Religion;** names of churches, denominations
Greene — *Revol. See* index p.461
Hofstadter — *Amer.* p.180-216

Sloane — *Spirits* p.42-43
Tunis — *Living* p.153-154
Tunis — *Young* p.31-32
Wright — *New* p.204-209
- *Architecture*
  Morris — *Ency.* p.599
  Ross — *Taste* p.24-25
  Wright — *Cultural* p.202
- *Boston*
  Bridenbaugh — *Revolt* p.21
- *Charleston*
  Wertenbaker — *Golden* p.132-133
- *Choirs*
  Train — *Story* p.175
, *Dutch*
  Glubok — *Home* p.295-296
- *Exteriors*
  Gowans — *Images* p.190-192
, *German*
  Sweet — *Religion* p.36-39
- *Interiors*
  Gowans — *Images* p.193-196
- *Nationalization*
  Sweet — *Story* p.189-204
- *New York*
  Bridenbaugh — *Revolt* p.230
- *Non-English speaking*
  Sweet — *Religion* p.80-81
- *Pews*
  Glubok — *Home* p.288-289, 294
- *Philadelphia*
  Axtell — *18th* p.177-181
  Bridenbaugh — *Revolt* p.135-229
, *Post-Revolutionary*
  Carman — *History* p.222-224
, *Revolutionary*
  Morris — *Ency.* p.550
- *South*
  Glubok — *Home* p.293-294
  Tunis — *Living* p.153-154
, *Women in*
  Benson — *Women 18th* p.14, 64-65, 67, 119-122, 258-273

CHURNS
Gould — *Early* p.104-105

CIDER AND CIDER MAKING
Crèvecoeur — *Sketches* p.46, 49, 72, 102, 104-105, 134, 145, 149
Earle — *Customs* p.172-173
Earle — *Home* p.148-149, 161-163
Glubok — *Home* p.90-91
Gould — *Early* p.135-136
- *Massachusetts*
  Dow — *Every* p.95-96, 108
- *Tax, English*
  Morris — *American* p.56-58

CIRCUIT RIDERS
Speare — *Life* p.148-149
Sweet — *Religion* p.115-117
Wright — *Frontier* p.73

CIRCULAR LETTERS
Beach — *Samuel* p.140-142, 144
- *Massachusetts*
  Miller — *Origins* p.226, 257, 262
- *Virginia*
  Miller — *Origins* p.259-260

CIRCULATING LIBRARIES. ***See*** **Libraries — Circulating**

CITIES
See also **Towns;** names of cities
Bridenbaugh — *Revolt* p.3-4, 210-215
Bridenbaugh — *Wild.* p.303-329
Colbourn — *Colonial* p.118-127
Greene — *Revol.* p.10-11, 68
Langdon — *Every.* p.333-334
- *Civic consciousness*
  Bridenbaugh — *Wild.* p.298-300
- *Civilization*
  Adams — *Album* p.258
- *Congestion and confusion*
  Bridenbaugh — *Revolt* p.14, 24, 35, 243-244
- *Culture*
  Bridenbaugh — *Revolt* p.192, 215, 409
  Main — *Social* p.240
- *Economic role*
  Bridenbaugh — *Revolt* p.43-49, 260, 262, 419-420
- *Frontiers*
  Bartlett — *New* p.401-405
- *Independence*
  Bridenbaugh — *Revolt* p.425

CITIES (*continued*)
- *Life*
  Axtell — *18th* p.83-149
  Greene — *Revol.* p.2, 11, 78-79, 95-98, 161-162, 190-193, 412
  Miller — *First* p.122-134
  Speare — *Life* p.49-51
  Tunis — *Young* p.49-57
- *Mayor and common council*
  Bridenbaugh — *Wild.* p.145, 304
- *Mobility*
  Main — *Social* p.185-196, 282
- *Revolt*
  Bridenbaugh — *Revolt* p.114, 352, 392, 418-420, 425; *See also* index
- *Rural conflict*
  Bridenbaugh — *Revolt* p.7-8, 11-12, 149-150, 212, 219, 221
- *Society*
  Bridenbaugh — *Wild.* p.364-466
  Main — *Social* p.34-41, 44, 63-64, 278-279

CIVIL DISOBEDIENCE (1750)
Morris — *American* p.50-56

CIVIL RIGHTS
See also **Bill of Rights; *Rights of Man***
Life — *Making* p.37, 40, 105, 109, 137
Morison — *Oxford (1). See* index p.411

CLAMS
Handlin — *This* p.28

CLARK, ABRAHAM
Bakeless — *Signers* p.175-177
Malone — *Story* p.154-155
- *Biography*
  Lossing — *Biog.* p.90-92

CLARK, GEORGE ROGERS
Amer. Reader p.112-117
Collins — *Story* p.122
Davis — *Heroes* p.89-100
McDowell — *Rev.* p.138, 142-143, 145
200 Years p.128, 135, 295

CLARK, JONAS
Morris — *Voices* p.82-88

CLASSES
See also **Aristocracy; Lower class; Middle class; Servants; Society**
Bridenbaugh — *Wild.* p.96-100, 251, 256-257
Hofstadter — *Amer.* p.132-134, 136-137, 143-144, 158-159, 161-167
Main — *Social* p.5, 197, 215-219, 221-269
Sanderlin — *1776* p.xx-xxvi
, *Economic*
  Main — *Social* p.3, 5, 7-8, 43-67, 214, 224-236
- *Friction*
  Bridenbaugh — *Wild.* p.414-416
- *North*
  Main — *Social* p.7-43
- *Prestige*
  Social — *Main. See* index p.323
- *Revolutionary War*
  Main — *Social* p.197-220
- *Structure*
  Bridenbaugh — *Revolt* p.76, 136-138, 222, 282-286, 306, 313-314, 332, 351, 379, 398, 420-421
  Main — *Social* p.44-67
  Scott — *Trumpet* p.6, 8-9, 17-18, 117, 281-282

CLERGYMEN
Adams — *Provincial* p.62-63
Benson — *Women 18th* p.104-105, 110, 125, 250
Bridenbaugh — *Wild.* p.252, 289-290, 419-420
Greene — *Revol. See* index p.473
Morris — *American* p.5-9
Smith — *Colonial* p.348-364
Social — *Main. See* index p.319
Wilson — *Early* p.103-104
, *Itinerate*
  Dolan — *Yankee* p.214-223

- *Training*
Cable — *American* p.47
Sweet — *Religion* p.173-178
- *Views on women*
Benson — *Women 18th* p.104-105, 110, 125, 250
, *Wives of*
Smith — *Colonial* p.210-218

CLIFFORD, ANNA RAWLE
Evans — *Weather.* p.283-302

CLINTON, DE WITT
- *Biography*
Morris — *Ency.* p.644-645

CLINTON, SIR HENRY
Amer. Her. — *Rev. See* index p.381
Burt — *Phila.* p.289, 293
Life — *Making* p.9-10, 13-14, 17, 58, 60, 76, 81-82, 85-86
McDowell — *Rev. See* index p.197
Scott — *Trumpet. See* index p.302
Stember — *Middle* p.10, 52-53, 57, 61-65, 68-70, 72, 75, 137
Stember — *North* p.115-131; *See also* index p.378
Stember — *South. See* index p.210
200 Years p.73, 128-130, 133, 137, 139-140, 143-146, 152, 157-158
Wheeler — *Voices. See* index p.474
, *"Dumbbell code" of*
Treasury Amer. p.123

CLIPPERMEN
Wilson — *Early* p.77-78

"CLIVEDEN"
Burt — *Phila.* p.256-257

CLOCK-JACK
Earle — *Home* p.65

CLOCKS AND CLOCKMAKERS
Adams — *Album* p.306
Dolan — *Yankee* p.157-162
Earle — *Customs* p.123-124
Ross — *Taste* p.118
Speare — *Life* p.125
Train — *Story* p.159-160, 246, 255-256
Tunis — *Colonial* p.143-147
Tunis — *Living* p.119
Tunis — *Young* p.66

CLOSEN, BARON LUDWIG VON
Scott — *Trumpet* p.257, 259-260, 262, 265-266, 277

CLOTH. ***See* Fabrics**

CLOTHESPINS
Gould — *Early. See* index p.116-117

CLOTHING AND DRESS
See also **Accessories; Children and childhood;** names of articles
Adams — *Album* p.267
Adams — *Provincial* p.73-74, 89
Earle — *Customs* p.321-330
Earle — *Home* p.286-296
Glubok — *Home* p.270-283
Greene — *Revol.* p.177, 251-252, 326, 275-276, 358
Holliday — *Woman's* p.155-158, 159-171
Tunis — *Frontier* p.28-30
Tunis — *Living* p.103
Tunis — *Young* p.26-27
- *Baltimore*
Earle — *Home* p.293
- *Boston*
Dow — *Every* p.65-66, 68-70
- *Boys*
Train — *Story* p.164
Tunis — *Young* p.102-103
- *Children*
Speare — *Life* p.104-105
- *Cost*
Main — *Social* p.116-117, 119-120, 123-124, 132, 140, 151
, *Dutch*
Speare — *Life* p.59-60
- *Frontier*
Langdon — *Every.* p.119-121
- *Girls*
Earle — *Home* p.289-292
Tunis — *Young* p.104-105
- *Men*
Train — *Story* p.192
Tunis — *Living* p.140-144
Tunis — *Young* p.55, 99-102

CLOTHING AND DRESS (*continued*)
- *Middle Colonies*
  Train — *Story* p.190-194
- *Muffs*
  Earle — *Home* p.298, 386
- *New England*
  Train — *Story* p.160-164
- *Philadelphia*
  Tunis — *Young* p.54-55
- *Republic*
  Train — *Story* p.235-238
- *Richness of*
  Earle — *Home* p.292-294
- *South*
  Spruill — *Women's* p.116-125
  Train — *Story* p.211-213
- *Women*
  Benson — *Women 18th* p.296, 298-302
  Greene — *Revol.* p.13, 177, 326
  Holliday — *Woman's* p.155-171
  Miller — *First* p.119-120
  Speare — *Life* p.16, 59-60
  Train — *Story* p.192-194, 237-238
  Tunis — *Living* p.144-147
  Tunis — *Young* p.103
- *Women, Southern*
  Spruill — *Women's* p.133-134

CLUBS AND SOCIETIES
See also **Associations;** names of clubs and societies; special subjects
Adams — *Provincial* p.260-264
Bridenbaugh — *Revolt* p.162-163, 294, 363-364
Bridenbaugh — *Wild.* p.275, 436-437, 440-441
Cable — *American* p.48, 72-73
Ross — *Taste* p.47

CLYMER, GEORGE
Bakeless — *Signers* p.143-145
Malone — *Story* p.175-176
- *Biography*
  Lossing — *Biog.* p.114-118

COACHES
See also **Carriages**
Bridenbaugh — *Revolt* p.146, 340-342, 371
Speare — *Life* p.138
Wright — *Cultural* p.249
- *Coachmen*
  Wilson — *Early* p.133-137
- *New York*
  Earle — *Home* p.354-355

COAL
Bridenbaugh — *Revolt* p.26, 233-235
Speare — *Life* p.124
Tunis — *Young* p.71

COAST GUARD
- *Commandants (1790-1799)*
  Schemmer — *Almanac* p.234

COAT ROLL
Earle — *Home* p.248

COATS OF ARMS
, Making of
  Earle — *Child* p.322-325

COCKFIGHTING
Dulles — *History* p.33, 35
Life — *Growing* p.11
Speare — *Life* p.162
200 Years p.306
Wright — *Culture* p.189

CODFISH
Speare — *Life* p.116-117

COERCIVE ACTS. *See* **Intolerable Acts**

COFFEE
Belote — *Compleat* p.128-129
Earle — *Home* p.165
Gould — *Early* p.107
- *Scarcity*
  Earle — *Colonial* p.249-251
- *Substitutes*
  Earle — *Home* p.159

COFFEEHOUSES
Bridenbaugh — *Revolt* p.161-162
Bridenbaugh — *Wild.* p.266-269, 426, 430, 432

Tunis — *Tavern* p.57-58
Wright — *Cultural* p.248
, *First*
Dexter — *Colonial* p.12-15
- *Owners*
Wilson — *Early* p.58-59
- *Philadelphia*
Tunis — *Young* p.53

COINS. *See* **Currency; Money**

COLDEN, CADWALLADER
Bridenbaugh — *Wild.* p.186, 189-190, 245-247, 404-405, 461, 465-466
Greene — *Revol.* p.8, 49, 56, 79, 86, 132, 144, 149

COLDEN, JANE
Benson — *Women 18th* p.306-308
Earle — *Colonial* p.86-87

COLLEGE OF NEW JERSEY
See also **Princeton University**
Hofstadter — *Amer.* p.235, 242, 267, 285-287
Sweet — *Story* p.145

COLLEGE OF PHILADELPHIA
See also **University of Pennsylvania**
Greene — *Revol. See* index p.461-462
Hofstadter — *Amer.* p.286

COLLEGE OF RHODE ISLAND
Hofstadter — *Amer.* 285-286

COLLEGES AND UNIVERSITIES
See also **Libraries—College; Medical schools;** names of colleges and universities
Adams — *Album* p.286, 296
Alden — *Pioneer* p.50, 52-53, 58, 108
Bridenbaugh — *Revolt* p.177-178, 378-380
Carman — *History* p.101-104, 226
Greene — *Revol. See* index p.462
Langdon — *Every.* p.316, 318-319
Morison — *Oxford (1)* p.378-380
Morris — *Ency.* p.555
Speare — *Life* p.109-110
Tunis — *Young* p.130-132
- *Commencements*
Dulles — *History* p.31
, *Founding of*
Colbourn — *Colonial* p.93-102
Sweet — *Religion* p.166-167

COLONIES AND COLONISTS
See also **Middle Colonies; New England; North; Northeast; South;** names of colonies; special subjects
Kraus — *U.S. (1)* p.99-269
Miller — *Origins. See* index p.509
Tunis — *Living* p.104-156
- *Administration*
Carman — *History* p.121-144
- *Ancestry*
Alden — *Pioneer* p.59-60
- *Assemblies*
Alden — *Pioneer* p.43-44
Kraus — *U.S. (1)* p.124-126
Life — *New* p.144-145, 154
- *Character*
Axtell — *18th* p.13-81
- *Conflict of interest*
Carman — *History* p.145-193
- *Differences*
Carman — *History* p.145-150
- *Divisions among*
Alden — *Pioneer* p.47-48
- *Economy*
Earle — *Home* p.42, 185
- *Expansion and business*
Morison — *Oxford (1)* p.196-200
- *Exports*
Carman — *History* p.80-81
, *Fusing among*
Alden — *Pioneer* p.60-61
- *Growth and development*
- *1700*
Morison — *Oxford (1)* p.185 187
- *1713-1750*
Morison — *Oxford (1)* p.196 212
- *1763*
Morison — *Oxford (1)* p.234-243

COLONIES AND COLONISTS (*cont.*)
- *- Hardships*
  - Alden — *Pioneer* p.33-36
- *, Imperial system in*
  - Morison — *Oxford (1)* p.243-248
- *- Intercolonial relations*
  - Wertenbaker — *Golden* p.59-61, 73-74
- *- Life*
  - *See also* **Society;** special subjects
  - Belote — *Compleat* p.21-36
  - Main — *Social* p.115-163
  - Morison — *Oxford (1)* p.202-208
  - National — *History.* p.292-303
- *- Protest*
  - Carman — *History* p.164-166
  - Scott — *Trumpet* p.13, 53-55
- *- War debts*
  - Adams — *Provincial* p.318-319

COLUMBIA UNIVERSITY
- *See also* **King's College**
- Greene — *Revol.* p.379

COMBING MACHINES
- Earle — *Home* p.230

COMBS
- Dolan — *Yankee* p.169

COMMENCEMENT
- Earle — *Customs* p.223

COMMERCE
- *See also* **Industry; Retail trade; Ships and shipping; Trade and traders;** names of cities; etc.
- Bridenbaugh — *Revolt* p.43-49, 255-260
- Bridenbaugh — *Wild. See* index p.489
- Morris — *Ency.* p.484-488
- Tunis — *Young* p.85-86
- *200 Years* p.11, 16-17, 29, 179
- *, British restrictions*
  - Bridenbaugh — *Revolt* p.66-67, 251
- *, Illegal*
  - Bridenbaugh — *Revolt* p.47, 64-68, 258-260
- *, Intercolonial*
  - Bridenbaugh — *Revolt* p.44-45, 47-50, 53, 257-258
  - Kraus — *U.S. (1)* p.112-114
- *, Internal*
  - Morris — *Ency.* p.488
- *- Revival*
  - Morison — *Oxford (1)* p.368-372
- *- Rivalries*
  - Bridenbaugh — *Wild.* p.330-363

COMMITTEES OF CORRESPONDENCE
- Greene — *Revol.* p.198-199, 207
- Life — *New* p.154, 156, 159
- Miller — *Origins. See* index p.509
- Morris — *American* p.119-122
- Morris — *Ency.* p.80-81
- Sanderlin — *1776* p.71-73, 250
- *200 Years* p.26, 29, 50
- *, and Samuel Adams*
  - Ingraham — *Album* p.25

COMMON SENSE.* See Paine, Thomas, and *Common Sense

COMMUNICATION
- *See also* **Postal service; Transportation; Travel and travelers;** types of communication
- Cable — *American* p.39-40
- Greene — *Revol.* p.37, 208, 232, 341-342, 407-408, 436-437

COMMUNITARIANISM
- Sweet — *Religion* p.192-300

COMMUNITY LIFE. *See* name of locality, subdivision **Life; Cities—Life; Colonies and colonists—Life; Country life**

COMPOSERS
- *, Foreign in America*
  - Morris — *Ency.* p.614

CONCERTS
- Bridenbaugh — *Revolt* p.195, 360, 401-403
- Howard — *Our* p.22-23
- Morris — *Ency.* p.612
- Speare — *Life* p.164-165

Wright — *Cultural* p.193
- *Boston*
Dulles — *History* p.49-50
- *Halls, and outdoor*
Morris — *Ency.* p.612
- *New York*
Dulles — *History* p.53
Howard — *Our* p.31-34

CONCORD, MASSACHUSETTS
, Battle of
Adams — *Album* p.368-369
Amer. Her. — *Rev.* p.99, 101-105, 113-115
Collins— *Story* p.103
Ingraham — *Album* p.34-36
Kraus — *U.S. (1)* p.213-215
McDowell — *Rev.* p.41-45, 48-49
Miller — *Origins* p.219, 407-411, 415, 420, 428, 462
Morison — *Oxford (1)* p.285-286, 288, 302
Morris — *Ency.* p.85-86
Morris — *Voices* p.88-90
National — *History.* p.189-193
Sanderlin — *1776* p.145-147, 150, 154-161, 251
Stearns — *Story* p.84-85
Stember — *North* p.289, 297, 303, 305, 310-319
200 Years p.36-41
- *Hymn*
Davie — *Profile* p.55

CONCORD COACHES
Earle — *Home* p.352-353

CONESTOGA MASSACRE
Burt — *Phila.* p.176

CONESTOGA WAGONS
Adams — *Album* p.340
Bartlett — *New* p.291-293
Dolan — *Yankee* p.63-65
Earle — *Home* p.339-344
Glubok — *Home* p.338-340
Morris — *Ency.* p.535
Speare — *Life* p.140-141
Train — *Story* p.197-198
Tunis — *Living* p.119
Tunis — *Tavern* p.49-51
Wright — *Cultural* p.250

CONFEDERATION
Carman — *History* p.228-268
Life — *Making. See* index p.156

CONFIDENCE MEN
Bridenbaugh — *Wild.* p.381-382

CONGREGATIONALISTS
Alden — *Pioneer* p.43, 54-57, 66, 105-106, 166
Bridenbaugh — *Revolt* p.151-152, 355-357
Bridenbaugh — *Wild.* p.258-259, 264-265
Greene — *Revol. See* index p.462
Hofstadter — *Amer. See* index p.iv
Life — *New* p.122, 124-125
Main — *Social* p.187n; 193
Miller — *Origins* p.187, 189, 192-194
Morison — *Oxford (1)* p.208-212, 241-242, 380-388
Sweet — *Religion* p.3-13, 54-56, 198-199
Sweet — *Story* p.176-178; 203-204, 210-212, 214, 221

CONGRESS
See also House of Representatives; Senate
Greene — *Revol. See* index p.462
Morris — *Ency.* p.121

CONJURERS
Wilson — *Early* p.122-124

CONNECTICUT
See also names of cities
Glubok — *Home. See* index p.350
Hofstadter — *Amer.* p.145, 147, 149-150, 205, 208-212, 214, 226, 262-263, 284
Life — *New* p.100-101
Main — *Social. See* index p.309
Morison — *Oxford (1)* p.186, 189, 236, 385-388
Morris — *Voices* p.59-61, 134-136
Scott — *Trumpet* p.34, 87, 121, 150, 195, 242, 250-251, 262
Stember — *North* p.25, 212, 252, 321, 343-371

CONNECTICUT (*continued*)
, and Declaration of Independence
Bakeless — *Signers* p.193-209
Malone — *Story* p.125-134
- Eighth regiment
Scott — *Trumpet* p.215-216, 222
- View of French traveler
Handlin — *This* p.79-81

"CONNECTICUT WITS"
Morris — *Ency.* p.564-565

CONSCIENTIOUS OBJECTORS
See also **Mennonites; Moravians; Quakers;** etc.
Sweet — *Story* p.185-188

CONSERVATIVES
Alden — *Pioneer* p.101-102, 111-114, 122, 125
Miller — *Origins. See* index p.509
, versus radicals
Kraus — *U.S. (1)* p.198-200

CONSTABLES AND SHERIFFS
Bridenbaugh — *Revolt* p.107-109, 114, 120, 297
Bridenbaugh — *Wild.* p.215-216, 374-375

***CONSTITUTION.* See Old Ironsides**

CONSTITUTION — UNITED STATES
Alden — *Pioneer* p.97-100, 104
Angle — *By* p.100-115
Baldwin — *Ideas* p.190-205
Butterfield — *Amer.* p.11-13
Greene — *Revol. See* index p.465
Kraus — *U.S. (1)* p.257-259
Life — *Making. See* index p.156
Life — *100 Events* p.45
Linton — *Bicentennial* p.430-437
Lossing — *Biog.* p.329-370
Morison — *Oxford (1)* p.244n, 259, 265, 394-493
Morris — *Ency.* p.451
Morris — *Voices* p.158-169
Tunis — *Young* p.58-59
Wright — *New* p.14-16
- Adoption, urged by Franklin
Amer. Reader p.130-133
- Amendments, Articles I-XI
Angle — *By* p.118
Carman — *History* p.775-777
Morris — *Ency.* p.126, 458
- Celebration, New York
Collins — *Story* p.135
- Comments
Davie — *Profile* p.62-66
- Excerpts
Davie — *Profile* p.62-66
- Immutability
Baldwin — *Ideas* p.203-205
- Preamble
Butterfield — *Amer.* p.12
- "Pro and con"
Baldwin — *Ideas* p.192-193
- Ratification
Alden — *Pioneer* p.122-124
Angle — *By* p.62-78
Butterfield — *Amer.* p.13
Kraus — *U.S. (1)* p.260-264
Morison — *Oxford (1)* p.403-408
Morris — *Ency.* p.118-120
Morris — *Voices* p.167-169
- Signing
Collins — *Story* p.134
Morris — *Voices* p.165-167
- Text
Carman — *History* p.764-765

CONSTITUTIONAL CONVENTION
Alden — *Pioneer* p.91-100, 114-121
Butterfield — *Amer.* p.11
Carman — *History* p.250-260
Greene — *Revol.* p.123, 340, 353, 363-365, 406
Kraus — *U.S. (1)* p.254-260
Life — *Making. See* index p.156
Morison — *Oxford (1)* p.394-403
Morris — *Ency.* p.116-117
Morris — *Voices* p.158-169
Tunis — *Young* p.57
200 Years p.161-173

CONSTITUTIONAL GAZETTE
Scott — *Trumpet* p.98-100, 103, 120

CONTINENTAL ARMY
Greene — *Revol. See* index p.463
Sanderlin — *1776* p.182-188, 192-194, 238

Scott — *Trumpet. See* index p.302
Stember — *Middle. See* index p.166
Stember — *North* p.26, 53, 73, 84, 120, 134-135, 170-171, 185, 203-210, 302-303, 341, 343, 345, 348
Wheeler — *Voices. See* index p.474

- Commissary
Tunis — *Tavern* p.83
- Song
Scott — *Trumpet* p.221
- Uniforms
Amer. Her. — *Rev. See* index p.384
Earle — *Home* p.247-248
Speare — *Life* p.90
Train — *Story* p.236-237
Tunis — *Tavern* p.82-83

CONTINENTAL ASSOCIATION
Greene — *Revol.* p.23, 202-203, 206, 211, 216, 259-260
Morris — *American* p.135-140

CONTINENTAL CONGRESS (First and Second)
Alden — *Pioneer* p.78, 83, 87-88, 92
Amer. Her. — *Rev. See* index p.381
Amer. Reader p.95-99
Angle — *By* p.46-51
Baldwin — *Ideas* p.175-178
Beach — *Samuel* p.19, 259-260, 262-271, 281, 285-288, 296-300
Brodie — *Jefferson. See* index p.788-789
Burt — *Phila.* p.170-171, 180, 230, 243, 266-267, 275
Colbourn — *Colonial* p.342-345
Collins — *Story* p.99-100
Forbes — *Paul* p.209, 217-218, 237, 277
Ingraham — *Album* p.31-32
Kraus — *U.S. (1)* p.211-213, 216
Life — *Making* p.34, 37; *See also* index (under Second C. C.) p.159
Miller — *Origins. See* index p.509
Morison — *Oxford (1). See* index p.1129
Morris — *Ency.* p.53, 86-87
Morris — *Voices* p.90, 97
Sanderlin — *1776* p.90, 119, 126-128, 130, 251; *See also* index p.261
Scott — *Trumpet* p.73-74, 87, 91, 120-122, 140, 183-184, 205, 229, 234-235, 240
Whitney — *Abigail* p.87, 98, 120, 162, 191, 196, 216, 239-241, 273
Stember — *Middle. See* index p.166
200 Years p.29, 31, 296
Wright — *New* p.16-17
- Delegates
Lossing — *Biog.* p.383-384

CONTINENTAL NAVY. *See* **Navy**

CONVICTS
- Immigrants
Alden — *Pioneer* p.39-40
Dolan — *Yankee* p.114
Earle — *Colonial* p.8-10

CONWAY CABAL
Burt — *Phila.* p.277n, 278

COOK, EBENEZER
Miller — *Colonial* p.372-376

COOKERY
See also **Food;** special subjects
Belote — *Compleat* p.2, 37-53, 57-63, 65-83, 101-102
Earle — *Home* p.158-159
Gould — *Early* p.95-96
Tunis — *Living* p.135-139
, French
Belote — *Compleat* p.2
- Massachusetts
Dow — *Every* p.92-93, 98
- Philadelphia
Burt — *Phila.* p.303-304
- Roasting
Gould — *Early* p.70-72
- Utensils. See **Kitchen utensils**

COOPER, WILLIAM
- Colony
Morris — *Voices* p.150-152

COOPERS
Main — *Social* p.22, 76, 80, 191, 274-275
Tunis — *Colonial* p.22-23, 80

COOPERSTOWN, NEW YORK
Morris — *Voices* p.150-152

COPLEY, JOHN SINGLETON
Adams — *Provincial* p.309
Bridenbaugh — *Revolt* p.196-198, 335, 347, 403, 405-407
Burt — *Phila.* p.235, 237
Earle — *Child* p.37, 49-50, 52-53, 55
Forbes — *Paul* p.53, 67, 107-109, 298-299
Morris — *Ency.* p.596-597
Wertenbaker — *Golden* p.33-34, 97, 155
Wright — *Cultural* p.212

COPPER AND COPPERSMITHS
Forbes — *Paul* p.376-379, 384, 409-410
Train — *Story* p.169, 199
Tunis — *Colonial* p.76-80

CORBIN, MARGARET ("Captain Molly")
Cook — *What* p.228-231
Somerville — *Women* p.12-17
Stember — *Middle* p.70-71.

CORN
See also **Husking Bees**
Belote — *Compleat* p.88-89
Crèvecoeur — *Sketches* p.56, 86, 114-118, 120-121, 123, 142-143, 150
Gould — *Early* p.89-90, 133-134
Life — *New* p.60, 101
, Indian
Earle — *Home* p.456
- Prices
Earle — *Home* p.138
- Use in games
Earle — *Home* p.139

CORNWALLIS, LORD CHARLES
Amer. Her. — *Rev.* p.381
Brodie — *Jefferson* p.167, 170-171, 177-178, 180-181, 184-185
Burt — *Phila.* p.286-287, 296
Greene — *Revol.* p.127, 291, 395
Life — *Making* p.17, 56-57, 68-69, 82-86, 90, 99-101
McDowell — *Rev. See* index p.197
Morison — *Oxford (1)* p.293, 318, 322, 337-348, 350
Morris — *American* p.246-249
Morris — *Voices* p.107, 121-123, 158
Scott — *Trumpet* p.257-277
Stember — *Middle. See* index p.166
Stember — *South. See* index p.210
200 Years. See index p.346
- Song
Scott — *Trumpet* p.274-275

CORPORATIONS
Morris — *Ency.* p.504
- Beginnings
Greene — *Revol.* p.355

COSBY, WILLIAM
Scott — *Settlers* p.120-121, 126, 128-129, 131-132

COSMETICS
See also **Beauty—Aids**
Ross — *Taste* p.225
Spruill — *Women's* p.283

COST OF LIVING. ***See*** **Standard of living**

COSTUME. ***See*** **Clothing and dress**

COTILLIONS. ***See*** **Dances and dancing**

COTTON
Cable — *American* p.94
Dolan — *Yankee* p.50-56
Earle — *Home* p.206-210
Glubok — *Home* p.251-253
Speare — *Life* p.131-132
Train — *Story* p.241-242, 252-253
Tunis — *Young* p.60-61
- South
Life — *Growing* p.134, 138-139
Morris — *Ency.* p.479

COTTON GIN
Davie — *Profile* p.198-199
Tunis — *Young* p.64-65

COUNTRY LIFE
See also **Farmers and farming**
Crèvecoeur — *Sketches* p.79-100
Greene — *Revol. See* index p.480-481
National — *History.* p.292-303

COUNTRY STORES
Speare — *Life* p.44-46

COURTSHIP
Earle — *Colonial* p.203-205
Earle — *Customs* p.55-66
Gould — *Early* p.85
Miller — *Colonial* p.132-140
Miller — *First* p.189-199
Speare — *Life* p.60
- South
Spruill — *Women's* p.136-162
- Virginia
Downey — *Our* p.11-29

COVERED BRIDGES
Tunis — *Young* p.77

COVERLETS
Earle — *Home* p.242-246

COWHERDS
Earle — *Home* p.400-401
Glubok — *Home* p.316-317

CRAFTS, THOMAS, JR.
Forbes — *Paul* p.156, 190, 227, 305-306, 312-313, 323, 330

CRAFTS AND CRAFTSMANSHIP
See also **Artisans;** names of articles and types
Adams — *Provincial* p.273-274
Amer. Her. — *Rev.* p.78-79
Bridenbaugh — *Revolt* p.272-274
Earle — *Colonial* p.234-235
National — *History.* p.156-157
Speare — *Life* p.124-133
Wilson — *American* p.10-11
, Country
Tunis — *Colonial* p.18-38
, Group
Tunis — *Colonial* p.111-131
, Home
Wilson — *Early* p.62-65
- Masters
Tunis — *Colonial* p.15-16
- Middle Colonies
Train — *Story* p.179-202
- Quality and honesty
Tunis — *Colonial* p.16-17

CRANCH, MARY SMITH
Whitney — *Abigail. See* index p.353

CRANCH, RICHARD
Whitney — *Abigail. See* index p.353

CREEK INDIANS
Morison — *Oxford (1)* p.192, 237, 264-265

CRÈVECOEUR, J. HECTOR ST. JOHN (pseud.)
Crèvecoeur — *Sketches* p.1-35; *See also* index, under special subjects
Hofstadter — *Amer. See* index p.iv, v
Life — *New* p.112, 129
Morris — *Voices* p.101-102
Sanderlin — *1776* p.1-4
Scott — *Trumpet* p.6-9, 13-18
, on Americans
Morris — *American* p.195-204
200 Years p.304
, on customs
Crèvecoeur — *Sketches* p.122-137
, on farmers
Handlin — *This* p.36-59
Miller — *Colonial* p.479-498

CRIME AND CRIMINALS
See also types of crime; **Prisons and prisoners; Punishment**
Bridenbaugh — *Revolt* p.110-113, 299-304
Bridenbaugh — *Wild.* p.220-224, 379-384
Downey — *Our* p.115-124
Greene — *Revol. See* index p.463

CRIME AND CRIMINALS (*continued*)
Miller — *First* p.259-265
Ross — *Taste* p.120
- *Boston*
Bridenbaugh — *Revolt* p.112, 301-302
- *Charlestown*
Bridenbaugh — *Revolt.* p.112, 303
- *Massachusetts*
Dow — *Every* p.210, 214
- *New York*
Bridenbaugh — *Revolt* p.113, 136, 241, 302-303
Newport, R.I.
Bridenbaugh — *Revolt* p.112, 300-301
- *Philadelphia*
Bridenbaugh — *Revolt* p.36, 112-113, 302
- *Women*
Benson — *Women 18th* p.226-232
- *Women, Southern*
Spruill — *Women* p.323-339

CROPS AND GRAINS
See also **Cereal farming;** names of crops; names of localities
Tunis — *Living* p.104-105
, *Harvesting*
Gould — *Early* p.133-134
, *New England*
Train — *Story* p.165

CROWN POINT, NEW YORK
Stember — *North* p.4, 12, 15, 19-22, 27, 47-48, 51-52, 54, 57, 280

CROWS
Crèvecoeur — *Sketches* p.26, 86, 114-116

CULTURE
See also **Art; Books and reading; Cities—Culture; Drama; Libraries; Music;** names of various types of education
Bridenbaugh — *Revolt* p.5, 140, 192, 372-373, 416, 422-423
Bridenbaugh — *Wild.* p.288-297, 451-465; *See also* index p.490
Burt — *Phila.* p.144-145
Greene — *Revol.* p.12-13
Life — *New* p.122, 125-129
Main — *Social* p.6, 242-269, 285-286
Wertenbaker — *Golden* p.151-152, 157-158
, *Colonial*
Adams — *Provincial* p.258-292
Carman — *History* p.85-118
Morison — *Oxford (1)* p.202-208, 234-243
, *Crucibles of*
Wertenbaker — *Golden* p.1-17
- *Definition*
Sweet — *Religion* p.160
, *Democratic*
Kraus — *U.S. (1)* p.173-176
, *Literary*
Bridenbaugh — *Revolt* p.188-191, 393-398
Bridenbaugh — *Wild.* p.453-454, 457-458, 463
- *Boston*
Bridenbaugh — *Revolt* p.190, 395
- *Charlestown*
Bridenbaugh — *Revolt* p.190, 395-396
- *New York*
Bridenbaugh — *Revolt* p.189, 396
- *Newport, R. I.*
Bridenbaugh — *Revolt* p.396
- *Philadelphia*
Bridenbaugh — *Revolt* p.190, 394-395
, *Native*
Kraus — *U.S. (1)* p.160-180
- *Patterns and classes*
Main — *Social* p.240-269
, *Post-Revolutionary*
Morison — *Oxford (1)* p.368-384
, *Pre-Revolutionary*
Greene — *Revol.* p.117-154
- *Uniformity*
Adams — *Provincial* p.165

CUPBOARDS
Earle — *Customs* p.111-112
Gould — *Early* p.25, 62

CUPS
Earle — *Home* p.90, 93-96

CURES. *See* Medicine; Remedies

CURRENCY
Adams — *Album* p.303
Bridenbaugh — *Wild.* p.205, 360-361
Carman — *History* p.81-83, 140-142, 147, 163, 172, 188, 200, 245
Greene — *Revol. See* index p.463
, and politics
Kraus — *U.S. (1)* p.132-135
- Controversies
Morison — *Oxford (1)* p.200-202
- South
Adams — *Provincial* p.209-210
- Stabilization
Adams — *Album* p.282

CUSHING, THOMAS
Beach — *Samuel. See* index p.325

CUSTOMS (duties)
Miller — *Origins* p.83-86, 266
Tunis — *Living* p.102-103

CUTLER, MANASSEH
Dolan — *Yankee* p.223

CUTLERS
Tunis — *Colonial* p.50-52

D

DALE, RICHARD
Morris — *Voices* p.116-118

DAME SCHOOLS
Earle — *Customs* p.29-30

DANBURY RAID
Stember — *North* p.345-356

DANCES AND DANCING
Benson — *Women 18th* p.292-293, 295-297
Bridenbaugh — *Revolt* p.149, 163-165
Bridenbaugh — *Wild.* p.277, 277n, 279, 435, 437-439, 441
Cable — *American* p.62-63
Earle — *Child* p.103, 109-111
Earle — *Colonial* p.210-216
Earle — *Customs* p.240
Gould — *Early* p.32-33
Greene — *Revol.* p.5, 95, 114, 255, 285, 326-327, 406
Ross — *Taste* p.82-83
Speare — *Life* p.157-158
Train — *Story* p.222-224
Tunis — *Living* p.150-151
200 Years p.306
Wright — *Cultural* p.190-191
, and music
Dannett — *Yankee* p.235-248
- Assemblies
Bridenbaugh — *Revolt* p.140, 164-165, 366-367
- "Corsino"
Earle — *Colonial* p.216
- Cotillions
Dannett — *Yankee* p.241-244
, Country
Dulles — *History* p.37-39
- "Innocent maid"
Earle — *Colonial* p.216
- South
Spruill p.91-92, 94-99, 101, 103-104, 107, 110-111, 204-205
- "Stony Point"
Earle — *Colonial* p.215-216
- "Successful campaign"
Earle — *Colonial* p.214-215
- Virginia
Cable — *American* p.43-44

DARRAGH, LYDIA
Burt — *Phila.* p.284-286
Dexter — *Colonial* p.73-76
Ellet — *Eminent* p.114-120
Somerville — *Women* p.56-61

DARTMOUTH COLLEGE
Greene — *Revol.* p.115, 127-128, 377
Stearns — *Story* p.71

DATES. *See* Chronology; 1700's

DAUGHTERS
- South
Spruill — *Women's. See* index p.403

DAUGHTERS OF LIBERTY
Benson — *Women 18th* p.250
Earle — *Colonial* p.240-257
Earle — *Home* p.183-184
Glubock — *Home* p.238-239
Miller — *Origins* p.139, 271, 396

DAUGHTERS OF THE AMERICAN REVOLUTION
- Markers
Stember — *North* p.35, 49, 100, 243, 269, 272, 338, 359, 361

DAVIES, SAMUEL
Sweet — *Story* p.148-149, 168

DAWES, WILLIAM
Morris — *Voices* p.82-83

DE LA LUZERNE, CHEVALIER
Morris — *Voices* p.118-119

DE PEYSTER, JOHANNES, III
Cable — *American* p.50

DEANE, SILAS
Stember — *North* p.371

DEARBORN, HENRY
Wheeler — *Voices* p.60-61, 65-66, 271-276

DEATH
See also **Cemeteries; Funerals**
Burner — *America* p.121-122
Cable — *American* p.45
Pettengill — *Yankee* p.170-173

DEBT
Main — *Social* p.132, 151, 154, 159-160
, and imprisonment
Bridenbaugh — *Revolt* p.118-119, 255, 304

DECATUR, STEPHEN
- Biography
Morris — *Ency.* p.649-650

"DECLARATION OF COLONIAL RIGHTS AND GRIEVANCES"
Morris — *American* p.130-135

DECLARATION OF INDEPENDENCE
See also names of signers; names of thirteen colonies
Adams — *Album* p.377-378
Alden — *Pioneer* p.63, 86-89, 105
Amer. Her. — *Rev.* p.145-152
Angle — *By* p.56-61
Beach — *Samuel* p.297-300
Brodie — *Jefferson. See* index p.789
Burt — *Phila.* p.44, 114, 174, 207, 279-281, 283, 286
Butterfield — *Amer.* p.x-xi
Carman — *History* p.190-192, 226, 230-231, 233, 251, 262, 267
Davie — *Profile* p.55-58
Greene — *Revol.* p.195, 302, 396, 416
Ingraham — *Album* p.48-50
Kraus — *U.S. (1)* p.218-221
Life — *Making. See* index p.157
Life — *100 Events* p.45
Linton — *Bicentennial* p.428-429
Lossing — *Biog.* p.244-309
McDowell — *Rev.* p.72-73, 82-83, 85-88, 90-91, 109
Miller — *Origins. See* index p.510
Morison — *Oxford (1)* p.218, 244n, 246, 280, 292-297, 310, 367
Morris — *American* p.186-190
Morris — *Ency.* p.91-92
Morris — *Voices* p.94, 96-97, 100, 158
Sanderlin — *1776. See* index p.257
Scott — *Trumpet. See* index p.302-303
200 Years p.70-72, 76-81, 162, 296
Wheeler — *Voices* p.154-156, 293
Whitney — *Abigail* p.126-127
- Abigail Adams, views of
Amer. Reader p.102-103
- Adoption
Collins — *Story* p.130
Miller — *Origins* p.491-493
- Analysis
Alden — *Pioneer* p.88-89
, and servants
Earle — *Customs* p.103
- Anniversary, first
Burt — *Phila.* p.281, 294

, as sacred document
Malone — *Story* p.248
- Background
Alden — *Pioneer* p.86-88
- Causes
Malone — *Story* p.5-8
- Drafting
Malone — *Story* p.67-78
Sanderlin — *1776* p.224-226
- Proclamation
Collins — *Story* p.131
Malone — *Story* p.79-83
- Signers and signing
Adams — *Album* p.378-380
Angle — *By* p.60-61
Carman — *History* p.762-763
Life — *Making* p.36-39, 42-53
Malone — *Story* p.93-245
Sanderlin — *1776* p.230-235
- Text
Carman — *History* p.759-763
Sanderlin — *1776* p.227-234
, Travels of
Malone — *Story* p.249-251
, Women's place in
Spruill — *Women's* p.245
- Writing
Sanderlin — *1776* p.216-217

DECLARATION OF RIGHTS (1774)
See also **Continental Congress**
- Adoption
Sanderlin — *1776* P.127-128

"DECLARATION OF THE CAUSES AND NECESSITY OF TAKING UP ARMS"
Sanderlin — *1776* p.176-178

DECLARATORY ACT (1766)
Baldwin — *Ideas* p.168-169
Beach — *Samuel* p.107-108, 110-111, 118, 131, 174
Miller — *Origins. See* index p.510
Morris — *American* p.86-87

DEER
Glubok — *Home* p.56-58
, as food
Earle — *Home* p.109
- Georgia
Earle — *Home* p.109

DEERFIELD, MASSACHUSETTS
- Massacre
Adams — *Album* p.269
National — *History* p.92-95
Stearns — *Story* p.62

DEFENSE, COMMON
See also **Blockhouses; Forts**
Speare — *Life* p.83-96

DEISM
Bridenbaugh — *Wild.* p.423-424
Greene — *Revol.* p.94, 109-110, 116, 137, 282, 285, 368-369
Morris — *Ency.* p.551
Sweet — *Religion* p.91-92
Tunis — *Young* p.32

DELAWARE
Greene — *Revol.* p.32-33, 121, 288, 358, 363, 375
Main — *Social* p.26-27, 32-33, 36-37, 107
Morison — *Oxford (1)* p.184, 240, 296, 383-384, 405
200 Years p.70, 77, 80, 166, 176
, and Declaration of Independence
Bakeless — *Signers* p.249-261
Malone — *Story* p.181-188

DELAWARE INDIANS
Burt — *Phila.* p.16, 47, 167-172, 177
- "Declaration of Independence"
Burt — *Phila.* p.169

DELAWARE RIVER
McDowell — *Rev.* p.99-101
Morris — *Voices* p.108-110
Scott — *Trumpet* p.154, 157, 205, 211, 215-216, 222-223, 232, 261, 265
Wheeler — *Voices* p.203-204, 244, 282-286, 440
, Crossing of
See also **Washington, George**
Adams — *Album* p.391
Amer. Her. — *Rev.* p.189-203
Kraus — *U.S. (1)* p.227-228
Stember — *Middle* p.21-26
Wheeler — *Voices* p.197, 203-204, 301

DEMING, SARAH WINSLOW
Benson — *Women 18th* p.170

DEMOCRACY
Main — *Social* p.3, 17, 43, 236-237, 250, 270-271, 277-278, 283, 287
, Colonial
Miller — *Origins* p.54-55, 57-58, 497-505
- Reform
Kraus — *U.S. (1)* p.238-245

DEMOCRATIC-REPUBLICAN PARTY
Alden — *Pioneer* p.128, 130-131, 138-140

DENOMINATIONS. *See* **Religion—Denominations;** names of denominations

DENTISTRY
Forbes — *Paul* p.122-127, 444
Train — *Story* p.177
, Birthplace of modern
Burt — *Phila.* p.220-221
, Itinerant
Dolan — *Yankee* p.206
, Postwar
Greene — *Revol.* p.383-384

DEPRESSIONS. *See* **Business depressions**

DERBY, ELIAS HASKET
Adams — *Album* p.298-299

DESIGN. *See* **Art—Design**

D'ESTAING, COMTE CHARLES HECTOR
Scott — *Trumpet* p.236, 238-239, 241, 279
Stember — *North* p.325, 327-328, 335
Wheeler — *Voices* p.308-311, 314, 353-354, 357, 359-361

DIALECT
Boorstin — *Americans* p.273-274
Kraus — *U.S. (1)* p.178-179

DIARIES AND DIARISTS
Adams — *Provincial* p.265-267
Dexter — *Colonial* p.15-17
Earle — *Child* p.166-172
Glubok — *Home* p.163-167
, Value and location of
Main — *Social* p.296-297

DICKINSON, JOHN
Amer. Hist. — *Rev.* p.61-62, 65, 71, 139, 149, 217
Beach — *Samuel* p.134-135, 271, 290, 298, 303
Miller — *Origins. See* index p.510
Sanderlin — *1776* p.54-55, 60, 74, 120, 177, 210-211, 215
200 Years p.22, 67-68, 71, 73, 77, 80, 165, 290
- on Townshend Acts
Morris — *American* p.95-98

DIET. *See* **Cookery; Food;** etc.

DINING ROOMS
Tunis — *Living* p.135

DINING TABLES
Earle — *Customs* p.133-139, 142-144
Speare — *Life* p.73-75

DINNERS
Earle — *Customs* p.161-162
Earle — *Home* p.104-106
Forbes — *Paul* p.382, 397-398
Gould — *Early* p.90-91, 94
- Adams, John
Earle — *Home* p.159-160
- New England
Earle — *Home* p.104-106, 122, 159
- South
Spruill — *Women's* p.72-73

DISEASES
See also **Medicine; Remedies;** names of diseases
, Children's
Glubok — *Home* p.96, 98
- Frontier
Wright — *Frontier* p.72

- *Immunity and resistance*
Hofstadter — *Amer.* p.68-69
- *Slave ships*
Hofstadter — *Amer.* p.84-86
, *Tropical*
Hofstadter — *Amer.* p.69-77

DISHES AND UTENSILS
See also **Kitchen utensils;** names of articles
Speare — *Life* p.74
- *Frontier*
Langdon — *Every.* p.121
- *Newspaper advertising*
Earle — *Home* p.106

DISPENSARIES
See also **Apothecaries**
Morris — *Ency.* p.541

DISTILLERIES AND BREWERIES
Greene — *Revol.* p.42, 45, 60, 359
Main — *Social* p.77n, 78, 81-82, 132, 186, 275
- *Boston*
Bridenbaugh — *Revolt* p.74, 269-270
- *Charlestown*
Bridenbaugh — *Revolt* p.74, 272
- *New York*
Bridenbaugh — *Revolt* p.74, 271
- *Newport, R.I.*
Bridenbaugh — *Revolt* p.74, 270
- *Philadelphia*
Bridenbaugh — *Revolt* p.74, 269

DIVERSIONS. ***See*** **Amusements; Sports and games;** etc.

DIVORCE
Benson — *Women 18th* p.233-234
Greene — *Revol.* p.73-74, 371
Holliday — *Woman's* p.264-268
- *New England*
Earle — *Customs* p.81

DOAN BROTHERS
Burt — *Phila.* p.294

DOCK, SAMUEL
Glubok — *Home* p.136-137

DOCKS. ***See*** **Wharves and docks**

DOCTORS. ***See*** **Physicians**

DOCUMENTS
See also names of documents
, *"Excerpts" of founding*
200 Years p.296-297
- *Texts*
200 Years p.289-297

DOGS
See also **"Turnspit dogs"**
Crèvecoeur — *Sketches* p.31, 119, 127, 132-133, 243-244

DOLLS
Adams — *Album* p.336
Earle — *Child* p.363-365, 384, 390
Speare — *Life* p.102

DOORWAYS
Gowans — *Images* p.182-183

DOUGLASS, DAVID
Wright — *Cultural* p.183-185

DOUGLASS, WILLIAM
Wright — *Cultural* p.162-163

DOUGLASS COMPANY (dramatic company)
Dexter — *Colonial* p.159-161

DOVE, DAVID
Burt — *Phila.* p.233

DOWRIES
Benson — *Women 18th* p.235-238
Train — *Story* p.254

DOWSERS
Wilson — *Early* p.113-114

"DRAGONS" (chaperones)
Wilson — *Early* p.110-112

DRAINAGE
- *Streets and houses*
Bridenbaugh — *Wild.* p.158-161, 318-319

DRAKE, DANIEL
Wright — *Frontier* p.59-64

DRAMA
See also **Theater**
Adams — *Provincial* p.276
Earle — *Customs* p.246
Greene — *Revol.* p.127, 139, 141, 153, 318, 394-395
Wright — *Cultural* p.186
- *New York*
Wright — *Cultural* p.179-180
- *Philadelphia*
Wright — *Cultural* p.179
- *Women*
Benson — *Women 18th* p.201-209

DRAMATIC COMPANIES
See also **Douglass Company; Hallam Company**
Wright — *Cultural* p.181-186

DRAMATISTS
Morris — *Ency.* p.589-590

DRAPER, MARY
Ellet — *Eminent* p.65-69

DRESS. *See* **Clothing and dress**

DRESS MATERIALS. *See* **Fabrics**

DRESSMAKING
Dexter — *Colonial* p.40-42
- *"Sempstresses"*
Wilson — *Early* p.78-79

DRING, THOMAS
Scott — *Trumpet* p.170-177

DRINKER, ELIZABETH SANDWITH
Evans — *Weather.* p.152-184
, *on anniversary of Declaration of Independence*
Burt — *Phila.* p.281

DRINKER, HANNAH
Benson — *Women 18th* p.170, 267n

DRINKS. *See* **Beverages**

DRUDGERY
Kraus — *U.S. (1)* p.171-173

DRUGS. *See* **Medicine; Remedies**

DUCHÉ, JACOB
Burt — *Phila.* p.242-245

DUCKS
Glubok — *Home* p.69-70

"DUDES"
Wilson — *Early* p.161-162

DUELS
Burt — *Phila.* p.81-83
Tunis — *Young* p.108-109

DUER, WILLIAM
Locke — *Birth* p.134-148

DULANY FAMILY
Wright — *Cultural* p.14

DUNBAR, WILLIAM
Morris — *Ency.* p.530

DUNKERS (Dunkards, German Baptists, Taufers)
Morris — *Ency.* p.549
Sweet — *Religion* p.44-45
Sweet — *Story* p.103-104

DUNMORE, JOHN MURRAY, EARL OF
Greene — *Revol.* p.7-8, 176, 220-222, 236
200 Years p.70
- *Proclamation (1775)*
Morris — *American* p.349-350

DUTCH
See also special subjects, subdivision **Dutch**
Alden — *Pioneer* p.51, 57-58
Greene — *Revol. See* index p.464
Hofstadter — *Amer.* p.11, 16, 18, 36-37, 71, 74, 99, 151, 189, 201-202
Life — *New* p.120
Speare — *Life* p.52-62
- *Houses. See* **Architecture, Dutch**

- *Influence, in New York*
Wertenbaker — *Golden* p.40-41
- *Literature*
Wertenbaker — *Golden* p.46-48
- *Women*
Benson — *Women 18th* p.104, 134-135, 281, 306

"DUTCH CROWNS"
Gould — *Early* p.80

DUTCH OVENS
Earle — *Home* p.65-66
Glubok — *Home* p.34-35
Gould — *Early* p.72, 74

DUTCH REFORMED CHURCH
Greene — *Revol.* p.12, 71, 102, 111, 118, 284-285, 366-367, 378
Sweet — *Religion* p.39-40, 80-81
Sweet — *Story* p.146-147, 181, 200

DWIGHT, TIMOTHY
Greene — *Revol.* p.120, 125, 285, 290, 292, 298, 325, 368, 390, 393
Sweet — *Religion* p.147-148
, on women
Benson — *Women 18th* p.117, 145, 151, 165, 273n, 302, 304, 312

DYES
Earle — *Home* p.250-251
Glubok — *Home* p.86, 245-246
Gould — *Early* p.113
Speare — *Life* p.79
- *Barberry root*
Earle — *Home* p.194
, Domestic
Earle — *Home* p.155, 193-194, 250-251
- *Washington, Martha*
Earle — *Home* p.237-238

E

EAGLE (symbol)
Adams — *Album* p.406
Tunis — *Young* p.99

EARL, RALPH
Morris — *Ency.* p.597

EAST INDIA COMPANY
Carman — *History* p.175, 177-178, 181
Greene — *Revol.* p.199-200, 217, 350-351
Miller — *Origins. See* index p.510
Scott — *Trumpet* p.63-65, 70-71

EATING. *See* **Food; Meals; Menus;** names of meals

ECONOMY (economics)
- *Creation*
Carman — *History* p.60-84
- *Development*
Bridenbaugh — *Wild.* p.175-205
, during Revolution
Life — *Making* p.156
- *Post-Revolutionary*
Life — *Making* p.110-111

"EDENTON TEA-PARTY" (N.C.)
Earle — *Colonial* p.251-255

EDUCATION
See also **Children and childhood; Girls;** special subjects
Adams — *Provincial* p.131-136
Alden — *Pioneer* p.50, 52-54, 57-58
Boorstin — *Americans* p.169-188
Bridenbaugh — *Wild. See* index p.490
Dreppard — *Pioneer* p.216-221
Glubok — *Home* p.120-128
Greene — *Revol. See* index p.464
Kraus — *U.S. (1)* p.166-171
Main — *Social. See* index p.310
Miller — *First* p.227-228, 235-236
Morris — *Ency.* p.554-558
Tunis — *Living* p.155-156
Wertenbaker — *Golden* p.152-153
Wright — *New* p.187-190
- *Annapolis*
Wertenbaker — *Golden* p.88-90
- *Boston*
Wertenbaker — *Golden* p.21-23
- *Charleston*
Wertenbaker — *Golden* p.136-140

EDUCATION (continued)
, Colonial
Life — *New* p.97, 124-125
- Connecticut
Morison — *Oxford (1)* p.236
- "Dark days"
Train — *Story* p.177
, Demand for
Main — *Social* p.249-253
, Elementary
Main — *Social* p.241-243
, Higher
See also **Colleges and universities**
Main — *Social* p.246-247
- Kentucky frontier
Wright — *Frontier* p.74-75
- New York
Bridenbaugh — *Wild.* p.286-289
Wertenbaker — *Golden* p.43-46
, of children. See **Children and childhood—Education; Education, Elementary**
- Pennsylvania
Morison — *Oxford (1)* p.185
- Quakers. See **Quakers—Education**
- Revolution, effects on
Kraus — *U.S. (1)* p.244
- South
Benson — *Women 18th* p.309-311
- South Carolina
Morison — *Oxford (1)* p.238
- Virginia
Morison — *Oxford (1)* p.238-239
Morris — *American* p.345-348
Wertenbaker — *Golden* p.106-109
- Women
Benson — *Women 18th. See* index p.337
Bridenbaugh — *Revolt* p.176-177, 377-378
Greene — *Revol.* p.120, 324-325
Holliday — *Woman's* p.72-74, 82-86
- Dutch, in New York
Holliday — *Woman's* p.72-73
- New England
Benson — *Women 18th* p.108-112, 145-154
- New York
See also **Education—Women—Dutch, in New York**
Benson — *Women 18th* p.134-135
- Philadelphia
Benson — *Women 18th* p.133-134, 137-144
- Views of Benjamin Franklin
Holliday — *Woman's* p.73-74
- Zeal
Wright — *Cultural* p.106-125

EDWARDS, JONATHAN
Adams — *Provincial* p.282-283
Alden — *Pioneer* p.54-55
Cable — *American* p.46
Carman — *History* p.100-101
Hofstadter — *Amer. See* index p.v
Morison — *Oxford (1)* p.209-212, 225-226
Morris — *Ency.* p.562
Scott — *Settlers* p.151-158, 160-162, 164-165
Stearns — *Story* p.67-68
Sweet — *Story* p.128-133
, and social welfare
Baldwin — *Ideas* p.125-130
, as "highbrow"
Baldwin — *Ideas* p.130-131
- Biography
Morris — *Ency.* p.655
- "Personal narrative"
Miller — *Colonial* p.212-219
- "Sinners in the hands of an angry God"
Miller — *Colonial* p.207-211
- Views on women
Benson — *Women 18th* p.19, 51, 114, 117, 125, 259, 261, 276

ELECTIONS
See also **Politics**
Earle — *Customs* p.225-226
200 Years p.164

ELECTRICITY
Adams — *Album* p.344

Boorstin — *Americans* p.251-259
, before Franklin
Wilson — *American* p.18-19
- Discoveries by Franklin
Wertenbaker — *Golden* p.69

ELIOT, JARED
Morris — *Ency.* p.535
Wright — *Cultural* p.234

ELLERY, WILLIAM
Bakeless — *Signers* p.216-219
Malone — *Story* p.124
- Biography
Lossing — *Biog.* p.47-49

ELLIOTT, SUSANNAH
Ellet — *Eminent* p.334-341

ELLIS, HENRY
, on "Proclamation of 1763"
Morris — *American* p.17-20

EMANCIPATION
See also **Freedom; Liberty**
Greene — *Revol.* p.288-289, 316, 322-323, 328, 333-334

EMBROIDERY
Adams — *Album* p.308-309
Earle — *Home* p.267-268
Glubok — *Home* p.219-225

EMERSON, WILLIAM
Morris — *Voices* p.88-90

ENGLAND AND ENGLISH
See also **George III; Great Britain**; names of Englishmen; etc.
Amer. Her. — *Rev.* p.10-47
Crèvecoeur — *Sketches* p.173-175
Life — *New. See* index p.173
, Cultural inheritance of
Kraus — *U.S. (1)* p.122
- in America
Axtell — *18th* p.229-232

ENTERTAINERS
Wilson — *Early* p.120-121

ENTERTAINMENT. *See* **Amusements; Sports and games**; etc.

EPHRATA CLOISTER
Adams — *Album* p.277
Burt — *Phila.* p.232
Morris — *Ency.* p.549
Sirkis — *Reflect.* p.89-90
- Buildings
Langdon — *Every.* p.76-78
- Handwork
Langdon — *Every.* p.74-86
- Industries
Langdon — *Every.* p.82
- Music
Langdon — *Every.* p.82-86
Morris — *Ency.* p.612
Rublowsky — *Music* p.27-31
Wright — *Cultural* p.194
- Women
Benson — *Women 18th* p.269-270

EPIDEMICS
See also **Smallpox**; etc.
Bridenbaugh — *Wild.* p.239-241
Evans — *Weather.* p.24, 34, 101, 108-109, 113, 179, 181

EPISCOPALIANS
See also **Anglicans**
Sweet — *Religion* p.67-75
Sweet — *Story* p.176, 195-198, 221-222

EPITAPHS
Burner — *America* p.40-42
Earle — *Customs* p.381-387
- Negroes
Earle — *Customs* p.95-96

EQUALITY
Main — *Social. See* index p.311
- Backwoods
Sanderlin — *1776* p.xxv-xxvi

"ESTABLISHED CHURCH." *See* **Anglicans; Episcopalians**

ETIQUETTE
See also **Books and reading—Etiquette; Children and childhood—Etiquette**
Crèvecoeur — *Sketches* p.62-78
Tunis — *Young* p.105-106

ETIQUETTE (*continued*)
- *Food*
  Belote — *Compleat* p.157
  Spruill — *Women's* p.69-71
, *Lack of*
  Earle — *Colonial* p.200
- *Poise and carriage*
  Tunis — *Living* p.148
- *South*
  Benson — *Women 18th* p.284-290
- *Women*
  Benson — *Women 18th* p.274-275, 278-281, 291

EUROPE
See also names of countries, nationalities
- *Intrigues (1797-1799)*
  Butterfield — *Amer.* p.26-27

EVANGELISM. *See* Circuit riders; Clergymen; "Great Awakening"

EVANS, OLIVER
Morris — *Ency.* p.535
Tunis — *Young* p.62-64
Wilson — *American* p.54-58

EVE, SARAH
Benson — *Women 18th* p.283-308

EXECUTIONS
Earle — *Customs* p.252-254
Scott — *Trumpet* p.52, 138, 150-151, 153

EXECUTIVE DEPARTMENT
Morris — *Ency.* p.121-122

EXHIBITIONS (shows)
Earle — *Customs* p.242-245

EYEGLASSES
Earle — *Home* p.298
- *Franklin, Benjamin*
  Dolan — *Yankee* p.179
, *Sellers of*
  Tunis — *Colonial* p.48-50

F

FABRICS
See also types of fabrics, e.g. **Cotton, Wool**
Adams — *Album* p.309
Earle — *Customs* p.328-329
Tunis — *Young* p.25, 60-61
- *Dictionary (Massachusetts)*
  Dow — *Every* p.70-83
, *Oriental (names of)*
  Earle — *Customs* p.329-330
- *South*
  Spruill — *Women's* p.117-118, 281-282

FACTORIES
See also **"Manufactories"**
Tunis — *Young* p.60-71
- *Expansion*
  Morris — *Ency.* p.494
, *First successful*
  Wilson — *American* p.84-85

FAIRBANKS HOUSE
Gould — *Early* p.24, 29, 32, 48, 53

"FAIRHILL"
Burt — *Phila.* p.257

FAIRS
Bridenbaugh — *Wild.* p.195, 278, 353
Dulles — *History* p.30
Earle — *Home* p.190-191
Speare — *Life* p.162
Train — *Story* p.241
Tunis — *Living* p.150
- *South*
  Spruill — *Women's* p.110

FALLEN TIMBERS
, *Battle of*
  Morris — *Ency.* p.420

FAMILIES AND FAMILY LIFE
Greene — *Revol.* p.68-69, 151, 177-178, 220, 227, 370-371, 439-440
- *Size*
  Axtell — *18th* p.212-213
  Glubok — *Home* p.98-99
  Holliday — *Woman's* p.114-116

FANEUIL HALL
Adams — *Album* p.283

FANS
- *South*
Spruill — *Women's* p.124

FARM IMPLEMENTS
Crèvecoeur — *Sketches* p.137-151
Dreppard — *Pioneer* p.56
Tunis — *Young* p.20
- *Frontier*
Kraus — *U.S. (1)* p.142
- *Inventions*
Morris — *Ency.* p.535
, *Wooden*
Tunis — *Living* p.105-106

FARMERS AND FARMING
See also **Agriculture; Plantations and planters**
Greene — *Revol.* p.79-80, 159, 219-224, 236
Main — *Social. See* index p.311-312
Morison — *Oxford (1)* p.200, 205, 239, 390-393
Sanderlin — *1776* p.2-7
Sloane — *Spirits* p.45-46
Tunis — *Young* p.15-27
Wilson — *Early* p.151-155
Wright — *New* p.139-144
- *Backwoods*
Boorstin — *Americans* p.259-265
- *Buildings*
Tunis — *Young* p.17-18
, *Colonial*
Carman — *History* p.61-69
, *Commercial*
Main — *Social. See* index p.309
- *Contribution*
Sloane — *Spirits* p.23
- *Enemies*
Crèvecoeur — *Sketches* p.100-102
- *Houses. See* **Houses, Farm**
, *Large*
See also **Land—ownership, Large; Plantations and planters**
Main — *Social* p.25, 27, 27n, 29, 31, 34
, *Life*
Crèvecoeur — *Sketches* p.122-137
- *Middle Colonies*
Carman — *History* p.53
- *New England*
Carman — *History* p.52-53
- *Pennsylvania*
Axtell — *18th* p.62-69
, *Poor*
Main — *Social* p.148-150, 157-158, 236, 272
, *Small*
Main — *Social. See* index p.311-312
, *South. See* **Plantations and planters**
, *Tenant*
Adams — *Provincial* p.199-201
- *Visitors*
Tunis — *Young* p.25-26

FASHION
See also **Clothing and dress;** articles of fashion
Ross — *Taste* p.170-171
- *Boston*
Speare — *Life* p.51
, *English, in South*
Spruill — *Women's* p.129-133

FEATHER WORK
Glubok — *Home* p.218-219

FEDERAL CONVENTION. *See* **Constitutional Convention**

FEDERAL JUDICIARY ACT
Morris — *Ency.* p.122

FEDERALIST, THE
Baldwin — *Ideas* p.193-201
Morris — *Ency.* p.119, 564

FEDERALISTS
Alden — *Pioneer* p.127, 130, 136, 138-140
Butterfield — *Amer.* p.1
Carman — *History* p.260-265
Kraus — *U.S. (1)* p.272-274
Life — *Making* p.37-38, 112-113, 132-136

FEDERALISTS (continued)
, and Antifederalists
Morris — *Voices* p.167, 181, 187, 194, 216
- Opposition
Butterfield — *Amer.* p.20-21
- Reign of terror
Butterfield — *Amer.* p.28-29

FEKE, ROBERT
Cable — *American* p.50
Wright — *Cultural* p.211

FENCES
Gould — *Early* p.110-112
Tunis — *Young* p.18-19
- Massachusetts
Dow — *Every* p.100

FERGUSON, ELIZABETH
Ellet — *Eminent* p.130-135

FERGUSON, ISABELLA
Ellet — *Eminent* p.667-673

FERGUSON, JANE YOUNG
Evans — *Weather.* p.271-282

FERRIES
Adams — *Album* p.272
Speare — *Life* p.138
Tunis — *Living* p.121
Tunis — *Young* p.37-38
- Bakers ferry
Tunis — *Tavern* p.11-17, 30-31, 35-36, 39
- Coryells ferry
Tunis — *Tavern* p.49, 80-81, 89, 93, 102
- Houses
Tunis — *Tavern* p.15-24
, Rope
Tunis — *Tavern* p.17
- Views by Alexander Hamilton
Miller — *Colonial* p.391-393, 396-397, 405-408, 415-417
- Women as keepers, Southern
Spruill — *Women's* p.303-304

FESTIVALS. *See* Holidays and festivals

FEVER
Scott — *Settlers* p. 183
, and ague
Handlin — *This* p.16-19

FICTION
See also **Novelists**
Benson — *Women 18th* p.188-201
- First
Earle — *Customs* p.268
- Patriotic adventure
Nye — *Unembar.* p.19-21
, Sentimental
Nye — *Unembar.* p.17-21
, Women as characters in
Benson — *Women 18th* p.188-201
, Women's
Benson — *Women's* p.44-54, 71, 78, 90, 164-165, 181, 188-201

"FIGHTING QUAKERS"
Burt — *Phila.* p.284-287

"FILCHERS" (outlaws)
Wilson — *Early* p.167-168

FINANCE
Greene — *Revol. See* index p.465
Life — *Making. See* index p.157
Life — *New* p.144-145
Morison — *Oxford (1)* p.289; 305-306, 365-366, 390-392
, Business
Life — *New* p.103-104
- Capital
Amer. Reader p.135-137
Bridenbaugh — *Wild.* p.202-203, 360
- Investment
Morris — *Ency.* p.493
, Public (1789)
Morris — *Ency.* p.501

FINE ARTS. *See* Art; Drama; Music; etc.

FIREARMS. *See* Guns

FIREPLACES
Earle — *Customs* p.129-130
Gould — *Early* p.44-66

- *Accessories*
  See also names of accessories
  Earle — *Home* p.61-62
  Gould — *Early* p.67-81
- *Crane*
  Gould — *Early* p.67
- *Massachusetts*
  Dow — *Every* p.91-92

FIRES AND FIRE FIGHTING
Bridenbaugh — *Wild.* p.206-213, 364-372
Dreppard — *Pioneer* p.148-150, 152-153, 155
Glubok — *Home* p.8-9
Speare — *Life* p.93-96
- *Associations*
  Greene — *Revol.* p.95-96
- *Equipment*
  Adams — *Album* p.330
- *Fire engines, first*
  Earle — *Home* p.19
- *Towns and cities*
  Tunis — *Young* p.51

FIRESIDE INDUSTRIES. ***See*** **Artisans; Spinning; Weavers and weaving;** names of industries

FIREWORKS
Dow — *Every* p.116-117

FISH (food)
Earle — *Home* p.123-125
Gould — *Early* p.98-100
- *Boston*
  Earle — *Home* p.123

"FISH HOUSE" (1732)
Burt — *Phila.* p.367-368

FISHERIES
Carman — *History* p.74-75
Greene — *Revol.* p.42-43, 232-233, 259, 352

FISHING AND FISHERMEN
Adams — *Provincial* p.42-43
Dulles — *History* p.24-26
Life — *New* p.104-105, 108-109, 145
Speare — *Life* p.116-117
Tunis — *Young* p.86-87
- *Parties, Philadelphian*
  Earle — *Colonial* p.216-218

FISHKILL, NEW YORK
Stember — *North* p.134, 149, 210-214

FITCH, JOHN
Greene — *Revol.* p.65-66, 345-346
Wilson — *American* p.52-53

FITHIAN, PHILIP VICKERS
Spruill — *Women's. See* index p.405
- *Views on women*
  Benson — *Women 18th* p.286, 288n, 290, 297, 310-311

FITZGERALD, ELLENOR
- *Views on men*
  Burt — *Phila.* p.242

FITZHUGH, ANNE
Ellet — *Eminent* p.547-553

FITZHUGH, WILLIAM
Adams — *Provincial* p.195, 201

FLAGS
Adams — *Album* p.406
McDowell — *Rev.* p.110
Quaife — *History. See* index
Sloane — *Spirits* p.12-14
- *Alliance*
  Quaife — *History* p.38, 42-44, 46, 100-101, 106
- *American Stripes*
  Quaife — *History* p.27, 37, 84
, *Bedford Company*
  Quaife — *History* p.22
- *Bennington*
  Quaife — *History* p.49-51, 61, 106
- *British East India Company*
  Quaife — *History* p.27, 32
- *Bunker Hill*
  Quaife — *History* p.22, 25
- *Congress*
  See also **Flags—Great or Grand Union**
  Quaife — *History* p.27, 44-45

FLAGS *(continued)*
- *Gadsen or South Carolina Rattlesnake*
  Quaife — *History* p.31
- *Great or Grand Union*
  Quaife — *History* p.11-12, 26-28, 30, 32-33, 44-45, 49, 58, 62, 97, 105
- *Green Mountain Boys*
  Quaife — *History* p.31
- *Hanover Association*
  Quaife — *History* p.22
- *Maryland, 3rd regiment (Revolutionary)*
  Quaife — *History* p.71, 106
- *Mercantile*
  Quaife — *History* p.44-45, 55
- *Meteor (Great Britain)*
  Quaife — *History* p.21, 24-27, 30
- *Mondhare flag sheet*
  Quaife — *History* p.44
- *Navy Jack ("Don't tread on me") (Revolutionary)*
  Quaife — *History* p.37
- *New England Pine Tree*
  Quaife — *History* p.31, 41
- *New Hampshire, 2nd regiment (Revolutionary)*
  Quaife — *History* p.31
- *North Carolina militia*
  Quaife — *History* p.71
- *Philadelphia City Cavalry (1st troop)*
  Quaife — *History* p.22
- *Prospect Hill ceremony (Somerville)*
  Quaife — *History* p.26-27
- *Resolution (1770)*
  Quaife — *History* p.33-34, 36, 39, 41-42, 44, 49, 51, 57-58, 60
- *Resolution (1780)*
  Quaife — *History* p.57-60
- *Rhode Island (Revolutionary)*
  Quaife — *History* p.31
- *Second*
  Quaife — *History* p.78
- *"Serapis"*
  Quaife — *History* p.38, 42-44, 99-101, 106
- *South Carolina Navy Flag. See* **Flags—Navy Jack ("Don't tread on me") (Revolutionary)**
- *"Stars and Stripes (first)*
  Quaife — *History* p.48-53
  - *at Yorktown*
    Quaife — *History* p.51-53, 72
- *"Stars and Stripes" (second)*
  See also **Flags—Resolution (1780)**
  Quaife — *History* p.54-62
- *Union. See* **Flags—Great or Grand Union**

FLAILERS
Wilson — *Early* p.152-154

FLATBOATS
- *Invention (1750)*
  Morris — *Ency.* p.535

FLAX
Earle — *Colonial* p.309-314
Glubok — *Home* p.229-236, 238
Speare — *Life* p.78-79
, and hemp
  Gould — *Early* p.131-133
- *Bates*
  Glubok — *Home* p.230-231
- *Brakes*
  Glubok — *Home* p.231-232
- *Culture*
  Glubok — *Home* p.228-235
- *Hackling*
  Glubok — *Home* p.232-233
- *Hetcheling*
  Glubok — *Home* p.232-233
- *South*
  Earle — *Home* p.182-183

FLINTLOCK RIFLES. *See* Guns

FLIP (rum)
Dolan — *Yankee* p.105-106
Gould — *Early* p.106

"FLIP DOGS" (hottles or loggerheads)
Gould — *Early* p.80

FLOGGING
Scott — *Trumpet* p.52-56

FLOORS
Tunis — *Living* p.129

FLORIDA
, Revolutionary War campaign in
  Wheeler — *Voices* p.323-325

FLORISTS
- *Women*
  Earle — *Colonial* p.85-87

FLOUR AND FLOUR MILLS
Bridenbaugh — *Wild.* p.183-184
Tunis — *Living* p.136-137
Tunis — *Young* p.62-63

FLOWERS
See also **Gardens**
- *Children's lore*
  Earle — *Child* p.377-403
- *Names*
  Earle — *Home* p.441-442
, Old-time
  Glubok — *Home* p.326-327
- *Oracles*
  Earle — *Child* p.380-381
- *Seeds*
  Glubok — *Home* p.327-328

FLOYD, WILLIAM
Bakeless — *Signers* p.187-188
Malone — *Story* p.143-144
- *Biography*
  Lossing — *Biog.* p.63-66

FOOD
See also names of food; names of localities
Adams — *Provincial* p.74-75, 90
Gould — *Early* p.82-107
Greene — *Revol.* p.127, 177, 252-254, 278-279
Ross — *Taste* p.55
Scott — *Trumpet. See* index p.303
Speare — *Life* p.69-72
Tunis — *Frontier* p.25-28
Tunis — *Living* p.135-139
Tunis — *Young* p.24-25
- *Abundance*
  Main — *Social* p.131
- *Albany, N.Y.*
  Axtell — *18th* p.135-136
, and drink
  See also **Beverages**
  Glubok — *Home* p.56-63, 67-74, 81, 83-93
  Miller — *First* p.182-188
  Scott — *Settlers* p.180-181
- *Appetite*
  Downey — *Our* p.183-193
- *Availability*
  Glubok — *Home* p.89-90
- *Backwoods, Southern*
  Spruill — *Women's* p.81-82, 82n
- *Children*
  Earle — *Customs* p.24-26
- *Colonial diet*
  Alden — *Pioneer* p.37
- *Cost*
  Main — *Social* p.115-117, 120, 122, 141, 151
  - *Boston*
    Earle — *Customs* p.157-160
- *Farm*
  Earle — *Home* p.158
- *Harvest*
  Earle — *Customs* p.231-232
- *Luxuries*
  Tunis — *Living* p.137
- *Middle Colonies*
  Train — *Story* p.194-195
- *New England*
  Earle — *Customs* p.153-154, 156-162
  Train — *Story* p.164-165
, of slaves
  Main — *Social* p.124
- *Pennsylvania recipes*
  Train — *Story* p.194-195
- *Philadelphia*
  Earle — *Home* p.160
- *Preservation*
  Earle — *Customs* p.156
- *Republic*
  Train — *Story* p.239
, Serving of
  See also **Etiquette**
  Glubok — *Home* p.54
- *Shortage*
  Bridenbaugh — *Wild.* p.196-197, 353-354
  Forbes — *Paul* p.274, 282, 295, 326-327
- *South*
  Spruill — *Women's* p.67-70
  Train — *Story* p.213-214
- *Substitutes*
  Earle — *Home* p.158-159
- *Women*
  Dexter — *Colonial* p.45-50

FOOTBALL
Dulles — *History* p.33

FOOTE, ABIGAIL
Glubok — *Home* p.199-200

FORCE, PETER
Morris — *Voices* p.99-100

FOREIGN AFFAIRS
See also names of countries, special subjects
Morris — *Voices* p.155-157

FOREST
Pettingill — *Yankee* p.37-41
- *Despoilment*
  Bartlett — *New* p.237-239
- *Industries*
  Morris — *Ency.* p.493

FORETELLERS
Wilson — *Early* p.121

FORGES
See also **Iron industry**
- *Pennsylvania, first*
  Burt — *Phila.* p.250

"FORTE-PIANERS." *See* **Pianos**

FORTS
Amer. Her. — *Rev. See* index p.381
Langdon — *Every.* p.117-119
Speare — *Life* p.84-85
Tunis — *Frontier* p.32-33
Wheeler — *Voices. See* index p.475
- *Chambly (Canada)*
  Stember — *North* p.30-33, 47
- *Clinton*
  Stember — *North* p.95, 117-120, 122, 124-125, 134-135, 137-140
, *Community*
  Tunis — *Young* p.47
- *Dorchester*
  Stember — *South* p.55-56
- *Duquesne*
  Adams — *Album* p.347
  Morris — *Voices* p.54-57
- *George*
  Stember — *North* p.257-264
- *Georgia*
  See also names of forts
  Stember — *South* p.25-29
- *Griswold*
  Stember — *North* p.363, 365-367, 370
- *Loudon*
  Adams — *Album* p.349
- *McHenry*
  Landmarks Liberty p.20-21
- *Mercer*
  Stember — *Middle* p.138-141
- *Mifflin*
  Scott — *Trumpet* p.211, 215-216
  Stember — *Middle* p.132-138
- *Montgomery*
  Stember — *North* p.95, 117-122, 124-125, 135-136, 144, 168-169, 185, 189, 197
- *Moultrie*
  Scott — *Trumpet* p.107-108, 110-111, 163, 248
- *Ontario*
  Stember — *North* p.60-63
- *Pownall*
  Stember — *North* p.264-265
- *Schoharie*
  Stember — *North* p.77-83
- *Stanwix*
  Stember — *North* p.63-67
- *Ticonderoga*
  Amer. Her. — *Rev. See* index p.381
  Amer. Reader p.91-93
  Collins — *Story* p.106
  Hale — *Through* p.116-127
  Life — *Making* p.11-12, 24-25, 57-59
  Morris — *Voices* p.90-97
  National — *History* p.196-197
  Stearns — *Story* p.86-89
  Stember — *North* p.7-19
  200 Years p.49-52, 122-125
  Wheeler — *Voices* p.39-47, 85, 177, 183, 198, 203, 223-226, 229-231, 240, 277
- *Tonyn*
  Stember — *South* p.25-27
- *Washington*
  Life — *Making* p.14-15, 30, 55, 93
  Stember — *North* p.253-256
- *William Henry, massacre at*
  Collins — *Story* p.92

FOSTER, HANNAH WEBSTER
Benson — *Women 18th* p.178, 181, 189-192, 201

FOX HUNTING
Speare — *Life* p.162-164
Tunis — *Living* p.149

FRANCE
See also **French; French and Indian War; French Revolution**
Greene — *Revol. See* index p.465
Life — *Making. See* index p.157
Life — *New. See* index p.173
Miller — *Origins. See* index p.511
Morris — *Voices* p.111, 121, 125-129, 183-187
200 Years. See index p.347
Wheeler — *Voices* p.221, 296, 308-315

- Fleet
Scott — *Trumpet* p.230, 234, 236-239, 263-264, 266, 268, 281

, in American Revolution
Adams — *Album* p.399
Amer. Her. — *Rev. See* index p.381
Forbes — *Paul* p.323, 325-331
Ingraham — *Album* p.67
Kraus — *U.S. (1)* p.230-233, 280-285
McDowell — *Rev.* p.109-110, 121, 134-135, 148-149, 171, 173, 186-189
Morison — *Oxford (1)* p.331-337
Morris — *Ency.* p.91-92, 98-99, 128
Sanderlin — *1776* p.22-24, 207, 238-239, 242, 249, 252
Scott — *Trumpet* p.228-230, 234-235
Stember — *North* p.13, 101, 114-115, 120, 147, 321, 323-329, 348-351

- Influence on American life
Forbes — *Paul* p.405-406

- Loss of empire
Amer. Reader p.65-79

, Naval war with
Morris — *Ency.* p.128-129

- Post-Revolutionary relations
Wright — *New* p.29-30, 46

FRANCISCO, PETER
Cook — *What* p.179-214

FRANKLIN, ANN
Dexter — *Colonial* p.168-169

FRANKLIN, BENJAMIN
Alden — *Pioneer* p.36, 47, 58, 67, 83, 88, 92, 94, 115, 131
Amer. Her. — *Rev. See* index p.381
Bakeless — *Signers* p.107-126
Benson — *Women 18th. See* index p.338
Bridenbaugh — *Wild. See* index p.491
Brodie — *Jefferson. See* index p.791
Cable — *American* p.76-77
Carman — *History. See* index p.x
Colbourn — *Colonial* p.157-166
Collins — *Story* p.65
Dannett — *Yankee* p.18, 28, 73-78, 105, 191, 218, 229
Davis — *Heroes* p.64-78
Earle — *Home. See* index p.458
Forbes — *Paul. See* index p.490
Glubok — *Home. See* index p.351
Greene — *Revol.* p.465-466
Hofstadter — *Amer.* p.vi
Ingraham — *Album* p.87
Life — *Making* p.14, 36-38, 45, 60-61, 80, 88-89, 105, 130-132
Life — *New. See* index p.173
McDowell — *Rev. See* index p.197
Malone — *Story* p.161-164; *See also* index p.280
Miers — *American* p.67-74
Miller — *Colonial* p.154-155
Miller — *Origins. See* index p.511
Morison — *Oxford (1). See* index p.413
Sanderlin — *1776 See* index p.258
Train — *Story* p.101-102
Tunis — *Tavern* p.36, 55, 62-63, 65, 73
Tunis — *Young* p.55-56
200 Years. See index p.347

FRANKLIN, BENJAMIN (*continued*)
Wertenbaker — *Golden* p.3, 14-15, 24, 62, 65, 68-70, 72-74
Wheeler — *Voices* p.118, 169-170, 261-262, 343
Whitney — *Abigail. See* index p.354
Wilson — *American* p.16-23
- "Advice to a young man"
Downey — *Our* p.171-182
Miller — *Colonial* p.384-385
, and Declaration of Independence
Amer. Her. — *Rev.* p.143-144
, and Stamp Act
Morris — *American* p.81-86
, and the American psyche
Baldwin — *Ideas* p.118-124
, as ambassador
Hale — *Through* p.108-112
, as "lowbrow"
Baldwin — *Ideas* p.130-131
, as meteorologist
Wilson — *American* p.23
, as physicist
Wilson — *American* p.23
, as scientist
Wilson — *American* p.18
Wright — *Cultural* p.231-233
, Attack on
Morris — *American* p.110-113
- Autobiography
Miller — *Colonial* p.419-436
Morris — *Ency.* p.564
- Biography
Lossing — *Biog.* p.104-111
Morris — *Ency.* p.661
- Broad interests
Burt — *Phila.* p.145-154
Wilson — *American* p.22-23
- Doctrines
Wright — *New* p.97-98
- Education, interest in
Burt — *Phila.* p.215-220
- Examination, by House of Commons
Morris — *American* p.84-86
- "Grand design"
Treasury Amer. p.88-95
- Leyden-jar experiments
Wilson — *American* p.20-21
- Libraries
Burt — *Phila.* p.206-210
Wright — *Cultural* p.148-149
- Musical interest
Rublowsky — *Music* p.41
, on American life, immigration
Morris — *Voices* p.137-140
, on character, etc.
Baldwin — *Ideas* p.124-125
, on Treaty of Paris
Morris — *Voices* p.124-129
, on wealth
Burner — *American* p.66-72
Miller — *Colonial* p.377-384
, on wives
Belote — *Compleat* p.15
, on women
Benson — *Women 18th. See* index p.338
- Philadelphia
Morris — *Voices* p.65-70
- Pro and con
Baldwin — *Ideas* p.118-119
- Proverbs
Burt — *Phila.* p.140-141
- Seal, design for
Amer. Her. — *Rev.* p.151
- "The speech of Polly Baker"
Miller — *Colonial* p.156-158
- Speech to Constitutional Convention
Morris — *Voices* p.165-167
- Vision of America (1767)
Morris — *American* p.191-195
- Writings
Wright — *Cultural* p.174-175

FRANKLIN, DEBORAH READ ROGERS
Holliday — *Woman's* p.85, 147-148

FRANKLIN, SARAH. *See* Bache, Sarah Franklin

FRANKLIN FAMILY
Burt — *Phila.* p.146, 155, 175
Earle — *Colonial* p.65-66

FRANKLIN STOVE
Adams — *Album* p.324
Dolan — *Yankee* p.154-156
Earle — *Home* p.70
Glubok — *Home* p.38
Morris — *Ency.* p.535
Ross — *Taste* p.121-122
Tunis — *Living* p.134

FRANKS, REBECCA
Benson — *Women 18th* p.283
Burt — *Phila.* p.282-283
Ellet — *Eminent* p.121-129

FRAUDS
Bridenbaugh — *Revolt* p.83-84

"FREE QUAKERS." *See* **"Fighting Quakers"**

FREEDOM
See also **Independence; Liberty**
, *Shock of*
Wilson — *American* p.37-39
, *Striving for greater*
Kraus — *U.S. (1)* p.123-129
, *Surge of*
National — *History* p.264-272

FREEDOM OF SPEECH AND ASSEMBLY
Adams — *Album* p.361

FREEDOM OF THE PRESS
Adams — *Album* p.288
Angle — *By* p.22-29
- *Fight for (1736)*
Davie — *Profile* p.95-97
- *New England*
Wertenbaker — *Golden* p.24-25

FREEDOM TO WORSHIP. *See* **Religious freedom**

FREEMAN'S FARM
, *Battles of*
Amer. Her. — *Rev.* p.244-247, 253-254
Stember — *North* p.91, 93-97, 100

FREEMASONRY. *See* **Masonic order**

FREIGHT SERVICE
Bridenbaugh — *Wild.* p.333-336

FRELINGHUYSEN, THEODORUS J.
Adams — *Provincial* p.280-281
Hofstadter — *Amer.* p.40, 231-233, 255
Sweet — *Story* p.139-140

FRENCH
See also **Canada and Canadians—French; France**
Greene — *Revol. See* index p.466
, *before Revolution*
Crèvecoeur -- *Sketches* p.175-177
, *in American Revolution. See* **France, in American Revolution**
, *in colonies*
Axtell — *18th* p.162-166
, *in Illinois*
Amer. Her. — *Rev.* p.299-301
, *in interior*
Kraus — *U.S. (1)* p.148-149
, *in Philadelphia*
Burt — *Phila.* p.303
, *on Mississippi River, expansion*
Morris — *Ency.* p.63

FRENCH AND INDIAN WAR (Seven Years' War)
Adams — *Provincial* p.293, 295
Alden — *Pioneer* p.32, 66, 70
Amer. Reader p.69-72
Carman — *History* p.71, 154-156
Colbourn — *Colonial* p.281-291
Ingraham — *Album* p.14-15
Kraus — *U.S. (1)* p.154-158
Miers — *American* p.63-67
Miller — *Origins* p.39-49, 54, 69-73, 89-94, 429, 432
Morison — *Oxford (1)* p.224-234, 282, 326
Morris — *Ency.* p.67-70, 413-414
Morris — *Voices* p.49, 54-57
National — *History* p.170-175
Stearns — *Story* p.68-69, 77, 84, 86
Stember — *North* p.12, 20, 22, 40, 63, 119, 227, 268, 299-300
Tunis — *Frontier* p.41
200 Years p.13

FRENCH LANGUAGE, STUDY OF
, *for women*
Benson — *Women 18th* p.32, 49, 73, 114, 133, 146, 162-163, 166

FRENCH REVOLUTION
Butterfield — *Amer.* p.19
Morris — *Voices* p.102, 134, 174, 181
Wright — *New* p.23-29
, *Impact of*
Morris — *Ency.* p.125

FRIENDLY SOCIETIES
Bridenbaugh — *Revolt* p.127-128, 322-323, 325

FRIENDS, SOCIETY OF. *See* Quakers

FRIES, JOHN
- *Uprising*
Morris — *Ency.* p.130

FRONTIER
See also **Allegheny Mountains; Ohio Valley; West and westward movement; Wilderness;** special subjects and localities
Baldwin — *Ideas* p.132-139
Carman — *History* p.54-58
Greene — *Revol. See* index p.466
Life — *Making* p.62-63, 110-114, 117-123, 126-127
Life — *New* p.60, 64, 101, 122, 145-146, 149-150
, *and abundance*
Baldwin — *Ideas* p.145-154
, *and American character*
Baldwin — *Ideas* p.141-144
- *Culture*
Main — *Social* p.240
, *Deepwater*
Tunis — *Frontier* p.13
- *Expansion*
Morris — *Ency.* p.409-411
- *Individualism on*
Kraus — *U.S. (1)* p.143-144
- *Life*
Kraus — *U.S. (1)* p.142-149
Miller — *First* p.135-142
Tunis — *Young* p.45-48
-*Morality*
Main — *Social* p.172-176, 193-194, 196, 281
- *Myths*
Bartlett — *New* p.3-18
- *Society*
Main — *Social* p.277
, *Wealth, distribution of*
Main — *Social* p.276n

FRONTIERSMEN
Axtell — *18th* p.234-235
Tunis — *Frontier* p.17-18
Tunis — *Living* p.101-104
Wilson — *Early* p.14
, *as soldiers*
Scott — *Trumpet* p.87, 90-91
Tunis — *Frontier* p.17-18

FRUGALITY. *See* Thrift

FRUIT
See also names of fruits
Tunis — *Young* p.20-21, 109

FUEL
See also **Coal; Wood;** etc.
Bridenbaugh — *Revolt* p.25-27, 232-235
Bridenbaugh — *Wild.* p.151-153, 311-313
- *Boston*
Bridenbaugh — *Revolt* p.25-26, 129, 234
, *Charlestown*
Bridenbaugh — *Revolt* p.27, 234-235
- *New York*
Bridenbaugh — *Revolt* p.26-27, 233-234
- *Newport, R.I.*
Bridenbaugh — *Revolt* p.27, 232-233, 310
- *Philadelphia*
Bridenbaugh — *Revolt* p.27

FULLERS
Tunis — *Colonial* p.35-36

FULTON, ROBERT
Wilson — *American* p.64-65
- *Biography*
Morris — *Ency.* p.662-663

FUNERALS
See also **Cemeteries; Epitaphs; "Mourning pieces"; Tombstones**
Bridenbaugh — *Revolt* p.128-129, 274
Bridenbaugh — *Wild.* p.255, 387, 412
Cable — *American* p.45
Earle — *Customs* p.365-387

Glubok — *Home* p.301
Sirkis — *Reflect.* p.23
, as recreations
Holliday — *Woman's* p.193-197, 216-217
- Cost
Holliday — *Woman's* p.216
- Dinners, Bostonian
Downey — *Our* p.207-215
- Elegies, poetical
Earle — *Customs* p.365-367
- Gifts
Earle — *Home* p.298-299
Train — *Story* p.164
- Gloves
Earle — *Customs* p.374-376, 379
Earle — *Home* p.298-299
- Pallbearers, girls as
Earle — *Colonial* p.205
- Rings
Earle — *Customs* p.376-379
Earle — *Home* p.298
- Sermons, on women
Benson — *Women 18th* p.105, 107, 124, 179-180
- Tributes
Earle — *Colonial* p.41-42

FUR TRADE
See also **Hunting and trapping**
Carman — *History* p.69, 71
Greene — *Revol.* p.168, 173, 399, 416
Kraus — *U.S. (1)* p.119-120, 148
Life — *Making* p.122-123, 125
Tunis — *Young* p.90-91
- South
Adams — *Provincial* p.208

FURNITURE
See also **Cabinetmakers;** names of pieces of furniture
Adams — *Album* p.322-323
Dolan — *Yankee* p.123-125
Dreppard — *Pioneer* p.243-246, 250, 252-258, 260-265
Gould — *Early* p.43
Langdon — *Every.* p.147-157
Ross — *Taste* p.103, 107-110
Tunis — *Living* p.130-131
Wertenbaker — *Golden* p.42-43, 75-77, 100-101, 117-119, 133-134, 157
Wright — *Cultural* p.205-206
- Adam style-Federal
Gowans — *Images* p.164-172
- Age of transition
Gowans — *Images* p.124-136
- Charleston
Wertenbaker — *Golden* p.133-134
- Chippendale-Georgian
Gowans — *Images* p.151-163
Train — *Story* p.184-187
- Classical
- Four phases
Gowans — *Images* p.120-123
, Colonial
Life — *New* p.105, 113, 128
- Diversity
Gowans — *Images* p.173-223
- Duncan Phyfe
Train — *Story* p.230-231
- Frontier
Kraus — *U.S. (1)* p.142-143
- Heppelwhite
Train — *Story* p.231-233
- History
Gowans — *Images. See* index p.495
, Homemade
Tunis — *Frontier* p.23
- Materials
Gowans — *Images. See* index p.195
- Middle Colonies
Train — *Story* p.184-190
- Personal expression
Gowans — *Images* p.224-239
- Philadelphia
Wertenbaker — *Golden* p.168
- Queen Anne
Gowans — *Images* p.137-150
Train — *Story* p.157-160, 184-185, 210
- Regional forms
Gowans — *Images. See* index p.495-496
- Republic
Train — *Story* p.230-235
- Sheraton
Train — *Story* p.230-231
- South
Train — *Story* p.209-211
- Styles
Gowans — *Images. See* index p.195

FURNITURE (*continued*)
- *Virginia*
Wertenbaker — *Golden* p.117-119
- *William and Mary*
Gowans — *Images* p.124-136

G

GAGE, THOMAS
Alden — *Pioneer* p.68, 77, 79, 83-84
Forbes — *Paul. See* index p.490
Life — *Making* p.8-11, 17-18
Miller — *Origins. See* index p.511
Sanderlin — *1776* p.91, 122, 141, 145-147, 164-165, 188
Scott — *Trumpet* p.71-72, 76-77, 79, 84, 93
200 Years p.18, 21-30, 34-35, 42, 61

GALLATIN, ALBERT
- *Biography*
Morris — *Ency.* p.603

GALLITZIN, DEMETRIUS
Dolan — *Yankee* p.223

GALLOWAY, GRACE GROWDON
Evans — *Weather.* p.185-244

GALLOWAY, JOHN
Sanderlin — *1776* p.120-124, 127

GALLOWAY, JOSEPH
Beach — *Samuel* p.269-270

GALLOWAY PLAN
Colbourn — *Colonial* p.227-233
Morris — *American* p.128-130
Morris — *Ency.* p.83-84
Sanderlin — *1776* p.123-125, 251

GAMBLING
Bridenbaugh — *Revolt* p.120, 315, 364-366
Bridenbaugh — *Wild.* p.78, 227-228, 389-390
Cable — *American* p.67

GAME
See also **Hunting**
Gould — *Early* p.98
Tunis — *Living* p.104

GAMES. *See* Amusements; Boys—Games; Children and childhood—Games; Sports and games

GANNETT, DEBORAH SAMPSON. *See* Sampson, Deborah

GAOLS. *See* Prisons and prisoners

GARDEN, ALEXANDER
Wright — *Cultural* p.230-231

GARDENS
See also **Flowers**
Bridenbaugh — *Revolt* p.143, 145, 339-340
, Flower
Glubok — *Home* p.327-329
Speare — *Life* p.82
- *New York*
Earle — *Home* p.439-440
- *Pennsylvania*
Earle — *Home* p.439-440
- *Pieces (accessories)*
Dreppard — *Pioneer* p.192
- *Rhode Island*
Earle — *Home* p.437-438
- *South*
Earle — *Home* p.438-439
Spruill — *Women's. See* index p.406
- *Virginia*
Earle — *Home* p.439
Wertenbaker — *Golden* p.115-116

***GASPEE* (affair)**
Amer. Reader p.84-86
Ingraham — *Album* p.24
Miller — *Origins* p.325-329

GATES, HORATIO
Amer. Her. — *Rev.* p.143, 247-248, 254, 324-327, 339, 342
Life — *Making* p.57-59, 65, 70-71, 82-83, 85
McDowell — *Rev.* p.14, 57, 114, 116-117, 120-122, 130, 153, 155, 165, 192

Scott — *Trumpet* p.195-196, 199, 201
Stember — *North. See* index p.380
200 Years p.69, 120, 123-125, 129, 133-134, 138-140
Wheeler — *Voices. See* index p.475

GATES
- *Wrought-iron*
Langdon — *Every.* p.165-167

GEESE PLUCKING
Gould — *Early* p.125

GENÊT, EDMOND
Life — *Growing* p.15-16
Morris — *Ency.* p.125-126
Wright — *New* p.30

GENLIS, MADAME DE
Benson — *Women 18th* p.79, 81-84, 89, 156, 164

"GENTLEMEN"
, *Books owned by*
Main — *Social* p.257
- *Definition*
Main — *Social* p.217-218
- *New York*
Bridenbaugh — *Wild.* p.275

GEOGRAPHY
Wertenbaker — *Golden* p.44, 68, 137
, *and Geology*
Greene — *Revol.* p.145-146, 293-294, 384-385

GEORGE III
Alden — *Pioneer. See* index p.iv
Carman — *History. See* index p.xi
Colbourn — *Colonial* p.270-281
Ingraham — *Album* p.23
Kraus — *U.S. (1)* p.208-210, 216
Life — *Making* p.17, 19, 34-35, 57, 59, 87, 89
Life — *New* p.142, 144, 147-148, 151, 155-156
Miller — *Origins. See* index p.511
Morris — *American* p.167-175
Morris — *Ency.* p.74, 84-85, 88-91, 110, 113
Morris — *Voices* p.155-157
Sanderlin — *1776. See* index p.258
Scott — *Trumpet. See* index p.303
200 Years. See index p.347

GEORGETOWN, SOUTH CAROLINA
Stember — *South* p.42, 66-68

GEORGIA
Greene — *Revol. See* index p.466
Hofstadter — *Amer. See* index p.vi
Life — *New* p.60-61, 66, 139
Main — *Social* p.92, 112, 118-119
Miller — *Origins* p.53, 141, 402, 479
Morison — *Oxford (1)* p.193, 196, 213-216, 283, 313, 336
National — *History* p.166-169
Stember — *South* p.5-38
200 Years p.29, 68, 70, 80, 139, 176
, *and Declaration of Independence*
Bakeless — *Signers* p.285-298
Malone — *Story* p.239-245
- *Founding*
Kraus — *U.S. (1)* p.151-152
Morris — *Ency.* p.64
- *Revolutionary War*
Amer. Her. — *Rev.* p.322-323, 337
- *Settlers*
Boorstin — *Americans* p.71-96

GEORGIAN ARCHITECTURE. ***See*** **Architecture, Georgian**

GERARD, LOUIS
Scott — *Trumpet* p.234-236, 240

GERMAN BAPTISTS. ***See*** **Dunkers**

GERMAN REFORMED CHURCH
Greene — *Revol.* p.366-367, 377
Morris — *Ency.* p.550
Sweet — *Religion* p.82-84
Sweet — *Story* p.111-112, 181, 200-201

GERMANS
See also **Palatinates**
Alden — *Pioneer* p.45, 49, 57-58
Bridenbaugh — *Wild.* p.232, 250, 334, 409-410
Greene — *Revol. See* index p.466-467
Kraus — *U.S. (1)* p.104-106
Miller — *Origins* p.53, 61-63
Morison — *Oxford (1)* p.187, 196-199, 214, 240-241, 293, 303, 313, 317, 319-321, 324, 337
Wright — *Cultural* p.250
- Craftsmen
Wright — *Cultural* p.215
- Culture
Wertenbaker — *Golden* p.14-15
- Frontier
Carman — *History* p.56-57
Kraus — *U.S. (1)* p.142-143
- Immigrants
Adams — *Provincial* p.175-184
Bridenbaugh — *Revolt* p.14, 51, 87, 135-136, 231, 261-262, 322, 332-333
Hofstadter — *Amer.* p.6, 11-12, 17-24, 28, 36-37, 163, 168, 170, 175-176, 181, 183
Morris — *Ency.* p.444
Scott — *Settlers* p.68-76, 80-81
Sirkis — *Reflect.* p.89-90
- Pennsylvania
See also **Pennsylvania Dutch**
Tunis — *Living* p.100
- Mercenaries
Amer. Her. — *Rev.* p.172-173
- Soldiers
See also **Hessians**
Amer. Her. — *Rev. See* index p.382
Ingraham — *Album* p.42
Stember — *North* p.84, 86-88
- Views on women
Benson — *Women 18th* p.281, 299-300
- Women
Benson — *Women 18th* p.302-304

GERMANTOWN, PENNSYLVANIA
, Battle of
Amer. Her. — *Rev.* p.213-216, 226
Burt — *Phila.* p.256, 274-275
Collins — *Story* p.116
Handlin — *This* p.25
Stember — *Middle* p.126-132

GERRY, ELBRIDGE
Bakeless — *Signers* p.59-64
Malone — *Story* p.118-120
Morris — *Voices* p.159-161, 164, 183-187
- Biography
Lossing — *Biog.* p.40-43

GIBBES, SARAH REEVE
Ellet — *Eminent* p.142-153

GINSENG
Burt — *Phila.* p.118

GIRARD, STEPHEN
Burt — *Phila.* p.326-327, 329-332

GIRLS
- Amusements
Tunis — *Living* p.149
- Beauty
Handlin — *This* p.98
- Clothing and dress
Spruill — *Women's* p.133
- Colchester, Conn.
Earle — *Home* p.253
- Complexions
Glubok — *Home* p.278-279
- Education
See also **Schools, Girls'**
Earle — *Child* p.91-116
Glubok — *Home* p.123-129
Speare — *Life* p.112-113
- Occupations
Earle — *Home* p.252-256

GLASS
Earle — *Customs* p.143-144
Langdon — *Every.* p.200-210
Train — *Story* p.187
Wright — *Culture* p.214-215
- Blowers
Tunis — *Colonial* p.136-141

- *Making*
Hale — *Through* p.85-91
Speare — *Life* p.125
Tunis — *Living* p.115-116
Tunis — *Young* p.69
, *Stiegel*
Adams — *Album* p.321
Burt — *Phila.* p.231-232
- *Uses*
Glubok — *Home* p.24, 49-50
, *Window*
Dolan — *Yankee* p.185-186

GLOVES
- *Funeral*
Earle — *Customs* p.374-376, 379
Earle — *Home* p.298-299
- *South*
Spruill — *Women's* p.123-124

GOBLETS
Earle — *Home* p.96

GOD, WORSHIP OF. See Religion

GODDARD, ANNA
Earle — *Colonial* p.61-62

GODDARD, JOHN
Train — *Story* p.157-158, 186

GODDARD, MARY KATHARINE
Earle — *Colonial* p.59-60
Spruill — *Women's* p.266-267

GODDARD, SARAH
Earle — *Colonial* p.57-58

GODDARD, WILLIAM
Earle — *Colonial* p.57-61

GODDARD FAMILY
Dexter — *Colonial* p.171-173
Earle — *Colonial* p.57-62

"GOLDEN HILL" RIOT
Morris — *Ency.* p.79

GOLDSMITH, OLIVER
Glubok — *Home* p.172-174, 178-179

GOLDSMITHS
Main — *Social* p.29, 81, 275

GOSHEN, CONNECTICUT
Gould — *Early* p.131

GOVERNESSES
Dexter — *Colonial* p.95-97

GOVERNMENT
See also names of federal departments, localities, etc.
Bridenbaugh — *Wild. See* index p.492
Life — *New. See* index p.173
- *Contracts*
Bridenbaugh — *Revolt* p.68-69, 252
- *Establishment*
Miers — *American* p.94-98
- *Fear of strong*
Morris — *American* p.219-222
- *First three systems*
Miers — *American* p.94
, *Frames of*
Morison — *Oxford (1)* p.358-362
, *Local*
Bridenbaugh — *Revolt* p.6-11, 217-224
- *Need for central*
Morris — *American* p.219

GOVERNORS
See also names of governors
, *Royal*
Miller — *Origins* p.32-35, 38
, *versus Assembly*
Kraus — *U.S.(1)* p.126-127

GRAIN
See also **Cereal farming;** names of grain
Crèvecoeur — *Sketches* p.336
Tunis — *Young* p.19
- *Frontier*
Kraus — *U.S. (1)* p.144-145

GRAMMAR
Glubok — *Home* p.145-147

GRAMMAR SCHOOLS. *See* Schools, Grammar

GRANARIES
Bridenbaugh — *Revolt* p.81, 83, 280, 324

GRANT, ANNE MacVICAR
Benson — *Women 18th* p.104, 281-282, 305-306

GRASS
Pettengill — *Yankee* p.42-50

GRASSE, FRANÇOIS J. P. DE, MARQUIS
200 Years p.143-150, 158

GRAVESTONES. *See* Tombstones

GRAY, ROBERT
Wright — *New* p.163-164

GRAYDON, ALEXANDER
Amer. Reader p.104-106

GREAT AND GENERAL COURT
Beach — *Samuel. See* index p.325-326

"GREAT AWAKENING"
Adams — *Album* p.273
Adams — *Provincial* p.279-283
Alden — *Pioneer* p.55-58
Bridenbaugh — *Revolt* p.151-152, 162, 164
Cable — *American* p.45-47
Carman — *History* p.98-101
Dulles — *History* p.43
Hofstadter — *Amer. See* index p.vi
Kraus — *U.S. (1)* p.137-139
Morison — *Oxford (1)* p.208-212
Morris — *Ency.* p.549
Scott — *Settlers* p.150-151, 154-162, 164-165
Treasury Amer. p.120
- *Middle and Southern colonies*
Sweet — *Story* p.138-154
- *New England*
Sweet — *Story* p.127-137
- *Virginia*
Sweet — *Story* p.147-148

"GREAT AWAKENING," SECOND
Sweet — *Religion* p.146-149
- *Western phase*
Sweet — *Story* p.226-227

GREAT BRITAIN
See also **British; England and English**; etc.
Greene — *Revol. See* index p.467
Life — *Making. See* index p.156 (under Britain)
Miller — *Origins. See* index p.512
- *Costs of empire*
Kraus — *U.S. (1)* p.184-187
- *Imperial policy*
Morris — *American* p.49-77
- *Strategy*
Ingraham — *Album* p.61
- *Strength and weaknesses*
Ingraham — *Album* p.43

GREAT PHILADELPHIA WAGON ROAD
Wright — *Cultural* p.250

GREAT SEAL OF THE UNITED STATES. *See* Seal of the U.S.

GREATNESS
- *Definition*
Sloane — *Spirits* p.43

GREEN, ANNE CATHERINE
Spruill — *Women's* p.264-265

GREEN, NANCY
Ellet — *Eminent* p.588-625

GREEN FAMILY
Dexter — *Colonial* p.174-176

GREEN MOUNTAIN BOYS
Miller — *Origins* p.318, 481-482
Morison — *Oxford (1)* p.287, 302, 324-325
National — *History.* p.196-197
Stember — *North* p.13-14, 84-85, 87, 281

GREENE, CATHARINE
Ellet — *Eminent* p.46-57

GREENE, CHRISTOPHER
Amer. Her. — *Rev.* p.123-125, 216, 265

GREENE, NATHANAEL
Amer. Her. — *Rev. See* index p.382
Davis — *Heroes* p.113-126
Life — *Making* p.9, 15, 55, 64-65, 82-85
McDowell — *Rev. See* index p.197
Scott — *Trumpet* p.237, 261, 275
Stember — *Middle. See* index p.167
Stember — *North* p.241, 254-255, 325, 328, 333
Stember — *South. See* index p.212
200 Years p.87, 90, 95-96, 98, 138, 140
Wheeler — *Voices. See* index p.475
- *Biography*
Morris — *Ency.* p.668

GREENE, POLLY
Glubok — *Home* p.217

GREENWICH, CONNECTICUT
Stember — *North* p.360-364

GRENVILLE, GEORGE
Beach — *Samuel* p.4, 8, 50, 53, 68, 90, 95, 106-109, 127, 217, 247
Carman — *History* p.158-166
Miller — *Origins. See* index p.512

GRIDDLES
Gould — *Early* p.78-79, 98

GRIDIRONS
Gould — *Early* p.77-78

GRIFFITH, ELIZABETH
Benson — *Women 18th* p.92-94, 214

GRINDING
Gould — *Early* p.134

GROCERS AND GROCERY STORES
Bridenbaugh — *Revolt* p.278-279
Dexter — *Colonial* p.24-27
- *Women, Southern*
Spruill — *Women's* p.276-277

GUESS BOOKS
Glubok — *Home* p.175-176

GUIDEBOOKS
, *First (1732)*
Adams — *Provincial* p.259

GUILFORD COURTHOUSE, NORTH CAROLINA
, *Battle of*
Stember — *South. See* index p.212

GUNDALOWS (gondolas)
Tunis — *Young* p.16-17

GUNPOWDER
Forbes — *Paul* p.289-290

GUNS
See also **Ballistics**
Adams — *Album* p.374
Greene — *Revol.* p.231, 240, 259-260, 264-265
Sirkis — *Reflect.* p.27-28
Tunis — *Living* p.104
Tunis — *Young* p.65
- *Artillery*
Amer. Her. — *Rev.* p.158-159
- *Cannon*
Speare — *Life* p.91-92
- *Flintlock rifles*
Tunis — *Frontier* p.16-17
- *Muskets*
Life — *100 Events* p.79
Speare — *Life* p.90-91
- *Rifles*
See also **Guns—Flintlock rifles**
Speare — *Life* p.91
, *Long*
Burt — *Phila.* p.250
Morris — *Ency.* p.535
- *Manufacture*
Langdon — *Every.* p.104-107
- *Traps, snares, and hooks*
Dreppard — *Pioneer* p.38-39, 42, 44-45

GUNSMITHS
Tunis — *Colonial* p.63-65
, *German*
Dolan — *Yankee* p.139-140

GUY FAWKES DAY
Beach — *Samuel* p.75-76
Earle — *Customs* p.229-231
Forbes — *Paul* p.89-93
Speare — *Life* p.161

GWINNETT, BUTTON
Bakeless — *Signers* p.290-296
Malone — *Story* p.242-243
- *Biography*
Lossing — *Biog.* p.227-229

H

HADDONFIELD, ELIZABETH
Earle — *Colonial* p.49-50

"HAIL COLUMBIA"
Howard — *Our* p.118-121

HAIRDRESSING
See also **Headdress**
Earle — *Customs* p.291-296
Ross — *Taste* p.203-204
Speare — *Life* p.17
Tunis — *Living* p.144-145
, Long, objection to
Earle — *Customs* p.289-290
, Men's
Tunis — *Young* p.100, 102

HAIRPINS
Ross — *Taste* p.221-222

HALE, NATHAN
Ingraham — *Album* p.56
McDowell — *Rev.* p.92-93, 97-98
Scott — *Trumpet* p.150-153
- *Execution*
Collins — *Story* p.110
- *Song*
Scott — *Trumpet* p.152-153

HALL, LYMAN
Bakeless — *Signers* p.287-290
Malone — *Story* p.240-241
- *Biography*
Lossing — *Biog.* p.229-233

HALLAM, SARAH
Wertenbaker — *Golden* p.54, 95

HALLAM COMPANY (dramatic company)
Dexter — *Colonial* p.158-159
Morris — *Ency.* p.589
Wright — *Cultural* p.182-183

"HALLIARDS" (songs)
Rublowsky — *Music* p.76

HALLS
Gould — *Early* p.24
Sirkis — *Reflect.* p.25

HAMILTON, ALEXANDER
Alden — *Pioneer. See* index p.iv
Amer. Her. — *Rev.* p.192, 219-220, 264, 358
Baldwin — *Ideas* p.206-239
Bridenbaugh — *Revolt* p.36-37, 121, 127, 144, 159-160, 163, 170, 180, 200
Bridenbaugh — *Wild.* p.308, 460, 466
Brodie — *Jefferson. See* index p.791-792
Burt — *Phila. See* index p.387
Greene — *Revol.* p.140, 308, 354, 381, 393
Life — *Growing* p.13, 15, 18-19, 39-40
Life — *Making. See* index p.157
McDowell — *Rev.* p.34, 104-105, 109, 131, 134, 178, 183, 193
Miers — *American* p.88-93
Miller — *Origins* p.29, 182, 184, 291, 373-374, 427-428, 430, 483
Morison — *Oxford (1). See* index p.414
Morris — *Voices* p.163-164, 167, 181, 187
Stember — *North* p.166-168, 173-174, 205, 213, 234, 248
200 Years p.96, 104, 153-154, 162-163, 165, 169-170, 173, 176
Whitney — *Abigail* p.226-227, 250, 253, 275, 281, 283-285, 287-293, 296
Wright — *New* p.18-19
, and Thomas Jefferson
Brodie — *Jefferson. See* index p.157
Butterfield — *Amer.* p.16-17
Morris — *Voices* p.173-174

- *Bank*
Butterfield — *Amer.* p.18
Morris — *Amer.* p.261-266
- *Biography*
Morris — *Ency.* p.669-670
- *Diary (1744)*
Burner — *America* p.91-97
- *Financial program*
See also **Hamilton, Alexander—Bank**
Butterfield — *Amer.* p.18
Kraus — *U.S. (1)* p.274-280
Morris — *Ency.* p.122
- *"Itinerarium"*
Miller — *Colonial* p.389-418
, *on manufactures*
Baldwin — *Ideas* p.242-245
, *on profiteers*
Morris — *Amer.* p.258-261
- *Relations with Burr*
Locke — *Birth* p.101-132

HAMILTON, ANDREW
Bridenbaugh — *Wild.* p.204-205, 307, 426, 456, 461
, *on Peter Zenger*
Angle — *By* p.25-29

HAMILTON, ELIZABETH
Brooks — *Colonial* p.215-244
Holliday — *Woman's* p.104-105, 273-274
Life — *Growing* p.14

HAMMOND HOUSE
Wertenbaker — *Golden* p.5, 98-99

HAMPDEN-SYDNEY ACADEMY
Greene — *Revol.* p.122, 289, 369, 378, 380

HANCOCK, DOROTHY
Ellet — *Eminent* p.93-96

HANCOCK, JOHN
Amer. Her. — *Rev.* p.62, 99, 101, 109, 139
Bakeless — *Signers* p.33-45
Beach — *Samuel. See* index p.326
Bridenbaugh — *Revolt* p.242, 258, 285, 288, 307, 335, 347
Collins — *Story* p.127
Forbes — *Paul. See* index p.491
Greene — *Revol.* p.41, 47, 134, 226, 247, 285, 291
Malone — *Story* p.106-108; *See also* index p.281
Miller — *Origins. See* index p.512
Morison — *Oxford (1)* p.261, 271, 286-287, 289-290, 404-405
Morris — *Voices* p.81-84
Stearns — *Story* p.76-77, 82-83, 91
Whitney — *Abigail* p.50, 52-54, 65, 72, 77-78, 80, 86, 111, 115, 120, 123, 154
- *Biography*
Lossing — *Biog.* p.22-26
Morris — *Ency.* p.670
, *and sloop "Liberty"*
Morris — *American* p.98-100

HANCOCK FAMILY
Wright — *Cultural* p.39-40

HANCOCK HOUSE
Glubok — *Home* p.14-15

HANDICRAFTS. ***See*** **Artisans; Crafts and craftsmanship;** names of crafts

HANDIWORK. ***See*** **Needlework; Spinning; Weavers and weaving;** etc.

HANDWRITING. ***See*** **Penmanship**

HARADEN, JONATHAN
Cook — *What* p.305-335

HARDWARE STORES
- *Women, as managers*
Dexter — *Colonial* p.30-32

HARLEM HEIGHTS, NEW YORK
, *Battle of*
Collins — *Story* p.111
Stember — *North* p.66, 239-241, 255-256

HARMONICAS
- *Invention of B. Franklin*
Rublowsky — *Music* p.41-42

HARNESS MAKERS
Wilson — *Early* p.65

HARPE, WILEY AND MICAJAH
Locke — *Birth* p.53-76

HARPSICHORDS
Earle — *Child* p.112-113

HARRISON, BENJAMIN
Bakeless — *Signers* p.87-90
Malone — *Story* p.210-211
200 Years p.67, 77, 81
- *Biography*
Lossing — *Biog.* p.184-187

HARRISON, JEMIMA CONDICT
Evans — *Weather.* p.33-51

HARRISON, PETER
Bridenbaugh — *Revolt* p.20-21, 23, 25, 41, 81, 140, 143, 180, 247, 282, 309, 335, 404
Wright — *Cultural* p.202-203

HARRISON, WILLIAM HENRY
- *Biography*
Morris — *Ency.* p.672-673

HART, JOHN
Bakeless — *Signers* p.173-174
Malone — *Story* p.146-147
- *Biography*
Lossing — *Biog.* p.87-89

HART, NANCY MORGAN
Cook — *What* p.238-244
Ellet — *Eminent* p.444-449
McDowell — *Rev.* p.169
Somerville — *Women* p.42-45

HARTFORD, CONNECTICUT
Handlin — *This* p.79-80
Morris — *Voices* p.134-135

HARVARD COLLEGE
Bridenbaugh — *Revolt* p.177, 182, 318-319
Greene — *Revol. See* index p.467
Hofstadter — *Amer.* p.212, 228, 288-289
Main — *Social* p.95, 98, 144, 187n, 193, 246
Wertenbaker — *Golden* p.18, 22-23
Whitney — *Abigail* p.3, 68, 120, 124, 214-215, 231, 284
- *Amusements*
Adams — *Album* p.328
- *Library*
Wright — *Cultural* p.151-152

HAT ACT OF 1732 (England)
Carman — *History* p.138
Morris — *Ency.* p.485

HATS AND HATTERS
Adams — *Album* p.311
Colbourn — *Colonial* p.262
Gould — *Early* p.142
Speare — *Life* p.16-17
Tunis — *Colonial* p.46-48
, *Beaver*
Carman — *History* p.138
Dolan — *Yankee* p.73
Speare — *Life* p.133
- *Export restrictions*
Miller — *Origins* p.20-21
- *South*
Spruill — *Women's* p.284, 286

HAUNTED HOUSES
- *Philadelphia*
Burt — *Phila.* p.325-326

HAY
Crèvecoeur — *Sketches* p.138, 142, 183, 233, 239-241

"HAYSEEDS" (bumpkins)
Wilson — *Early* p.162-163

HAYWOOD, ELIZA
Benson — *Women 18th* p.12, 41-44

HEADDRESS
See also **Hairdressing**
- *Philadelphia*
Tunis — *Young* p.54-55
- *South*
Spruill — *Women's* p.119-122, 129, 132-134

HEATH, WILLIAM
Wheeler — *Voices* p.30, 81, 120, 123, 125, 158, 163, 188-193, 440

HEATING
See also **Fireplaces; Franklin stove**
Earle — *Customs* p.129-130
Pettengill — *Yankee* p.90-93

Tunis — *Living* p.133-135
- *Engineering of B. Thompson*
Wilson — *American* p.30-31

HECK, BARBARA RUCKLE
Dexter — *Colonial* p.148-150

HEELPEGS
Glubok — *Home* p.215-216

HENDEE, HANNAH HUNTER
Somerville — *Women* p.52-55

HENRY, JOHN JOSEPH
Wheeler — *Voices* p.86-87, 92-93, 96-102, 104-106, 174

HENRY, PATRICK
Adams — *Album* p.366-367
Alden — *Pioneer* p.37, 73, 78, 88, 106, 114-115, 124, 189
Brodie — *Jefferson. See* index p.794
Greene — *Revol. See* index p.468
Life — *Making* p.9, 34, 40, 105-106, 117, 130, 135
McDowell — *Rev.* p.15-16, 19-20, 139, 174
Miller — *Origins* p.42, 76, 126, 139, 169, 175, 374, 381, 392, 478, 483
Sanderlin — *1776* p.xvi, 29-31, 91, 113, 136-137, 250-251
Scott — *Trumpet* p.29-31, 72
200 Years p.18, 20-21, 176
, *and First Continental Congress*
Collins — *Story* p.100
, *at Virginia Assembly*
Collins — *Story* p.129
Morris — *American* p.71-72
- *Biography*
Morris — *Ency.* p.675

HERKIMER, NICHOLAS
Stember — *North* p.59, 61, 64, 68-71
Wheeler — *Voices* p.233-234, 238, 318

HERMITS
Wilson — *Early* p.118-120

HESSELIUS, GUSTAVUS
Dolan — *Yankee* p.133-134
Sirkis — *Reflect.* p.86-87
Wertenbaker — *Golden* p.96

HESSIANS
See also **Germans—Soldiers**
Alden — *Pioneer* p.85-87, 89-91
Morris — *Voices* p.106-108
Scott — *Trumpet. See* index p.303
Stember — *Middle. See* index p.168
Stember — *North* p.113, 182, 220, 235-236, 242-243, 254-255, 282, 329
Wheeler — *Voices. See* index p.475

HEWES, GEORGE
Forbes — *Paul. See* index p.491
Morris — *Voices* p.77-79
Sanderlin — *1776* p.78-79
- *Biography*
Lossing — *Biog.* p.205-207

HEWES, JOSEPH
Bakeless — *Signers* p.267-270
Malone — *Story* p.222-223

HEWITT, JAMES
Howard — *Our* p.81-90

HEYWARD, THOMAS, JR.
Bakeless — *Signers* p.275-277
Malone — *Story* p.232-233
- *Biography*
Lossing — *Biog.* p.215-218

HIGHER EDUCATION. *See* Colleges and universities

HIGHWAYS
Bridenbaugh — *Revolt* p.28, 56, 236, 238, 265-266
Kraus — *U.S. (1)* p.270-272
, *Colonial*
See also **Roads**; etc.
Kraus — *U.S. (1)* p.161-163
, *King's*
Langdon — *Every.* p.246

HIRED MEN
Wilson — *Early* p.154-155

HISTORIANS
, and annalists
Morris — *Ency.* p.561, 564

HISTORIC LANDMARKS AND SHRINES
See also names of houses, etc.
- in eighteen states
Early Amer. Life — *Yrbk. 1970* p.40-47

HISTORIES
- Writing
Wright — *Cultural* p.163-169

HITCHCOCK, ENOS
, on women
Benson — *Women 18th* p.61, 79, 101, 136, 143, 145, 148, 155-157, 159-160, 164, 167-168, 168n

HOAXES, LITERARY
Miller — *Colonial* p.156-158

HOE CAKES
Gould — *Early* p.74

HOGS
Crèvecoeur — *Sketches* p.82, 102, 112, 142, 145, 232, 235
Gould — *Early* p.101-103
- Butchering
Gould — *Early* p.138-139
Tunis — *Living* p.108-109
- Races and pig runs
- Massachusetts
Dow — *Every* p.113

HOG'S PUDDING
Gould — *Early* p.102

HOLIDAYS AND FESTIVALS
See also names of holidays, etc.
Bridenbaugh — *Wild.* p.276, 435, 437
Earle — *Customs* p.220-233
Gould — *Early* p.142
Speare — *Life* p.159-162
Tunis — *Young* p.120-121
Wright — *Cultural* p.188

HOLLOWWARE
Gould — *Early* p.68

HOME FURNISHINGS
See also **Furniture; Houses—Interiors**
Adams — *Provincial* p.71-73
Earle — *Customs* p.107-131
Greene — *Revol.* p.147-148, 425
Ross — *Taste* p.112
Sirkis — *Reflect.* p.26-27
Wright — *Cultural* p.203-204
- Inventory (1720)
Earle — *Customs* p.118-119
- Massachusetts
Dow — *Every* p.46-52
- South
Spruill — *Women's* p.36-37

HOME RULE
See also **Freedom;** special subjects
Boorstin — *Americans* p.359-362

HOMES. *See* Houses; Log cabins; Mansions

HOMESICKNESS
Speare — *Life* p.82

"HONESTUS" (pseud.)
- Lawyers' role
Morris — *American* p.341-345

HOOKS
Gould — *Early* p.68

HOOP-PETTICOATS
Train — *Story* p.162
Tunis — *Living* p.146-147
- South
Spruill — *Women's* p.116

HOOPER, WILLIAM
Bakeless — *Signers* p.265-267
Malone — *Story* p.225-227
- Biography
Lossing — *Biog.* p.201-204

HOPE
Sloane — *Spirits* p.62-64

HOPKINS, SAMUEL
Sweet — *Story* p.168, 171

HOPKINS, STEPHEN
Bakeless — *Signers* p.213-216
Greene — *Revol.* p.44, 61, 140, 226, 247
Malone — *Story* p.122-123
- Biography
Lossing — *Biog.* p.44-46

HOPKINSON, FRANCIS
Bakeless — *Signers* p.169-173
Bridenbaugh — *Revolt* p.190, 197, 365, 394, 398, 400-401
Dannett — *Yankee* p.121, 147-148, 153, 251, 278, 283
Greene — *Revol.* p.135, 141, 182, 299, 380, 394
Howard — *Our* p.37-44
Malone — *Story* p.156-157
Morris — *Ency.* p.613
Quaife — *History* p.37, 39-40, 180
Scott — *Trumpet* p.183-184, 223-228
Wright — *Cultural* p.195
, and "Stars and Stripes"
Life — *Making* p.41
- Biography
Lossing — *Biog.* p.85-87

HORN
, Uses of
Glubok — *Home* p.47, 50-51, 139

HORNBOOKS
Earle — *Child* p.119-125

HORNSMITHS
Tunis — *Colonial* p.54-56

"HORNSWOGGLERS"
Wilson — *Early* p.174-175

HORSE FAIRS
- Massachusetts
Dow — *Every* p.114

HORSE RACING
Bridenbaugh — *Revolt* p.166-167, 364-365
Bridenbaugh — *Wild.* p.275-276, 435, 441
Dulles — *History* p.35
Earle — *Customs* p.242
Morison — *Oxford (1)* p.205-207
Wright — *Culture* p.189-190
- Massachusetts
Dow — *Every* p.112-113

HORSES
Crèvecoeur — *Sketches* p.337
Earle — *Customs* p.186-191
Earle — *Home* p.336-339
Forbes — *Paul* p.183-186, 204
Langdon — *Every.* p.288-291
Morison — *Oxford (1)* p.197, 205-206, 371-372
Tunis — *Living* p.106-107
, Famous
Downey — *Our* p.195-206
- Handlers and riders
Wilson — *Early* p.125-138

HOSE
Spruill — *Women's* p.123

HOSPITALITY
Speare — *Life* p.20-22

HOSPITALS
Bridenbaugh — *Revolt* p.129-131, 326-329
Morris — *Ency.* p.541
- Bethlehem, Pa.
Langdon — *Every.* p.102-103
- New York
Bridenbaugh — *Revolt* p.230, 330-331
- Philadelphia
Burt — *Phila.* p.283
Wright — *Cultural* p.235

HOTELS. *See* Inns and innkeepers

HOUSE OF REPRESENTATIVES
Beach — *Samuel. See* index p.326
Morris — *Ency.* p.121

HOUSE RAISING
Earle — *Home* p.408-409

HOUSE RENTS. *See* Housing—Rentals

HOUSEHOLD ARTICLES
See also **Kitchen utensils;** names of articles
Tunis — *Frontier* p.24-25
, Handmade
Adams — *Provincial* p.145

HOUSEKEEPERS
- *Qualifications*
Glubok — *Home* p.198-199
- *South*
Spruill — *Women's* p.312-313

HOUSES
See also **Architecture; Log cabins; Mansions;** names of famous houses
Adams — *Provincial* p.67-71, 91-92
Dreppard — *Pioneer* p.15
Glubok — *Home* p.2-15
Sirkis — *Reflect.* p.24
Tunis — *Living* p.109-110
Tunis — *Young* p.38-39
- *Backwoods, Southern*
Spruill — *Women's* p.40-41
- *Charm*
Holliday — *Woman's* p.95-105
, *Colonists*
Alden — *Pioneer* p.36
- *Cost*
Main — *Social* p.119-120, 122, 132, 135, 159
, *Dutch*
Axtell — *18th* p.133-136
- *Entrances*
Gould — *Early* p.41
- *"Entries"*
Sirkis — *Reflect.* p.26
Tunis — *Living* p.110-111
- *Exteriors*
Adams — *Album* p.264-265
, *Farm*
Dow — *Every* p.92-100
Tunis — *Young* p.21-24
- *Georgia*
Spruill — *Women's* p.39-40
, *Interest in*
Holliday — *Woman's* p.141-142
- *Interiors*
Sirkis — *Reflect.* p.25-28
- *Middle Colonies*
Train — *Story* p.179-184
- *New England*
Train — *Story* p.151-159
- *North Carolina*
Spruill — *Women's* p.28-29, 34-35
- *"on the green"*
Speare — *Life* p.43-45
, *Pennsylvania German*
Tunis — *Living* p.100-101
- *Philadelphia*
Axtell — *18th* p.91
Burt — *Phila.* p.258-259
National — *History.* p.212-213
Tunis — *Young* p.50
- *Plantations*
Spruill — *Women's* p.29-37
- *"Republic period"*
Train — *Story* p.225-231
- *South*
Train — *Story* p.203-209
- *South Carolina*
Spruill — *Women's* p.30-31
- *Wilderness cabins*
Langdon — *Every.* p.115-117

HOUSEWARMINGS
Tunis — *Frontier* p.24

HOUSEWIVES
Benson — *Women 18th* p.24-25
Earle — *Colonial* p.15-16
Morris — *Voices* p.36-37
Speare — *Life* p.68-82
- *Attainments, Southern*
Spruill — *Women's* p.83-84
- *Backwoods, Southern*
Spruill — *Women's* p.81-83
, *Dutch*
Smith — *Colonial* p.108-122
- *Duty*
Belote — *Compleat* p.5-7
- *Kentucky*
Tunis — *Frontier* p.48-50
- *Life*
Crèvecoeur — *Sketches* p.41, 43, 45-46, 49, 71-73, 96, 102-104, 122, 142, 144-145
Early Amer. Life — *Yrbk. 1970* p.128
- *Management*
Belote — *Compleat* p.8
, *Revolutionary*
Earle — *Colonial* p.258-275
- *South*
Spruill — *Women's* p.64-84

HOUSEWRIGHTS
Tunis — *Colonial* p.24-25
Tunis — *Young* p.30-31

OUSING
Miller — *First* p.175-181
- *Boston*
Bridenbaugh — *Revolt* p.17-18, 228
- *Charlestown*
Bridenbaugh — *Revolt* p.18-19, 227-228
- *New York*
Bridenbaugh — *Revolt* p.16, 226
- *Newport, R.I.*
Bridenbaugh — *Revolt* p.17, 226-227, 232
- *Philadelphia*
Bridenbaugh — *Revolt* p.13-15, 224-225
- *Rentals*
, Cost of
Main — *Social* p.117-118, 131, 131n, 135
- *New York*
Bridenbaugh — *Revolt* p.16, 226
- *Philadelphia*
Bridenbaugh — *Revolt* p.15, 225

OWE, RICHARD
Ingraham — *Album* p.52-53
200 Years p.45, 82-83, 87, 90, 92, 99, 104, 117, 122, 125, 128, 134
Wheeler — *Voices* p.154-156, 167, 243, 293, 298, 308-311, 324

OWE, WILLIAM
Amer. Her. — *Rev. See* index p.382
Burt — *Phila. See* index p.387
Greene — *Revol.* p.217, 232, 234, 236, 261, 296, 299
Life — *Making* p.10-15, 28, 56-58, 68, 75-76
McDowell — *Rev. See* index p.197
Morison — *Oxford (1)* p.229, 293, 304, 316-324, 328-329
Morris — *Voices* p.104-106, 111, 121
Sanderlin — *1776* p.191, 197-198, 200-201, 238, 252
Scott — *Trumpet. See* index p.304
Stember — *North. See* index p.381
Wheeler — *Voices. See* index p.476

HUBBARDTON, VERMONT
, Battle of
Stember — *North* p.280-283

HUDSON RIVER, NEW YORK
Scott — *Trumpet* p.131, 180, 189, 194-197, 199, 204, 247, 264
Stember — *North. See* index p.381
Treasury Amer. p.175-176, 182-183
, during Revolution
Amer. Her. — *Rev.* p.82, 193, 200, 266-267
- *Valley*
McDowell — *Rev.* p.79, 94-95, 98, 110, 112, 114, 116-117, 155-157

HUDSON'S FERRY, GEORGIA
Stember — *South* p.29-31

HUGHES, JOAN
Miller — *Origins* p.114, 135-137, 152, 195-196, 227

HUGUENOTS
Bridenbaugh — *Wild.* p.250
Forbes — *Paul* p.4-6
Kraus — *U.S. (1)* p.103-104

HULTON, ANNE
Beach — *Samuel* p.136-137, 146-147
Benson — *Women 18th* p.292-293, 298, 301

HUMANITARIANISM
Greene — *Revol. See* index p.468

HUME, SOPHIA
Spruill — *Women's* p.252-253

HUMPHREYS, DAVID
Morris — *Voices* p.176-178

HUMPHREYS, JOSHUA
Burt — *Phila.* p.113, 124

HUNGER
Scott — *Trumpet* p.162-164, 166-167, 169, 171-172, 176, 178, 216-217, 241, 246, 269

HUNTING AND TRAPPING
Collins — *Story* p.137
Dulles — *History* p.24-26
Speare — *Life* p.154
Tunis — *Frontier* p.30

HUNTINGTON, SAMUEL
Bakeless — *Signers* p.202-204
Malone — *Story* p.132-134
- *Biography*
Lossing — *Biog.* p.53-55

HUSBANDS
- *South*
Spruill — *Women's. See* index p.410

HUSKING BEES
Downey — *Our* p.103-114
Dulles — *History* p.26-27
Earle — *Home* p.136
Gould — *Early* p.134, 142
Holliday — *Woman's* p.208-209
Speare — *Life* p.155
Train — *Story* p.174, 176, 224
Wright — *Frontier* p.64
- *Massachusetts*
Dow — *Every* p.117-118

HUTCHINS, THOMAS
Greene — *Revol.* p.294, 384-385
Wright — *Cultural* p.163

HUTCHINSON, THOMAS
Beach — *Samuel. See* index p.326
Forbes — *Paul. See* index p.492
Greene — *Revol.* p.8, 83, 136, 140-141, 201, 212, 216-217
Kraus — *U.S. (1)* p.200-201
Life — *New* p.129, 148, 151-154
Miller — *Origins. See* index p.512
Morison — *Oxford (1)* p.222, 253, 271-273
Morris — *Voices* p.74, 77, 79-80
200 Years p.24-26
- *"Exile's Lament"*
Morris — *American* p.216-218
- *Letters scandal*
Morris — *American* p.110-113
Morris — *Ency.* p.81-82
, *on Stamp Act repeal*
Morris — *American* p.87-93

HYLER, ADAM
Cook — *What* p.275-302

HYMNS
See also **Bay Psalm Book**
Morris — *Ency.* p.612
, *Presbyterian*
Rublowsky — *Music* p.73

I

ICE CREAM
- *First, in Philadelphia*
Burt — *Phila.* p.304

ILE-AUX-NOIX, FORT (Canada)
Stember — *North* p.23

ILLEGITIMACY
Benson — *Women 18th* p.225, 227-228, 230
- *South*
Spruill — *Women's* p.323-324

IMMIGRANTS AND IMMIGRATION
See also names of states; etc.
Alden — *Pioneer* p.37-41
Bridenbaugh — *Revolt* p.4, 134-136, 216, 332-334
Bridenbaugh — *Wild. See* index p.493
Davie — *Profile* p.51-52
Greene — *Revol. See* index p.468
Life — *Making* p.107, 110, 114, 117, 119-121, 126-127
Main — *Social* p.184, 187n, 188, 190-193
Morris — *Ency.* p.445
- *Hardships*
Wright — *New* p.39-47

- *Nationalities*
Adams — *Provincial* p.167-193
Axtell — *18th* p.217-229
Kraus — *U.S. (1)* p.101-102
Morris — *Ency.* p.445

IMORALITY
Bridenbaugh — *Wild.* p.226-227, 388-389

IPORTERS AND IMPORTS
Tunis — *Young* p.60
- *Women*
Dexter — *Colonial* p.33-34

IPRESSMENT
Bridenbaugh — *Revolt* p.26, 61, 114-116, 308-310

IAUGURATIONS
See also **Washington, George— Inauguration**
- *First (1789)*
Butterfield — *Amer.* p.2-3

ICOME
See also **Wages;** names of occupations
, and property
Main — *Social* p.68-114
- *Delaware*
Main — *Social* p.26-27, 32, 295
- *Influence on culture*
Main — *Social* p.240-241
- *Massachusetts lists*
Main — *Social* p.293
, of artisans
Main — *Social* p.75-78, 132
, of blacksmiths
Main — *Social* p.77
, of carpenters
Main — *Social* p.77
, of clergymen
Main — *Social* p.96-98, 139
, of distillers
Main — *Social* p.77n, 132
, of farmers
Main — *Social* p.104-109
, of founders
Main — *Social* p.81n
, of housewrights
Main — *Social* p.77
, of innkeepers
Main — *Social* p.90-91
, of landowners, large
Main — *Social* p.110-112
, of lawyers
Main — *Social* p.101-102, 146-147
, of mariners
Main — *Social* p.74
, of masons
Main — *Social* p.77
, of Massachusetts farms
Main — *Social* p.31
, of merchants
Main — *Social* p.87-88
, of millers
Main — *Social* p.82-83
, of physicians
Main — *Social* p.99-100
, of printers
Main — *Social* p.77n
, of rural laborers
Main — *Social* p.69-72
, of servants, indentured
Main — *Social* p.69
, of ship captains
Main — *Social* p.89
, of shipwrights
Main — *Social* p.77
, of shopkeepers
Main — *Social* p.87-88
, of slaves
Main — *Social* p.68-69
, of Southern overseers
Main — *Social* p.109
, of tailors
Main — *Social* p.77
, of teachers
Main — *Social* p.91-95
, of urban laborers
Main — *Social* p.73
, of weavers
Main — *Social* p.77

INDEPENDENCE
See also **Declaration of Independence; Freedom; Independence Day; Liberty**
Amer. Reader p.95-103
Kraus — *U.S. (1)* p.215-219
Sanderlin — *1776* p.207, 209-216, 253
Scott — *Trumpet* p.115-129

INDEPENDENCE (continued)
- *Caucuses*
Beach — *Samuel* p.293-294, 296
, *Coming of*
Morris — *American* p.151-190
, *Proclaimed by colonies*
Amer. Reader p.101-102
, *Torrent of*
Malone — *Story* p.55-65

INDEPENDENCE DAY
Bakeless — *Signers* p.1-13
Hale — *Through* p.115
Speare — *Life* p.161-162
- *First*
Amer. Reader p.150, 153
Hale — *Through* p.98-101
, *Spirit of*
Sloane — *Spirits* p.52-55

INDEPENDENCE HALL (State House, Philadelphia)
Adams — *Album* p.381
Collins — *Story* p.66
Landmarks Liberty p.40-42
Life — *Growing* p.23
McDowell — *Rev.* p.11, 84, 88, 90
Sanderlin — *1776* p.175-235
Sirkis — *Reflect.* p.90-91
Train — *Story* p.183
- *Architecture*
Gowan — *Images* p.117

INDEX OF AMERICAN DESIGN
Burner — *America* p.127-128

INDIAN CAMPING GROUND (Philadelphia)
Burt — *Phila.* p.49

INDIAN CHARITY SCHOOL (Lebanon, Connecticut)
Downey — *Our* p.125-134

INDIAN TRAILS
Burt — *Phila.* p.105
Dolan — *Yankee* p.30-35

INDIANS
See also names of special subjects, tribes
Adams — *Album* p.350-351
Alden — *Pioneer. See* index p.v
Amer. Reader p.51-53
Axtell — *18th* p.235-237
Crèvecoeur — *Sketches. See* index p.337
Glubok — *Home. See* index p.352
Greene — *Revol. See* index p.468
Hofstadter — *Amer. See* index p.vii
Life — *New. See* index p.174
Morison — *Oxford (1). See* index p.414
Scott — *Trumpet* p.9, 18, 20-23, 29, 182-184, 189, 195, 242-243
Speare — *Life* p.84-85
Stember — *North. See* index p.382
Tunis — *Frontier* p.32
Tunis — *Young. See* index p.154
200 Years. See index p.348

, *and liquor*
Kraus — *U.S. (1)* p.286-287
, *and Revolutionary War*
Amer. Her. — *Rev. See* index p.382
Ingraham — *Album* p.70
Life — *Making* p.18, 57-58, 62-63, 67, 75, 109, 117
Miller — *Origins* p.429-430
, *and settlement of West*
Miller — *Origins* p.74-77
- *Babies*
Handlin — *This* p.13
- *Captures*
Burner — *America* p.84-91
- *Children*
Handlin — *This* p.14
Miller — *Colonial* p.250-251
- *Clothing and dress*
Handlin — *This* p.10-11
Miller — *Colonial* p.248-520
, *Colonists' struggles with*
Alden — *Pioneer* p.34-35
- *Conspiracies with Tories*
Wheeler — *Voices* p.316-322
- *Fighters*
Wilson — *Early* p.15
- *Food*
Handlin — *This* p.9-10
- *Houses and moving*
Handlin — *This* p.13-14
- *Invincibility misconception*
Bartlett — *New* p.16-18

- *Languages and learning*
  Miller — *Colonial* p.256
- *Life*
  Handlin — *This* p.9-14
  Miller — *Colonial* p.248-256
- *Marriage*
  Handlin — *This* p.11-12
  Miller — *Colonial* p.250-251
- *Massacres*
  See also names of massacres, localities
  Amer. Reader p.72-79
  Burt — *Phila.* p.170-171, 181-182
  Colbourn — *Colonial* p.180-186
- *Missions and missionaries*
  Sweet — *Religion* p.239-241
  Sweet — *Story* p.108-109, 160-167
- *Music*
  Howard — *Our. See* index p.787-788
  Rublowsky — *Music* p.53-55
- *Pennsylvania frontier*
  Morris — *American* p.27-31
- *Problem*
  Bartlett — *New* p.19-29
- *Servants*
  Earle — *Customs* p.84-87
- *Slaves*
  Adams — *Provincial* p.101
- *Towns, buildings, and fortifications*
  Miller — *Colonial* p.251-253
- *Trade*
  See also **Byrd, William**
  Adams — *Provincial* p.35-38, 93-95
  Wright — *Frontier* p.25-26, 39
- *Traveling and entertainment*
  Miller — *Colonial* p.253-256
- *Treaties*
  Burt — *Phila.* p.73-74
  , and Louisiana
    Tunis — *Frontier* p.68

NDIGO
Alden — *Pioneer* p.48
Colbourn — *Colonial* p.260
Dexter — *Colonial* p.120-122, 124
Dolan — *Yankee* p.121-122
Earle — *Colonial* p.78-83
Hofstadter — *Amer.* p.97-98, 164, 167
Life — *New* p.98, 101-102, 105, 114-115
Morris — *Ency.* p.485
Train — *Story* p.215
Wertenbaker — *Golden* p.144-145
- *South*
  Carman — *History* p.67
  Spruill — *Women's* p.309-311

INDUSTRY
See also **Artisans; Business; Commerce; Crafts and craftsmen; Manufacturing;** names of individual industries, etc.
Collins — *Story* p.55
Greene — *Revol.* See index p.469
Kraus — *U.S. (1)* p.114, 118-119
Life — *New* p.104-106
Morris — *Ency.* p.493-494
Speare — *Life* p.133
Tunis — *Living* p.112-118
- *Associations*
  Greene — *Revol.* p.40-41, 78-79, 273, 357
- *Middle Colonies*
  Train — *Story* p.198-200
- *New England*
  Train — *Story* p.168-174
- *Republic*
  Train — *Story* p.251-256
- *Revolution*
  Amer. Her. — *Rev.* p.14, 16-17, 30, 34
- *South*
  Train — *Story* p.217-218

INEQUALITY
See also **Classes**
Main — *Social* p.43, 45, 65, 221, 224-228, 236-238, 278-280, 286-287

INFLATION
Adams — *Provincial* p.318-319

INGERSOLL, JARED
, on Stamp Act debate (1765)
  Morris — *American* p.64-71

INK
Earle — *Child* p.154-155, 398

INNS AND INNKEEPERS
See also **Taverns;** names of inns
Earle — *Customs* p.196-197
Langdon — *Every.* p.252-253
Maine — *Social* p.22, 25, 90-91, 191, 222, 256
Speare — *Life* p.149-153
Tunis — *Living* p.122-123, 151-152
Tunis — *Tavern. See* index for subjects
Tunis — *Young* p.39-41
Wilson — *Early* p.54-57
- Bethlehem, Pa.
Langdon — *Every.* p.100-101
- Boston
Dolan — *Yankee* p.86
, Conversations at
Adams — *Provincial* p.290-291
- Names
Dexter — *Colonial* p.9
Earle — *Home* p.358-359

INOCULATION, SMALLPOX
See also **Mather, Cotton, on Inoculation; Smallpox**
Adams — *Provincial* p.269-270
Bridenbaugh — *Revolt* p.129-130, 327-329
Bridenbaugh — *Wild.* p.402, 404-406
Kraus — *U.S. (1)* p.169
Miller — *Colonial* p.118-131
Morris — *Ency.* p.541
-Washington, George, practice of
Handlin — *This* p.85

INSANE
, Care of
Bridenbaugh — *Revolt* p.126, 301, 320, 330

INSECTS
See also names of insects
Pettengill — *Yankee* p.126-130

INSURANCE
Bridenbaugh — *Revolt* p.61, 93, 103-104, 287, 322

INTELLECTUAL LIFE. ***See*** **Books and reading; Colleges and universities; Culture; Drama; Education; Libraries; Literary clubs; Literature; Music;** etc.

INTERIOR DECORATION. ***See*** **Furniture; Houses—Interiors; Wall decoration and wallpaper;** etc.

INTOLERABLE ACTS
Alden — *Pioneer* p.77-78
Beach — *Samuel* p.253-263
Carman — *History* p.179-180, 182-183, 185-187
Dannett — *Yankee* p.28
Ingraham — *Album* p.30
Miller — *Origins* p.369-376
Morison — *Oxford (1)* p.275-281, 290, 391
Morris — *American* p.125-128
Morris — *Ency.* p.82-83
Scott — *Trumpet* p.70-71, 74
200 Years p.22, 26, 29

INVENTIONS AND INVENTORS
See also names
Amer. Her. — *Rev.* p.16-17, 30
Glubok — *Home* p.28, 251-253
Greene — *Revol.* p.345-346
Morris — *Ency.* p.534-535
Speare — *Life* p.132
Tunis — *Young* p.60-71
Wilson — *American* p.48-49

INVENTORIES
Earle — *Colonial* p.294-295

IRELAND
See also **Irish**
, Emigration from
Adams — *Provincial* p.172
Greene — *Revol.* p.69-71
, Trade with
Greene — *Revol.* p.11, 48-49

IRISH
See also **Scotch-Irish**
Alden — *Pioneer* p.39, 59
Bridenbaugh — *Revolt* p.87, 134, 136, 333
Greene — *Revol.* p.158, 160, 247, 359
Life — *New* p.120, 122
Morison — *Oxford (1)* p.196, 231-232, 240-241, 313, 384
- Boston
Bridenbaugh — *Wild.* p.409-410

ON ACTS
Colbourn — *Colonial* p.245
Morris — *Ency.* p.485

ON INDUSTRY
See also **Ironmasters**
Carman — *History* p.138
Gould — *Early* p.68
Greene — *Revol.* p.60-62, 276-277, 358
Kraus — *U.S. (1)* p.119
Langdon — *Every.* p.161-168
Life — *New* p.104-105
Pettengill — *Yankee* p.134-141
Train — *Story* p.168, 199-200
Tunis — *Living* p.112-113
Tunis — *Tavern* p.26-30
Tunis — *Young* p.67-69
, and steel
Bridenbaugh — *Revolt* p.263, 268-269
Colbourn — *Colonial* p.260-261
- First
Train — *Story* p.168
- Forges
Adams — *Provincial* p.38-39
, Wrought, craft of
Langdon — *Every.* p.165

RON INDIANS"
Train — *Story* p.100

RONING
Gould — *Early* p.117-121

RONMASTERS
Morris — *Ency.* p.493-494
Tunis — *Colonial* p.147-154
- Pennsylvania
Burt — *Phila.* p.251-254

ROQUOIS INDIANS
See also **Sullivan, John—Expedition against Iroquois**
Burt — *Phila.* p.47, 167-168, 179
Greene — *Revol.* p.168-169, 235, 398
Kraus — *U.S. (1)* p.150
McDowell — *Rev.* p.138-139
Morison — *Oxford (1)* p.192-193, 197, 219, 225-227, 265, 282, 287, 323
Morris — *Ency.* p.55, 59-60, 101

"ISMS" (philosophical theories)
Tunis — *Young* p.33-34

ISOLATION
Pettengill — *Yankee* p.142-145

ISRAEL, HANNAH ERWIN
Ellet — *Eminent* p.102-113

ITINERANTS
See also **Clergymen; Judges; Peddlers;** etc.
Tunis — *Colonial* p.36
Wilson — *Early* p.37-51

J

JACKKNIVES. *See* Knives

JACKSON, ANDREW
- Biography
Morris — *Ency.* p.680-681

JAILS. *See* Prisons and prisoners

JAY, JOHN
See also **American Peace Commissioners**
Greene — *Revol. See* index p.469
Life — *Making* p.39-40, 80, 88, 104-108, 112, 130, 135-136
Morison — *Oxford (1). See* index p.414
Morris — *Voices* p.124-127, 156, 167-169
Whitney — *Abigail* p.162, 164, 166, 191, 216-217, 238, 255-257
- Biography
Morris — *Ency.* p.682
- Treaty
Butterfield — *Amer.* p.19
Life — *Growing* p.17-18
Morris — *Ency.* p.126-127
Morris — *Voices* p.174-176, 181
Wright — *New* p.45

JEFFERSON, MARIA ("Polly")
Brodie — *Jefferson. See* index p.795

JEFFERSON, MARTHA ("Patsy")
Brodie — *Jefferson. See* index p.795

JEFFERSON, MARTHA WAYLES SKELTON
Brodie — *Jefferson* p.86-100; *See also* index p.795-796

JEFFERSON, THOMAS
See also **Architecture—Jefferson, Thomas; Monticello**
Alden — *Pioneer. See* index p.v
Amer. Her. — *Rev.* p.143-144, 151, 272, 313, 349, 351
Bakeless — *Signers* p.71-79
Baldwin — *Ideas* p.206-239
Burt — *Phila. See* index p.388
Davis — *Heroes* p.43-55
Greene — *Revol. See* index p.469-470
Life — *Growing* p.12, 54
Life — *Making. See* index p.157
McDowell — *Rev.* p.34, 47, 72-73, 82-83, 85, 90-91, 163, 178, 193
Malone — *Story* p.205-209; *See also* index p.281
Miers — *American* p.83-88
Miller — *Origins* p.15, 175, 183, 259, 460, 491-493
Morison — *Oxford (1). See* index p.415
Morris — *Ency. See* index p.682-683
Morris — *Voices. See* index p.255
National — *History.* p.254-263
Sanderlin — *1776* p.91, 216-222, 227, 237, 242
Scott — *Trumpet* p.72, 121-124, 126
200 Years. See index p.348
Wertenbaker — *Golden* p.107-108, 110, 114, 121
Whitney — *Abigail. See* index p.355
Wright — *New* p.18-20

, and Declaration of Independence
Sanderlin — *1776* p.216-222, 237

, and Hamilton, Alexander
Butterfield — *Amer.* p.16-17
Morris — *Ency.* p.122-124
Morris — *Voices* p.170-172

, as governor
Brodie — *Jefferson. See* index p.797-798

, as revolutionary
Brodie — *Jefferson. See* index p.797

, as Secretary of State
Brodie — *Jefferson. See* index p.799

- Biography
Lossing — *Biog.* p.174-183
Morris — *Ency.* p.755
200 Years p.318-319

, Dining of
Belote — *Compleat* p.167-168

- Education
Morris — *American* p.345-348

- Eulogy of farm life
Main — *Social* p.210

- Family
Brodie — *Jefferson* p.39-52

- Hospitality
Earle — *Home* p.397

, Impoverishment of
Earle — *Home* p.397-398

- Land-tenure bill
Morris — *American* p.338-340

- Memorial
Landmarks Liberty p.76-79

, on agriculture
Davie — *Profile* p.172-175

, on women
Brodie — *Jefferson* p.796-797

- Parents
Brodie — *Jefferson* p.19-38

- Religious-freedom bill
Sweet — *Story* p.191-193

JEFFERSON NATIONAL EXPANSION MONUMENT
Landmarks Liberty p.50

JEMISON, MARY
Burner — *America* p.84-91

JERKY
Gould — *Early* p.103

ESUITS
Dolan — *Yankee* p.222-223

EWELRY
Dreppard — *Pioneer* p.80-83
Earle — *Home* p.297-298
Ross — *Taste* p.229

EWS
See also names of individuals
Adams — *Album* p.278
Alden — *Pioneer* p.37, 57, 106
Axtell — *18th* p.181-182
Bridenbaugh — *Revolt* p.20, 136, 140, 154
Kraus — *U.S. (1)* p.108
Life — *New* p.123
Tunis — *Young* p.32-33
, in Revolutionary War
Ingraham — *Album* p.72
- New York
Bridenbaugh — *Wild.* p.421
Handlin — *This* p.32-33
- Newport, R.I.
Adams — *Provincial* p.297
- Rhode Island
Stearns — *Story* p.73

OHNNYCAKES
See also **Bannocks**
Earle — *Home* p.135

OHNSON, SAMUEL
Miller — *Origins* p.82, 217, 219, 227, 340, 356, 359, 431

OHNSTON, HENRIETTA
Wright — *Cultural* p.210

OINERS
Main — *Social* p.22, 29, 52, 76
Tunis — *Colonial* p.26-28

OKE BOOKS
Glubok — *Home* p.175-176

ONES, JOHN PAUL
Amer. Her. — *Rev.* p.288-289, 292, 294
Davis — *Heroes* p.101-112
Life — *Making* p.62, 64, 90-91, 93, 137
McDowell — *Rev.* p.141, 146, 149-150
Morison — *Oxford (1)* p.291, 299, 311, 313, 336, 338, 364, 388
Morris — *Ency.* p.99
- Biography
Morris — *Ency.* p.684
- Defeat of "Serapis"
Collins — *Story* p.123
Morris — *Voices* p.116-118

JONES, THOMAS
Wheeler — *Voices. See* index p.476

JOUETT, JACK
, Ride of
Locke — *Birth* p.180-186

JOURNAL OF OCCURENCES
Scott — *Trumpet* p.42-43, 45-46, 49-53, 56

JOURNALISM
See also **Almanacs; Magazines; Newspapers**
Greene — *Revol.* p.388-391, 415
Ross — *Taste* p.36

JOURNEYMEN
Tunis — *Colonial* p.15

JUBILEES
Rublowsky — *Music* p.81-82

JUDGES
See also **Supreme Court of the U.S.—Chief justices**
, Itinerant
Dolan — *Yankee* p.224-226
- Prestige
Main — *Social* p.205-206
- Salaries
Main — *Social* p.103-104
- Tenure
Morris — *American* p.9-10

JUDICIARY
Kraus — *U.S. (1)* p.280
Life — *New* p.128-129, 144-145

JUGS
, as drinking vessels
Glubok — *Home* p.51-52

JUHAN, ALEXANDER
Howard — *Our* p.104-107

JUNTO CLUB
See also **Library Co. of Philadelphia**
Burt — *Phila.* p.147-148, 158, 205-206, 214-216, 220

JUSTICE
Tunis — *Frontier* p.34

JUSTICES OF THE PEACE
Main — *Social* p.205-206, 215

K

KALM, PETER
Handlin — *This* p.14-36

KELPIUS, JOHANNES
Wright — *Cultural* p.194

KENDRICK, JOHN
Wright — *New* p.162-165

KENNEBEC RIVER
Wheeler — *Voices* p.85-87, 90

KENT, JAMES
- Biography
Morris — *Ency.* p.684

KENTUCKY
See also **Boone, Daniel**
Amer. Her. — *Rev.* p.75, 298-299, 313
Axtell — *18th* p.233-234
Life — *Making* p.63, 107-109, 114, 117
Morison — *Oxford (1)* p.281-282, 349, 357, 361, 385
Tunis — *Frontier* p.43-59
- Exploration
Morris — *Ency.* p.414-415
- Life
Tunis — *Frontier* p.46-59
, Outdoor work in
Tunis — *Frontier* p.51-52
- Pioneers
Wright — *Frontier* p.46-76
- Population
Wright — *Frontier* p.77
, Saturdays in
Tunis — *Frontier* p.56-57
, Sundays in
Tunis — *Frontier* p.57
, Trades in
Tunis — *Frontier* p.55
- Villages
Tunis — *Frontier* p.54, 56-57
- Women
Ellet — *Eminent* p.463-475

KENTUCKY RESOLUTIONS
Baldwin — *Ideas* p.251-255
Brodie — *Jefferson* p.410-411
Butterfield — *Amer.* p.28

KETTLE CREEK, SOUTH CAROLINA
Stember — *South* p.33-35

KETTLES
Gould — *Early* p.68, 136-137

KIDD, WILLIAM
Kraus — *U.S. (1)* p.118

KING GEORGE'S WAR (War of the Austrian Succession)
Morris — *Ency.* p.65

"KING-HOOPER" HOUSE
Earle — *Home* p.30-31

KING'S BRIDGE, NEW YORK (Bronx)
Wheeler — *Voices* p.189-193, 437-439

KING'S COLLEGE
See also **Columbia University**
Bridenbaugh — *Revolt* p.22, 153, 178-179, 182, 230, 330, 375, 380, 384, 396
Colbourn — *Colonial* p.91-93
Greene — *Revol. See* index p.470
Wertenbaker — *Golden* p.44-46, 48

KING'S MOUNTAIN, SOUTH CAROLINA
, Battle of
Stember — *South* p.101-104, 112-113, 151
200 Years p.136, 140

KITCHEN UTENSILS
See also **"Hollowware"; Pewter and pewterers; Silverware; Woodenware**; names of utensils; etc.
Dreppard — *Pioneer* p.27-34

Earle — *Customs* p.142
Glubok — *Home* p.29-30
Gould — *Early* p.68-81
Tunis — *Living* p.139
- *Iron*
Glubok — *Home* p.28-32, 36
Gould — *Early* p.76-77

KITCHENS
Sirkis — *Reflect.* p.25-27
Speare — *Life* p.42-45
Tunis — *Living* p.137-139
Tunis — *Tavern* p.45-46
- *Fireside*
See also **Fireplaces**
Glubok — *Home* p.26-39
- *Paneling*
Gould — *Early* p.62
- *"Roasting"*
Glubok — *Home* p.34-35
Gould — *Early* p.73, 98
- *South*
Gould — *Early* p.40-41

KNIGHT, MADAME SARAH
, as teacher
Dexter — *Colonial* p.83-84
- *Travels and observations*
Benson — *Women 18th* p.279-280, 304-305
Bridenbaugh — *Wild.* p.180, 208, 267, 274, 292
Brooks — *Dames* p.75-101
Dexter — *Colonial* p.3-6, 133-134
Earle — *Colonial* p.135-159
Earle — *Home* p.8, 327-328, 332, 355
Langdon — *Every.* p.247-249
Morris — *Voices* p.58-61
Speare — *Life* p.145-147

KNITTING
Glubok — *Home* p.225
Wright — *Frontier* p.70

KNIVES
Dolan — *Yankee* p.172
Earle — *Home* p.307-308, 323-324
Glubok — *Home* p.194-195, 212-213
Speare — *Life* p.103

KNOCKERS
Earle — *Home* p.28-30

KNOTWORK
Glubok — *Home* p.158

KNOX, HENRY ("Little Ox")
Amer. Her. — *Rev. See* index p.382
Butterfield — *Amer.* p.17
Davis — *Heroes* p.30-41
Life — *Growing* p.12
McDowell — *Rev.* p.10, 58, 74-75, 79, 105-107, 129, 193
Stearns — *Story* p.89, 91-93
Stember — *North* p.15, 17, 145, 167, 172, 206-207, 232, 302
200 Years p.53, 90-91, 100, 104, 154, 158, 934-937

KNOX, LUCY
Ellet — *Eminent* p.508-524

KNYPHAUSEN, WILHELM VON
Stember — *Middle. See* index p.168
Wheeler — *Voices* p.192, 245, 363-364, 376-377

KOSCIUSZKO, THADDEUS
Stember — *North* p.92, 102, 134, 139, 141-142, 144, 304, 333

L

LA ROCHEFOUCAULD, FRANÇOIS DE
Benson — *Women 18th* p.231, 269-272, 274-275, 277, 290-301, 309

LABOR
See also **Apprentices; Children and childhood—Labor; Servants; Slaves and slavery**
Adams — *Provincial* p.95-97
Bridenbaugh — *Revolt* p.85-89
Bridenbaugh — *Wild. See* index p.493
Greene — *Revol.* p.19-21, 25-27, 65, 78-79, 438-439
Hofstadter — *Amer. See* index p.vii
Life — *New* p.62, 96-99
Main — *Social. See* index p.315-316
Miller — *First* p.143-162

LABOR (*continued*)
Morison — *Oxford (1). See* index p.415
Morris — *Ency.* p.517-518
Sloane — *Spirits* p.19-23
- *Combinations*
Morris — *Ency.* p.517-518
- *Conditions*
Kraus — *U.S. (1)* p.108-110
- *Laws and legislation*
Hofstadter — *Amer.* p.140-141
- *Unions, first*
Tunis — *Young* p.62

LACE MAKING
Glubok — *Home* p.227
- *South*
Spruill — *Women's* p.122

LADIES' BOOKS. *See* **Books and reading—Women**

LAFAYETTE, MARQUIS MARIE JOSEPH DE,
Amer. Her. — *Rev.* p.210-211, 213, 222-224, 230, 349-353, 356
Collins — *Story* p.117
Greene — *Revol.* p.245, 322, 416-417
Ingraham — *Album* p.64
Life — *Making* p.60-61, 66, 82, 85, 97, 104, 134, 150
McDowell — *Rev.* p.14, 110, 113-114, 136, 178, 183, 193, 195
Morris — *Voices* p.118-119, 121
Scott — *Trumpet* p.205, 207, 209, 263-264, 266
Stember — *North* p.18, 73, 167, 170, 172, 174, 210, 212, 323, 325, 328, 333, 350
Stember — *South* p.67, 84, 154-156, 158, 162, 181
Wheeler — *Voices. See* index p.476

LAMPLIGHTERS
Wilson — *Early* p.22-23

LAMPS
See also types of lamps
Earle — *Home* p.43-47
Glubok — *Home* p.22-24
- *Glass*
Earle — *Home* p.46-47
- *Pewter*
Earle — *Home* p.44-46

LANCASTER, PENNSYLVANIA
Greene — *Revol.* p.105, 161, 290, 375, 377

LAND
Adams — *Provincial* p.64-66, 109-112
Greene — *Revol. See* index p.470
Hofstadter — *Amer. See* index p.vii
Sanderlin — *1776* p.xvii-xx
- *Clearing*
Kraus — *U.S. (1)* p.144
Scott — *Settlers* p.175-176
- *Companies*
, Rivalry of
Morris — *Ency.* p.412-413
- *Grants*
, Inequities of
Kraus — *U.S. (1)* p.131-132
- *"Landless men"*
Main — *Social. See* index p.316-317
- *Laws and legislation*
Bartlett — *New* p.59-82
Morris — *Ency.* p.436
- *Women*
Benson — *Women 18th* p.238-239
- *Ownership*
Amer. Her. — *Rev.* p.51-52, 75, 81, 298, 313, 367
Pettengill — *Yankee* p.108-111
, Large
See also **Plantations and planters**
Main — *Social. See* index p.316
- *Women*
Dexter — *Colonial* p.101-12
- *Speculation*
Adams — *Provincial* p.298-299
Bartlett — *New* p.8, 28, 43, 59-60, 62

Carman — *History* p.57-58, 160
Morison — *Oxford (1)* p.363-364, 385-389, 393
Morris — *American* p.20-22
, North
Adams — *Provincial* p.243-247
- Systems
Bartlett — *New* p.66-72
Life — *New.* *See* index p.174
Morison — *Oxford (1). See* index p.415
- North, conflict in
Adams — *Provincial* p.240-243
, Post-Revolutionary
Carman — *History* p.221-222
- Tenure
Morris — *Ency.* p.476-477
- Jefferson, Thomas, bill of
Morris — *American* p.338-340

LAND BANKS
Adams — *Provincial* p.252-253
Beach — *Samuel* p.25-28
Carman — *History* p.140-142
Kraus — *U.S. (1)* p.134-135

LAND ORDINANCES
Carman — *History* p.237-238
Tunis — *Young* p.43

LANGSTON, DICEY
Ellet — *Eminent* p.214-224

LANGUAGES
See also names of languages
Greene — *Revol.* p.105, 121-122, 125, 130, 292, 379, 386-387
Tunis — *Young* p.106
, Non-English, percentages of
Life — *New* p.119-120
- Quest for standard
Boorstin — *Americans* p.277-283

LARDERS
Gould — *Early* p.38

LATIN LANGUAGE
Benson — *Women 18th* p.22-24, 50, 73, 153, 182
Wertenbaker — *Golden* p.21, 41, 68, 88-89, 107, 137-138
- Schools
Bridenbaugh — *Wild.* p.281, 284-287

LA TOURE, FRANCES MARY JACQUELINE
Brooks — *Colonial* p.31-58

LATROBE, BENJAMIN HENRY
- Biography
Morris — *Ency.* p.686

LATTEN WARE
Earle — *Customs* p.142

LAURENS, HENRY
- Denunciation of slavery
Morris — *American* p.351-352

LAW AND LAWYERS
See also **Judges; Women;** etc.
Adams — *Album* p.289
Adams — *Provincial* p.59-60
Bridenbaugh — *Revolt* p.95-96, 288-289, 312
Greene — *Revol. See* index p.470-471
Handlin — *This* p.75
Main — *Social. See* index p.317
Wilson — *Early* p.108-110
, and nature
Adams — *Provincial* p.277-278
, and politics
Boorstin — *Americans* p.202-205
, and religious doctrine
Adams — *Provincial* p.279
- Associations
Greene — *Revol.* p.84
- Boston
Axtell — *18th* p.148-149
- Enforcement
Bridenbaugh — *Revolt* p.107-121, 297-314
Wilson — *Early* p.30
- Massachusetts (1768)
Dolan — *Yankee* p.224
- Philadelphia
Burt — *Phila.* p.223-224

LAW AND LAWYERS (*continued*)
- *Political doctrine of contract*
Adams — *Provincial* p.278-279
- *Profession*
Life — *New* p.128-129
, *Role of (1786)*
Morris — *American* p.341-345
- *Unspecialized*
Boorstin — *Americans* p.195-202

LEATHER
Earle — *Colonial* p.235-239
Tunis — *Living* p.114-115
- *Tableware*
Earle — *Customs* p.143
Earle — *Home* p.94-96
- *Uses*
Glubok — *Home* p.50, 277
- *Utensils*
Earle — *Home* p.95-96

"LECTURE DAY"
Holliday — *Woman's* p.201-202

LECTURES
Bridenbaugh — *Revolt* p.200-201, 203, 206-208, 330, 386, 409, 416

LEDYARD, WILLIAM
Stember — *North* p.363, 366-370

LEE, ANN
Benson — *Women 18th* p.270, 272-273
Dexter — *Colonial* p.150-153
Evans — *Weather*. p.7-9
Sweet — *Religion* p.295-297

LEE, ARTHUR
, *on "Intolerable Acts"*
Morris — *American* p.125-128

LEE, CHARLES
Amer. Her. — *Rev. See* index p.382
Burt — *Phila.* p.277, 293
Life — *Making* p.56-57, 78-79, 82
McDowell — *Rev.* p.34, 57, 76, 80-81, 83, 98, 134, 136
Miller — *Origins* p.428, 430, 432, 472, 478, 485-486, 490, 500
Stember — *Middle. See* index p.168
Stember — *North* p.215, 246, 253, 332, 335
Wheeler — *Voices. See* index p.476

LEE, FRANCIS LIGHTFOOT
Bakeless — *Signers* p.91-92
Malone — *Story* p.214-215
- *Biography*
Lossing — *Biog.* p.194-196

LEE, HENRY ("Light-Horse Harry")
Brodie — *Jefferson. See* index p.803
Stember — *North* p.188-189
Stember — *South* p.36, 62, 67, 73, 80-83, 87, 95, 97, 138-140, 142, 146-147, 151, 192
Wheeler — *Voices* p.325, 340, 409-413, 415-417, 420-423, 426-432

LEE, JEREMIAH
- *Georgian home*
Train — *Story* p.153-154

LEE, LUCINDA
Benson — *Women 18th* p.19n, 78n, 297, 311

LEE, RICHARD HENRY
Bakeless — *Signers* p.79-87
Malone — *Story* p.203-204
Miller — *Origins* p.57-58, 114, 122, 125, 273-274, 381, 458, 489, 497
Scott — *Trumpet* p.72, 121, 132, 134
- *Biography*
Lossing — *Biog.* p.166-173

LENI-LENAPE INDIANS. *See* Delaware Indians

"LETITIA HOUSE" (home of William Penn)
Burt — *Phila.* p.46

LETTERS AND LETTER WRITING
See also names of diarists and letter writers
Earle — *Child* p.157-160
Earle — *Colonial* p.106-108, 195-199
Glubok — *Home* p.160-162

LEWIS, FRANCIS
Bakeless — *Signers* p.188-192
- Biography
Lossing — *Biog.* p.71-73

LEWIS, FRANK
Malone — *Story* p.136-137

LEXINGTON, MASSACHUSETTS
, Battle of
See also **Concord, Massachusetts, Battle of**
Adams — *Album* p.368
Amer. Her. — *Rev.* p.101-103, 113-115
Collins — *Story* p.102
Davie — *Profile* p.52-55
Forbes — *Paul* p.235, 241, 254-258, 431, 462, 472
Ingraham — *Album* p.34-36
Kraus — *U.S. (1)* p.213-215
McDowell — *Rev.* p.11, 32-33, 38, 40, 42-43
Miller — *Origins* p.219, 407-411, 415-420, 428, 462
Morison — *Oxford (1)* p.285-286, 288, 302
Morris — *American* p.161-163
Morris — *Ency.* p.85-86
Morris — *Voices* p.85-88
National — *History.* p.189-193
Sanderlin — *1776* p.151-154, 251
Scott — *Trumpet* p.79-82
Stearns — *Story* p.82-83, 85-86
Stember — *North* p.305-310; *See also* index p.382
Treasury — *Amer.* p.104-111
200 Years p.28, 34-36, 42

LEYDEN-JAR INVENTION
Greene — *Revol.* p.142

LIBERALS, REVOLUTIONARY
Alden — *Pioneer* p.101-102, 113, 122

LIBERTY
See also **Freedom; Independence**
Kraus — *U.S. (1)* p.176
200 Years. See index p.348
, Acclaimed by John Adams
Amer. Reader p.83-84
- "Excerpts," personal
200 Years p.290-291

***LIBERTY* (sloop)**
, Seizure of
Morris — *American* p.98-100

LIBERTY BELL
Burt — *Phila.* p.161-162
Landmarks Liberty p.44-45

LIBERTY POLES
McDowell — *Rev.* p.8-9
Stember — *North* p.232-233

"LIBERTY TEA"
Earle — *Colonial* p.255-256

LIBERTY TREE
Beach — *Samuel* p.74-75, 81-82, 110-111
Whitney — *Abigail* p.41, 55, 59, 77

LIBRARIES
Bridenbaugh — *Wild.* p.290-296, 458, 462
Main — *Social* p.260-261, 261n
Morris — *Ency.* p.565
Ross — *Taste* p.35
Speare — *Life* p.169
Wertenbaker — *Golden* p.70-71, 112-113
- Church
Bridenbaugh — *Revolt* p.182, 383
- Circulating
Greene — *Revol.* p.135-136, 391
Wright — *Cultural* p.150-151
- First, in Boston
Wertenbaker — *Golden* p.17-18, 26-28

LIBRARIES (continued)
- *College*
  - Bridenbaugh — *Revolt* p.182, 384-385
  - Greene — *Revol.* p.126-127, 377, 391
  - Wright — *Cultural* p.151-152
- *Institutional, largest*
  - Adams — *Provincial* p.116
- *Laws, earliest colonial*
  - Adams — *Provincial* p.118
- *New York*
  - Wertenbaker — *Golden* p.47-48
- *Newport, R.I.*
  - Wright — *Cultural* p.149
- *Philadelphia*
  - Wertenbaker — *Golden* p.70-71
  - Wright — *Cultural* p.148-149
- *Post-Revolution*
  - Greene — *Revol.* p.391
- *Private*
  - Bridenbaugh — *Revolt* p.95, 180, 182, 385
  - Earle — *Customs* p.272-273
  - Greene — *Revol.* p.136
  - Wright — *Cultural* p.144-145
  - *- Boston*
    - Bridenbaugh — *Wild.* p.290-291, 453
  - *, Largest*
    - Adams — *Provincial* p.115-116
- *, Provincial*
  - *, Earliest*
    - Adams — *Provincial* p.118
- *Public*
  - Adams — *Provincial* p.105, 117-118
  - Earle — *Customs* p.280
- *School*
  - Bridenbaugh — *Revolt* p.383
- *, Scientific*
  - Wright — *Cultural* p.145-146
- *South*
  - *, Largest*
    - Train — *Story* p.219
- *Subscription*
  - Bridenbaugh — *Revolt* p.181, 382
  - Carman — *History* p.105
- *Women*
  - Spruill — *Women's* p.230-231

LIBRARY COMPANY OF PHILADELPHIA
- Bridenbaugh — *Revolt* p.181, 383, 416
- Burt — *Phila.* p.147, 203, 206-212
- Wright — *Cultural* p.148-149

LIBRARY SOCIETY OF CHARLESTOWN
- Bridenbaugh — *Revolt* p.181, 384, 415

"LICKLADLES" ("apple polishers")
- Wilson — *Early* p.182-183

LIGHT AND LIGHTING
- *See also* **Candles and candlemaking; Lamps**
- Dreppard — *Pioneer* p.199-202, 204-205, 209
- Glubok — *Home* p.18-25
- Gould — *Early* p.124-125
- Pettengill — *Yankee* p.90-93
- Scott — *Settlers* p.181-182
- Tunis — *Living* p.133-135
- *Improvements*
  - Greene — *Revol.* p.96-97
- *Streets*
  - *See also* **Streets**
  - Bridenbaugh — *Revolt* p.33-34, 241-243

LIGHTHOUSES
- Bridenbaugh — *Revolt* p.20, 40-41, 247-248
- *Pennsylvania*
  - Burt — *Phila.* p.138

LIGHTNING RODS
- Bridenbaugh — *Revolt* p.99-100, 293

LIMNERS (painters)
- Tunis — *Colonial* p.109-110

LINCOLN, BENJAMIN
- Morris — *Voices* p.146-149
- Stember — *South* p.4-5, 8, 15-16, 21, 31-32, 34, 47-48, 50, 57, 64, 84, 196, 199

200 Years p.136, 139, 147, 150, 154-155, 157, 295
Wheeler — *Voices. See* index p.476

LINEN INDUSTRY
Earle — *Colonial* p.210-215
Kraus — *U.S. (1)* p.114, 119

LIQUOR
See also **Distilleries and breweries;** names of liquor
Bridenbaugh — *Revolt* p.157, 161, 256, 279
Greene — *Revol.* p.113, 170, 174, 253, 287, 337
- Philadelphia
Burt — *Phila.* p.130
- Taverns, licenses of
Bridenbaugh — *Wild.* p.493

LITERARY CLUBS
See also names of clubs
Smith — *Colonial* p.268-287
Wertenbaker — *Golden* p.92-93

LITERATURE
See also **Authors;** types of literature
Greene — *Revol. See* index p.471
Tunis — *Young* p.126-127
Wertenbaker — *Golden. See* index p.165
- Boston
Wertenbaker — *Golden* p.25-27
- Charleston
Wertenbaker — *Golden* p.140-141
- New York
Wertenbaker — *Golden* p.46-48
, Post-Revolutionary
Morison — *Oxford (1)* p.375-379
- Production
Wright — *Cultural* p.154, 162-175
- Prose
Dannett — *Yankee* p.72-120
- Virginia
Wertenbaker — *Golden* p.112-113

- Women
Benson — *Women 18th* p.188-222

LIVESTOCK
See also names of animals
Gould — *Early* p.100
Tunis — *Living* p.106-108
Tunis — *Young* p.18-19
- Branding
Gould — *Early* p.112, 127

LIVINGSTON, EDWARD
- Biography
Morris — *Ency.* p.688-689

LIVINGSTON, PHILIP
Bakeless — *Signers* p.181-184
Malone — *Story* p.138-140
- Biography
Lossing — *Biog.* p.67-70

LIVINGSTON, ROBERT
Morris — *Voices* p.125-127
Wilson — *American* p.61-63
- Biography
Lossing — *Biog.* p.238-243

LIVINGSTON, WILLIAM
Greene — *Revol. See* index p.471

LOBSTERS
Earle — *Home* p.118

LOCKE, JOHN
Carman — *History* p.148-149
Miller — *Origins* p.170-172, 187, 202, 349, 491-492

LOCKSMITHS
Tunis — *Colonial* p.61-63

LODGING HOUSES
Bridenbaugh — *Wild.* p.268-271, 427, 432-433

LOG CABINS
Pettengill — *Yankee* p.80-85
Tunis — *Frontier* p.20-24
Tunis — *Living* p.101-102
Tunis — *Young* p.46

LOG COLLEGE (Neshaminy, Pa.)
Hofstadter — *Amer.* p.234-235, 251, 265
- *Presbyterians*
Adams — *Album* p.275

LOG ROLLING
Glubok — *Home* p.313-314, 320

LOGAN, JAMES
Bridenbaugh — *Wild.* p.175, 177
Burt — *Phila.* p.145, 203
Cable — *American* p.51
Wright — *Cultural* p.145-146, 228-229

LOGANIAN LIBRARY (Philadelphia)
Burt — *Phila.* p.203-204

LONG ISLAND, NEW YORK
, Battle of
Amer. Her. — *Rev.* p.179-182, 196-197, 203
Collins — *Story* p.109
Ingraham — *Album* p.55
Morison — *Oxford (1)* p.303, 316-319
Morris — *Ency.* p.92
Stember — *North* p.53, 221, 226-230, 255-256
Wheeler — *Voices* p.34, 105-108, 158, 167-170

"LONG KNIVES"
, Campaign of
Amer. Her. — *Rev.* p.314-315

LONGEVITY
Handlin — *This* p.15, 97-98
Pettengill — *Yankee* p.158-169, 174-175
, Recipe for
Burner — *America* p.122-126

"LOST DECADE" (1781-1789)
Burt — *Phila.* p.297, 299

LOTTERIES
Bridenbaugh — *Revolt* p.9, 24, 30, 120, 178, 238-239
Bridenbaugh — *Wild.* p.147, 149, 198, 310, 348-349
Earle — *Customs* p.254-255
Greene — *Revol.* p.114, 287, 377
200 Years p.306

LOUISBOURG, CANADA
Adams — *Album* p.280-281
Amer. Reader p.65-68
Stearns — *Story* p.63-67

LOUISIANA
Morison — *Oxford (1)* p.192-193, 215, 219-220, 231
- *French settlement*
Morris — *Ency.* p.62-63
- *Life*
Holliday — *Woman's* p.238
- *Purchase*
Tunis — *Frontier* p.68

LOWER CLASS
See also **Poor relief; Servants; Slaves and slavery**
Bridenbaugh — *Revolt* p.86-89, 148, 284-285, 306, 420-421
Main — *Social* p.112-113, 235-236, 271-272, 279

LOYALISTS (Tories)
See also names of Loyalists
Adams — *Album* p.375-376
Alden — *Pioneer* p.81-82, 91, 95-96, 99, 102, 118
Amer. Her. — *Rev. See* index p.384
Burner — *America* p.103-106, 108-109
Carman — *History* p.192, 194, 197-200, 203, 211, 216, 221-222, 241-242
Colbourn — *Colonial* p.346-359
Forbes — *Paul. See* index p.498
Greene — *Revol. See* index p.483-484
Ingraham — *Album* p.45
Kraus — *U.S. (1)* p.240-241
Life — *Making* p.18, 39-41, 57-58, 68, 75, 81-83, 106-107
Miller — *Origins. See* index p.518 (Tories)
Morison — *Oxford (1)* p.311-314, 372-373
Morris — *American* p.205-218
Morris — *Voices* p.100-104
Scott — *Trumpet* p.98, 100-101, 140, 177, 212, 220-221, 223, 230, 232, 239-241
Sirkis — *Reflect.* p.29
Stember — *Middle. See* index p.172 (Tories)

Stember — *North* p.66, 97, 116, 118, 253, 259-260, 353, 360-361
Stember — *South. See* index p.216
Sweet — *Religion* p.16-24
Tunis — *Tavern* p.75-76, 80, 86, 89-94
200 Years p.72, 90, 137, 292-293
Wheeler — *Voices* p.35-36, 111-115
, and mutineers
Butterfield — *Amer.* p.8-9
, Brutality of
Scott — *Trumpet* p.161, 165, 167-168, 242-243, 260, 281
- "Excerpts," Personal
200 Years p.292-293
, Fate of
Ingraham — *Album* p.88
- Georgia
McDowell — *Rev.* p.142
- New England
Sweet — *Religion* p.15-16
- New York
Wheeler — *Voices* p.151-153
- North Carolina
McDowell — *Rev.* p.159-160
Wheeler — *Voices* p.411
- Pennsylvania
McDowell — *Rev.* p.135-136
, Post-Revolutionary
Wright — *New* p.39-41
- South Carolina
McDowell — *Rev.* p.79-80
- Southern Anglicans
Sweet — *Religion* p.24-26
- Versus patriots
Kraus — *U.S. (1)* p.219-221

LUCAS, ELIZA. ***See*** **Pinckney, Eliza Lucas**

LUDINGTON, SYBIL
Somerville — *Women* p.24-27

LUDWIG, MARY. ***See*** **"Pitcher, Molly"**

LUMBERING
Adams — *Provincial* p.297-298
Carman — *History* p.71-72, 138-139
Life — *New* p.103-105, 109

LUNENBURG COUNTY (Virginia)
Main — *Social* p.46-47, 95, 169-174, 177-180

LUTHERANS
Adams — *Album* p.275-276
Bridenbaugh — *Revolt* p.135, 153-154, 174
Greene — *Revol.* p.12, 104, 115, 150, 216, 367, 377
Hofstadter — *Amer.* p.20-21, 183, 203, 266-267
Life — *New* p.61, 66, 120, 123
Sweet — *Religion* p.81-82
Sweet — *Story* p.112-116, 181-182, 201
- Philadelphia
Axtell — *18th* p.178-179

LUXURY
, Outcry against
Earle — *Home* p.185
, Post-Revolutionary
Earle — *Home* p.159-160

LUZERNE, ANNE-CÉSAR, CHEVALIER DE LA
Burt — *Phila.* p.295

LYNCH, THOMAS, JR.
Bakeless — *Signers* p.282-284
Malone — *Story* p.236-237
- Biography
Lossing — *Biog.* p.219-222

LYON, JAMES
Howard — *Our* p.44-49

LYON, MATTHEW
Butterfield — *Amer.* p.29
Life — *Growing* p.37-38
Morris — *Voices* p.187-190

M

McCALLA, SARAH
Ellet — *Eminent* p.675-706

McCAULEY, MARY. ***See*** **"Pitcher, Molly"**

McCLANE, ALLAN
Burt — *Phila.* p.290
Cook — *What* p.21-81

McCLURE, MARY
Ellet — *Eminent* p.645-666

McCRAE, JANE
Collins — *Story* p.114
Ellet — *Eminent* p.438-443

McDONALD, FLORA
Ellet — *Eminent* p.379-386

McKEAN, THOMAS
Bakeless — *Singers* p.255-258
Malone — *Story* p.186-188
- Biography
Lossing — *Biog.* p.141-145

MacKENZIE, FREDERICK
Scott — *Trumpet. See* index p.304

MacPHERSON, JOHN
Burt — *Phila.* p.258-262

MACHINES, HOME
Dreppard — *Pioneer* p.85-87

MADEIRA
- Trade
Bridenbaugh — *Wild.* p.175-177

MADISON, DOLLEY
Hale — *Through* p.128-134

MADISON, JAMES
Alden — *Pioneer. See* index p.vi
Greene — *Rev. See* index p.472
Life — *Making* p.40, 105, 112-113, 130-131, 135
Miers — *American* p.95-98
Morris — *Voices* p.159-165, 167
200 Years p.162, 165-166, 169, 173, 176
- Biography
Morris — *Ency.* p.692
, on religious freedom
Sweet — *Story* p.190-193
, on Union
Butterfield — *Amer.* p.12

MADRIGALS
- Appalachia
Rublowsky — *Music* p.71-80

MAGAZINES
Adams — *Provincial* p.268-269
Carman — *History* p.107
Dannett — *Yankee* p.229-233
Greene — *Revol.* p.13, 93, 134-135, 192, 295, 385, 389-391, 430
Morris — *Ency.* p.580-582
Wright — *Cultural* p.246
- Philadelphia
Burt — *Phila.* p.241
- Women
Benson — *Women 18th* p.54, 209-222
- South
Spruill — *Women's* p.228-329

MAGNA CARTA
Sanderlin — *1776* p.103-105

MAIL-ORDER SERVICE
Bridenbaugh — *Revolt* p.52, 54, 263

MAIL SERVICE. *See* Postal service

MAINE
See also under special subjects
Greene — *Revol.* p.43, 155-156, 206, 399, 404, 408-409
Hofstadter — *Amer.* p.14, 22, 26, 149, 173
Stember — *North* p.255-277
Wheeler — *Voices* p.85-88, 337, 339-340
- Gentlemen
Adams — *Album* p.268

"-MAKERS"
Wilson — *Early* p.74

MAN. *See Rights of Man;* etc.

MANNERS. *See* Etiquette

MANORS. *See* Mansions

MANSIONS
Adams — *Album* p.266
- Maryland
Adams — *Album* p.265
Spruill — *Women's* p.31-34

- *New York*
Smith — *Colonial* p.198-204, 248-266
- *South*
Adams — *Provincial* p.211-214
Carman — *History* p.114-116

MANTUAMAKERS
- *South*
Spruill — *Women's* p.285-286

"MANUFACTORIES"
See also **Factories**
Tunis — *Colonial* p.132-154
Tunis — *Young* p.61-62

MANUFACTURING
See also **Industry;** names of individual types
Amer. Her. — *Rev.* p.76, 79, 82
Bridenbaugh — *Revolt* p.72-77, 267-274
Greene — *Revol. See* index p.472
Miller — *Origins* p.21-23, 271-276
Scott — *Trumpet* p.5, 21, 42, 278-279, 382
Speare — *Life* p.133
- *Beginnings*
Bridenbaugh — *Wild.* p.337-338
- *Boston*
Bridenbaugh — *Revolt* p.76, 269-270
- *Charlestown*
Bridenbaugh — *Revolt* p.76, 271-272, 274
- *English restricting acts*
Carman — *History* p.138
- *Home*
Bridenbaugh — *Revolt* p.268, 282, 284, 293-295, 390
Scott — *Trumpet* p.43, 45-48
- *New York*
Bridenbaugh — *Revolt* p.76, 271
- *Newport, R.I.*
Bridenbaugh — *Revolt* p.75
- *North*
Adams — *Provincial* p.232-234
- *Philadelphia*
Bridenbaugh — *Revolt* p.75, 268-269

MANUMISSION. *See* Antislavery movement

MAPLE SUGAR
Crèvecoeur — *Sketches* p.26, 98-99, 111
Earle — *Home* p.111-114
Glubok — *Home* p.61-63
Gould — *Early* p.86, 108-110

MAPS
Bridenbaugh — *Revolt* p.56, 145, 201-202, 266-267

MARBLES
Glubok — *Home* p.196-197

MARCHES, PATRIOTIC
Dannett — *Yankee* p.265-298

MARIETTA, OHIO
Collins — *Story* p.141
Greene — *Revol.* p.404, 406, 412-413
Tunis — *Young* p.48
- *Founding*
Morris — *Voices* p.152-155

MARINERS. *See* Sailors

MARINES
See also **Merchant Marine**
- *Birth, Philadelphia*
Burt — *Phila.* p.116
- *Commandants (1775-1799)*
Schemmer — *Almanac* p.233

MARION, FRANCIS ("Swamp Fox")
McDowell — *Rev.* p.172, 174, 177
Stember — *South. See* index p.213
Wheeler — *Voices* p.379, 395, 401, 420, 422, 426-428, 432
- *Biography*
Morris — *Ency.* p.693

MARITIME INDUSTRIES
Morris — *Ency.* p.493

MARKETS AND MARKETING
Belote — *Compleat* p.139-147
Bridenbaugh — *Revolt* p.24, 80-82, 278
Bridenbaugh — *Wild. See* index p.495
Gould — *Early* p.144

MARRIAGE
See also **Byrd, William—"Marriage"; Weddings**
Adams — *Provincial* p.309-310
Benson — *Women 18th* p.25-28, 38-39, 43-44, 50, 74-77, 96, 123, 130-133, 168-170, 182, 200, 287-288
Earle — *Customs* p.67-81
Greene — *Revol.* p.72-74, 167
Miller — *Colonial* p.141-153
Miller — *First* p.206-208
Spruill — *Women's* p.164-184
, Age at
Hofstadter — *Amer.* p.6-7
, and wealth
Hofstadter — *Amer.* p.139
- Banns and ceremony
Holliday — *Woman's* p.259-260
- Contracts, Southern
Spruill — *Women's* p.364-366
- Customs
Benson — *Women 18th* p.287-288
Cable — *American* p.37-39, 86-87
- Law
Benson — *Women 18th* p.229, 232-233
Evans — *Weather* p.2-4
- Rules
Holliday — *Women's* p.277-278

MARRINER, WILLIAM
Cook — *What* p.275-302

MARSHALL, MRS. CHRISTOPHER
Earle — *Colonial* p.258-275

MARSHALL, JOHN. ***See* XYZ Affair**

MARTIN, JAMES
Morris — *Voices* p.114-115

MARTIN, JOSEPH
Scott — *Trumpet* p.215-220, 222, 233, 246-247, 268-269, 277
Wheeler — *Voices* p.162-163, 171, 173, 220, 262, 284-286, 294, 304-305

MARTIN FAMILY
Ellet — *Eminent* p.204-210

MARYLAND
See also names of cities; special subjects
Adams — *Album* p.262
Greene — *Revol. See* index p.472
Hofstadter — *Amer. See* index p. viii
Life — *New* p.61, 68, 98, 101, 103, 120, 123, 143
Main — *Social* p.54, 97, 104, 107, 119, 137, 141, 212, 248-249, 254-255, 258
Miller — *Origins* p.14-16, 39-40, 44, 133, 175, 381, 416
Morison — *Oxford (1). See* index p.416
Morris — *Ency. See* index p.759
, and Declaration of Independence
Bakeless — *Signers* p.231-247
Malone — *Story* p.189-200
, Blocks Articles of Confederation
Morris — *American* p.231-235
- "Cavaliers"
National — *History.* p.148-155
- Culture
Wertenbaker — *Golden* p.102-104

MASKS
Earle — *Home* p.290
Train — *Story* p.211

MASON, GEORGE
Morris — *Voices* p.159-160, 187
200 Years p.70, 72, 162, 166, 173, 176, 265

MASON AND DIXON LINE
Adams — *Album* p.295

MASONIC ORDER
Bridenbaugh — *Wild.* p.389, 436-437, 440-441
Forbes — *Paul* p.58-59, 65, 140, 223, 383, 395-396, 455
Greene — *Revol.* p.94, 328
Stember — *North* p.176-177, 203
- First, in America
Adams — *Provincial* p.262-263
Burt — *Phila.* p.117

MASONS (artisans)
Main — *Social* p.76-77, 80, 191

MASSACHUSETTS
See also names of cities, especially **Boston;** special subjects, e.g. **Bill of Rights**
Axtell — *18th* p.77-81
Glubok — *Home. See* index p.353
Greene — *Revol. See* index p.472-473
Hofstadter — *Amer.* p.59, 149-150, 173, 205, 207-212, 214, 225-226
Life — *Growing* p.8, 56, 107
Life — *Making. See* index p.158
Life — *New. See* index p.174
Main — *Social. See* index p.318
Miller — *Origins. See* index p.514
Morison — *Oxford (1). See* index p.416
Morris — *Ency. See* index p.759
Sanderlin — *1776* p.116, 122-123, 207
Scott — *Trumpet. See* index p.304
200 Years p.14, 16-17, 19-26, 28-47, 162, 176, 276-277, 297
, and Declaration of Independence
Bakeless — *Signers* p.15-58
Malone — *Story* p.105-120
- Assembly dissolution
Amer. Her. — *Rev.* p.61
- "Circular letter," 1768
Baldwin — *Ideas* p.173-174
Morris — *American* p.116-119
Morris — *Ency.* p.76
- Constitution of 1778, rejection
Morris — *American* p.312-337
- Frontier
Main — *Social* p.12-14
- Laws
Glubok — *Home. See* index p.353
- Provincial Congress
Amer. Her. — *Rev.* p.99-100
Wheeler — *Voices* p.36, 58, 69, 74
- Suffolk Resolves
Amer. Her. — *Rev.* p.72

MASSACHUSETTS BAY
Beach — *Samuel. See* index p.327

MASSACHUSETTS COMMITTEE OF SAFETY
Wheeler — *Voices* p.40, 44, 47, 50, 57-58

MASSACRES
See also names of massacres
Burt — *Phila.* p.181-182
Morris — *Ency.* p.100

MATHEMATICS
See also **Arithmetic**
Morris — *Ency.* p.528-529

MATHER, COTTON
Benson — *Women 18th. See* index p.340
Bridenbaugh — *Wild. See* index p.494
Earle — *Customs* p.269-270
Wertenbaker — *Golden* p.13, 18-19, 22, 25, 27-29
, as music reformer
Rublowsky — *Music* p.21-22
, as scientist
Wright — *Cultural* p.226-228
- Books published
Earle — *Customs* p.267
- "The devil in the shape of a woman"
Miller — *Colonial* p.193-206
- Library
Earle — *Customs* p.271-272
Wright — *Cultural* p.145

MATHER, COTTON (continued)
, on inoculation
Miller — *Colonial* p.118-131
Train — *Story* p.177
, on women
See also **Mather, Cotton — "The devil in the shape of a woman"**
Benson — *Women 18th. See* index p.340

MATHER FAMILY
Forbes — *Paul* p.164

MAY, JOHN
Morris — *Voices* p.153-155

MAYHEW, JONATHAN
, on civil disobedience
Morris — *American* p.50-56

MEALS
See also **Food**; names of meals
Handlin — *This* p.96-97
, Serving of
Glubok — *Home* p.43-55

MEAT
Glubok — *Home* p.32-35, 46, 85
, and fish
Belote — *Compleat* p.65-83
- Massachusetts
Dow — *Every* p.91
- Preservation
Earle — *Home* p.153-155
Gould — *Early* p.55-56, 100

MEAT PIES
Tunis — *Living* p.137

MEDICAL SCHOOLS
Bridenbaugh — *Revolt* p.330, 380
Morris — *Ency.* p.541
Wright — *Culture* p.235

MEDICINE
See also **Remedies; related subjects**
Adams — *Album* p.332
Adams — *Provincial* p.60-62, 124-127
Boorstin — *Americans* p.207-238
Bridenbaugh — *Wild. See* index p.494
Colbourn — *Colonial* p.138-146
Greene — *Revol. See* index p.473
Kraus — *U.S. (1)* p.168-169
Morris — *Ency.* p.541-542
Train — *Story* p.219-220
Treasury Amer. p.97-103
Tunis — *Living* p.155
, and witchcraft
Tunis — *Frontier* p.33-34
- Associations
Greene — *Revol.* p.92, 293, 383
, Folk
Wright — *Frontier* p.71
, Lack of
Pettengill — *Yankee* p.146-151
- Massachusetts
Dow — *Every* p.99
- Practice
See also **Physicians;** etc.
Bridenbaugh — *Revolt* p.199-201
Miller — *First* p.237-238, 242-252
- Women, Southern
Spruill — *Women's* p.267-269

MEETINGHOUSES
See also **Churches**
Gowans — *Images* p.68-70, 78, 87-91, 145
Scott — *Trumpet* p.10, 38-40, 50, 66, 103, 137, 247
Smith — *Colonial* p.367-376
Train — *Story* p.174-175
Tunis — *Living* p.152-153

"MELTING POT"
See also **Nationalities**
Speare — *Life* p.67
Wright — *Cultural* p.48-71

MENIALS. ***See*** **Servants; Slaves and slavery**

MENNONITES
Adams — *Album* p.276
Hofstadter — *Amer.* p.20-21, 183
Sweet — *Religion* p.43-44
Sweet — *Story* p.102-103, 187
- Ideals
Greene — *Revol.* p.105

MENUS
See also **Food;** names of meals; names of holidays; etc.
Belote — *Compleat* p.157-162

MERCANTILISM
Miller — *Origins* p.14-18, 20-21, 152-153
Morris — *Ency.* p.483

MERCHANT MARINE
Morris — *Ency.* p.488

MERCHANT PRINCES
Adams — *Album* p.297-302
Wilson — *Early* p.59-61

MERCHANTS
See also **Shops and shopkeepers**
Bridenbaugh — *Revolt* p.51-52, 70-73, 77, 257-258, 261-263, 276-283
Bridenbaugh — *Wild. See* index p.494
Greene — *Revol. See* index p.473
Main — *Social. See* index p.319
Miller — *Origins* p.17-18, 89, 446-449, 453-454
- Homes
National — *History.* p.304-311
- New England
Train — *Story* p.151-178
- Philadelphia
Tunis — *Young* p.53-54
, Revolutionary
Amer. Her. — *Rev.* p.76-77

"MESHIANZA"
Burt — *Phila.* p.189-293

METALWORK
See also names of types of metalwork
Wright — *Culture* p.215

METHODISTS
See also **Circuit riders**
Bridenbaugh — *Revolt* p.353
Greene — *Revol. See* index p.473
Hofstadter — *Amer.* p.217, 229, 248, 268
Holliday — *Woman's* p.65-66, 68-69
Kraus — *U.S. (1)* p.242
Morison — *Oxford (1)* p.210, 381, 384
Morris — *Ency.* p.550
Sweet — *Religion* p.26-32, 62-66
Sweet — *Story. See* index p.484
Wright — *New* p.206-209
- Women leaders
Dexter — *Colonial* p.148-150

MICHAEL, DAVID MORITZ
Howard — *Our* p.29

"MID-CENTURY" (1745-1763)
Adams — *Provincial* p.293-323

MIDDLE CLASS
See also special subjects
Bridenbaugh — *Revolt. See* index p.xiii
Bridenbaugh — *Wild.* p.256, 412-415, 418
Hofstadter — *Amer.* p.131-179
Main — *Social* p.22, 42-43, 61, 66, 113, 158-160, 174, 234-235, 234n, 256, 273-275, 279

MIDDLE COLONIES
See also special subjects
Amer. Her. — *Rev.* p.82-83
Greene — *Revol. See* index p.473
Sirkis — *Reflect.* p.81-140
, French in
Kraus — *U.S. (1)* p.148-149
- Life
Belote — *Compleat* p.26-31
Train — *Story* p.201-202
, Struggle for
Kraus — *U.S. (1)* p.140-159

MIDDLETON, ARTHUR
Bakeless — *Signers* p.277-280
Malone — *Story* p.229-231
- Biography
Lossing — *Biog.* p.223-226

MIDDLETOWN, CONNECTICUT
Handlin — *This* p.81

MIDWAY, GEORGIA
Stember — *South* p.21-22

MIDWEST
- *Bicentennial*
Lawlor — *Bicen.* p.167-204

MIDWIVES
Dexter — *Colonial* p.58-68
Dolan — *Yankee* p.204-205
- *South*
Spruill — *Women's* p.272-275

MIGRATION
See also **West and westward movement;** etc.
Adams — *Album* p.409-411
Pettengill — *Yankee* p.73-79

MILESTONES
Earle — *Customs* p.202-206
Earle — *Home* p.335-336

MILITARY
See also **Continental Army; Militia;** etc.
Cable — *American* p.78-79

MILITARY UNIFORMS
See also **Continental Army — Uniforms**
Amer. Her. — *Rev. See* index p.384
Speare — *Life* p.90
Train — *Story* p.236-237

MILITIA
Scott — *Trumpet. See* index p.304-305
, *Colonial*
Speare — *Life* p.87-89
- *Control*
Morris — *American* p.149-150
- *Georgia*
Stember — *South* p.12, 18, 22, 32, 36
- *North Carolina*
Stember — *South* p.36, 113, 115, 118, 126, 142-143, 148-149
- *South Carolina*
Stember — *South* p.57-58, 69, 72, 74, 84-85, 97-99, 105-106
- *Virginia*
Stember — *South* p.100, 143, 157, 166, 176, 179, 181-182, 184, 192, 203

MILITIA ACT
Morris — *Ency.* p.124

MILK
Earle — *Home* p.148-149
Glubok — *Home* p.82-83
Gould — *Early* p.104

MILK PITCHERS
Earle — *Home* p.106

MILK ROOMS
Gould — *Early* p.37

MILKMAIDS
Wilson — *Early* p.151

MILLERS
Main — *Social* p.13-14, 17, 19, 29, 29n, 52, 76, 82-83
Tunis — *Colonial* p.29-32

MILLINERS. *See* **Hats and hatters**

MILLS AND MILLING
See also types of mills and products
Gould — *Early* p.134
Greene — *Revol.* p.30, 33, 59-60, 162
Treasury Amer. p.152-155
Tunis — *Tavern* p.16, 25-26
Tunis — *Young* p.29
- *Woolen, first*
Dolan — *Yankee* p.50

MINERAL WATERS
Ross — *Taste* p.129

MINERALS
See also names of minerals
Train — *Story* p.199-200

MINES AND MINING
See also types of mines
Adams — *Provincial* p.39-40

MINISINK, NEW YORK
, Battle of
Stember — *North* p.198-203

MINISTERS. *See* Clergymen

MINSTRELS
Morris — *Ency.* p.590
Nye — *Unembar.* p.162

MINUTEMEN
Adams — *Album* p.367
Amer. Her. — *Rev.* p.99-102, 113, 141
Amer. Reader p.86-91
Forbes — *Paul* p.219, 261-262, 267, 276, 282
Greene — *Revol.* p.207, 231, 240
McDowell — *Rev.* p.32-33, 37-38, 40-46
Morison — *Oxford (1)* p.284-286, 292
National — *History.* p.189-193
Sanderlin — *1776* p.138-140, 151-154, 163, 251
- Statue, Concord, Mass.
Landmarks Liberty p.60-63

MIRANDA, FRANCISCO DE
Axtell — *18th* p.13-16

MISCEGENATION
Bridenbaugh — *Wild.* p.388
Hofstadter — *Amer.* p.53, 101, 105, 115-116
- Laws
Adams — *Provincial* p.158

"MISFITS"
Wilson — *Early* p.163-164

MISSIONS AND MISSIONARIES
See also **Indians — Missions and missionaries; Moravians;** names of denominations
Greene — *Revol.* p.100, 104-105, 108, 111-112
Sweet — *Story* p.160-168
- California
Davie — *Profile* p.48-50
, Catholic
Sweet — *Story* p.164-166
, for Negroes
Sweet — *Story* p.167-168

MITTLEBERGER, GOTTFRIED
- "The crossing to Pennsylvania"
Miller — *Colonial* p.83-98

MOBILITY
Main — *Social* p.164-196
, Cultural
Main — *Social* p.268-269, 285-286
, Horizontal
Main — *Social* p.164-165, 170, 174, 176, 178, 183, 190n, 193-194, 280-281
, in social status
Main — *Social* p.282-284
, Vertical
Main — *Social. See* index p.319-320

MOBS
See also **Riots**
Bridenbaugh — *Revolt. See* index p.xiii
Bridenbaugh — *Wild.* p.223-224, 382-384, 388-389
Burner — *America* p.108-113
Morris — *American* p.145-149

MOHAWK INDIANS
Morison — *Oxford (1)* p.153, 323, 326
Stember — *North* p.63, 68-69, 71, 199, 246

MOHAWK VALLEY, NEW YORK
Amer. Her. — *Rev.* p.240-241, 265, 308-312, 316, 319
Evans — *Weather.* p.271-275

MOLASSES
Belote — *Compleat* p.55
Colbourn — *Colonial* p.246-253
Miller — *Origins* p.90, 95-96, 99, 235, 264, 278

MOLASSES ACT
Carman — *History* p.134-137
Colbourn — *Colonial* p.246
Greene — *Revol.* p.41, 45, 54
Miller — *Origins* p.84, 98-100
Morris — *Ency.* p.485

MONDHARE FLAG SHEET. *See* Flags — Mondhare flag sheet

MONEY
See also **Currency**
Adams — *Album* p.383-384
Adams — *Provincial* p.251-252
Carman — *History* p.134-137 140-142, 163, 200, 222, 245-247
Forbes — *Paul* p.10, 24-25, 277, 314, 347, 399
Langdon — *Every.* p.172 (facing), 314-315
Life — *Making* p.11, 63-64, 111, 132-133
Life — *New* p.103-104
Morison — *Oxford (1)* p.198-202, 305-306, 365, 390-391, 393, 399
Stearns — *Story* p.63-64
Tunis — *Living* p.125-126
Tunis — *Young* p.31, 72-74
- *Colonies*
Amer. Her. — *Rev.* p.14, 52-53, 56
- *Continental bills*
McDowell — *Rev.* p.148-149
- *Counterfeit*
Bridenbaugh — *Revolt* p.111-112
- *Paper*
Amer. Her. — *Rev.* p.22, 56, 270-271
Bridenbaugh — *Revolt* p.11, 90-92, 252
Dow — *Every* p.172-173
Greene — *Revol.* p.250-251, 261-262, 332, 338-339, 353
Langdon — *Every.* p.197-198
- *Revolutionary need*
Amer. Her. — *Rev.* p.270-272
- *Shortage*
Miller — *Origins* p.19-20

"-MONGERS"
Wilson — *Early* p.71-74

MONMOUTH, NEW JERSEY
, Battle of
Amer. Her. — *Rev.* p.222-224, 230-231
Burt — *Phila.* p.277n
Collins — *Story* p.119
Morison — *Oxford (1)* p.329-330
Morris — *Ency.* p.99
National — *History.* p.224-225
Stember — *Middle* p.59-73

MONROE, JAMES
Brodie — *Jefferson. See* index p.805
- *Biography*
Morris — *Ency.* p.696

MONTGOMERY, RICHARD
Wheeler — *Voices* p.85, 89, 94-95, 97-100, 102-104

MONTICELLO
Brodie — *Jefferson. See* index p.805
Life — *Growing* p.64-75
Train — *Story* p.227-229

MONTREAL, CANADA
Stember — *North* p.33-34
Wheeler — *Voices* p.46-47, 89, 94-95, 97-98

MONTRESOR, JOHN
, on New York rent riots
Morris — *American* p.32-33

MORALITY
See also **"Great Awakening"; Religion**
Adams — *Provincial* p.156-160
Benson — *Women 18th* p.226-230, 290
Bridenbaugh — *Revolt* p.119-122, 154-155, 314-315
Bridenbaugh — *Wild.* p.226-230, 387
Greene — *Revol. See* index p.474

MORAVIANS
See also **Beissel, Johann Conrad; "Bell House"; Bethlehem, Pa.; Ephrata Cloister**
Greene — *Revol. See* index p.474
Langdon — *Every.* p.87-109
Morison — *Oxford (1)* p.199, 312, 380
Morris — *Ency.* p.549-550
Sirkis — *Reflect.* p.89
Sweet — *Religion* p.43, 84
Sweet — *Story* p.105-109, 187-188, 201
Wright — *Cultural* p.194-195

- *Immigration*
Morris — *Ency.* p.444-445
- *Missions and missionaries*
Sweet — *Story* p.108-109, 163-164
- *Music*
Howard — *Our* p.28-30
Morris — *Ency.* p.612
Rublowsky — *Music* p.22-26
- *Philadelphia*
Axtell — *18th* p.180-181
- *Seminary, Bethlehem, Pa.*
Benson — *Women 18th* p.141, 163, 168, 268, 310
- *Travels of a bishop*
Handlin — *This* p.59-67
- *"Wachovia"*
Greene — *Revol.* p.104, 162-164, 166
- *Women*
Benson — *Women 18th* p.268-269

MOREAU DE SAINT-MERY, M.L.E.
Handlin — *This* p.88-103

MORE, HANNAH
Benson — *Women. See* index p.340

MORGAN, DANIEL
Amer. Her. — *Rev.* p.123, 125, 210, 222, 245-247, 253-254, 328-330, 332, 342
Morison — *Oxford (1)* p.299, 302, 308, 327, 341-342
Stember — *North* p.44-45, 91, 93, 97-98, 100-101, 105

MORRIS, GOUVERNEUR
Morison — *Oxford (1)* p.356, 394, 398-399, 401, 404
Morris — *American* p.141-144

MORRIS, LEWIS
Bakeless — *Signers* p.184-187
Malone — *Story* p.141-142
- *Biography*
Lossing — *Biog.* p.74-76

MORRIS, MARGARET HILL
Benson — *Women 18th* p.170, 267n
Ellet — *Eminent* p.481-483
Evans — *Weather.* p.73-109

MORRIS, ROBERT
Bakeless — *Signers* p.127-136
Burt — *Phila. See* index p.390
Greene — *Revol. See* index p.474
Malone — *Story* p.168-170
Morison — *Oxford (1)* p.287, 296, 305, 351, 359-360, 365, 369-370, 395
Morris — *Ency.* p.104
- *Biography*
Lossing — *Biog.* p.93-98

MORRISTOWN, NEW JERSEY
Stember — *Middle* p.42-52
Wheeler — *Voices* p.199, 218, 362-363, 373

MORSE, JEDIDIAH
Greene — *Revol. See* index p.474
- *on women*
Benson — *Women 18th* p.145, 152-153

MORTARS
Glubok — *Home* p.73-74

MORTON, JOHN
Bakeless — *Signers* p.141-143
Malone — *Story* p.165
- *Biography*
Lossing — *Biog.* p.112-113

MOTHERS
Spruill — *Women's* p.59-63

MOTTE, REBECCA
Ellet — *Eminent* p.322-331
McDowell — *Rev.* p.5, 177

MOULTRIE, WILLIAM
Scott — *Trumpet* p.104, 106-108, 110
Wheeler — *Voices* p.143-150, 326, 353, 356-357, 360-361, 366, 370-371, 401, 423, 425

MOUNT HOPE AND MOUNT DEFIANCE, NEW YORK
Stember — *North* p.53-57

"MOUNT PLEASANT" MANSION
Burt — *Phila.* p.259
Train — *Story* p.183-184

MOUNT VERNON
Earle — *Home* p.13, 237, 431
Glubok — *Home* p.262-263
Life — *Making* p.104, 138-139, 141-144, 146, 148-151
McDowell — *Rev.* p.4-5, 10, 30-31, 34, 178, 181, 192, 194-195
Wertenbaker — *Golden* p.106, 114-115, 117
Whitney — *Abigail* p.241, 283, 294-295, 303
- *Life*
Evans — *Weather.* p.335-337, 341-342
Train — *Story* p.221

"MOUNTAIN SOCIETY"
Evans — *Weather.* p.33-36

MOURNING PIECES
See also **Samplers, Mourning**
Earle — *Colonial* p.232-233
Glubok — *Home* p.219-221, 275

MUHLENBERG, FREDERICK
Life — *Growing* p.9

MUNITIONS. *See* **Guns**

MURDER
Scott — *Trumpet* p.190, 245-246

MURPHY, TIMOTHY
Cook — *What* p.87-139

MURRAY, JUDITH SARGENT
Benson — *Women 18th. See* index p.340

MURRAY, MARY
Ellet — *Eminent* p.755-756

MUSEUMS
See also names of localities
Stember — *North. See* index p.384

MUSIC
See also **Ballads; Concerts; Ephrata Cloister; Hymns; Indians — Music; Songs;** types of music
Adams — *Provincial* p.275-276
Bridenbaugh — *Revolt. See* index p.xiii
Earle — *Customs* p.250-251
Greene — *Revol.* p.105, 120, 150-152, 154, 182, 298, 446
Morris — *Ency.* p.611-614
Ross — *Taste* p.41
Tunis — *Young* p.128
Wertenbaker — *Golden* p.156-157
- *"Art"*
Rublowsky — *Music* p.44-45
- *Bethlehem, Pa.*
See also **Ephrata Cloister—Music; Moravians**
Howard — *Our* p.28-30
- *Books*
Nye — *Unembar.* p.307
- *Boston*
Bridenbaugh — *Wild.* p.290, 455
Wertenbaker — *Golden* p.35-36
- *Charleston*
Howard — *Our* p.30
Wertenbaker — *Golden* p.148-149
- *Charlestown*
Bridenbaugh — *Wild.* p.463-464
- *"Common"*
Rublowsky — *Music* p.20, 44-45
, *Dance*
Dulles — *History* p.39
- *Folk*
See also **Music, Negro**
Howard — *Our* p.613-642
, *Instrumental*
Spruill — *Women's* p.202-203
- *Moravians. See* **Moravians — Music**
, *Negro*
See also **Jubilees; Music — Plantation life**
Howard — *Our* p.623-625
Rublowsky — *Music* p.61-63, 67
- *New England*
Howard — *Our* p.58-70
Rublowsky — *Music* p.19
- *"New world"*
Rublowsky — *Music* p.20, 22

- *New York*
Bridenbaugh — *Wild.* p.295, 462
Howard — *Our* p.31-36
Wertenbaker — *Golden* p.55-57
- *Newport, R.I.*
Bridenbaugh — *Wild.* p.446, 460-461
, *Pennsylvania-German*
Speare — *Life* p.164
- *Philadelphia*
Bridenbaugh — *Wild.* p.294, 458-459
Burt — *Phila.* p.195-197
Howard — *Our* p.25-28
Morris — *Ency.* p.613
Wright — *Cultural* p.195
- *Plantation life*
Rublowsky — *Music* p.82-84
, *Scotch-Irish*
Rublowsky — *Music* p.72-80
, *Secular*
Howard — *Our* p.22-24
- *South*
Howard — *Our* p.30-31
Rublowsky — *Music* p.38-41
- *South Carolina*
Wright — *Cultural* p.194
- *"Traditionalist"*
Rublowsky — *Music* p.20-21
- *Virginia*
Wertenbaker — *Golden* p.121-122

MUSICAL INSTRUMENTS
Speare — *Life* p.164
- *French horns and oboes*
Morris — *Ency.* p.612
- *Imports*
Rublowsky — *Music* p.15
- *Indians*
Howard — *Our* p.621
, *Moravian*
Langdon — *Every.* p.94-96

MUSICAL SOCIETIES
Morris — *Ency.* p.613

MUSICIANS. *See* **Composers;** names of musicians

MUSTER DAY
Speare — *Life* p.160-161
Tunis — *Tavern* p.53

MUTINY ACT
Miller — *Origins* p.237-241, 248

N

NAILS
Speare — *Life* p.123
Train — *Story* p.168, 200, 267
Tunis — *Young* p.69
, *Wrought iron*
Langdon — *Every.* p.168

NAMES
, *Anglicization of*
Life — *New* p.119-120
, *Children's*
Glubok — *Home* p.98-99
- *Descriptive appellations*
Wilson — *Early* p.156-188
- *Surnames, unusual*
Burt — *Phila.* p.187-188
, *Unfavorable*
Wilson — *Early* p.161

NANTUCKET, MASSACHUSETTS
Handlin — *This* p.46-59
- *Women*
Benson — *Women* p.302-303

NARRAGANSETT BAY
Scott — *Trumpet* p.103, 185-186, 236, 238-239, 261

"NATION, NEW"
- *Creation*
Butterfield — *Amer.* p.14-15
Kraus — *U.S. (1)* p.181-265
Wright — *New* p.11-20

NATIONALISM
See also **Patriotism**
Bridenbaugh — *Revolt* p.64, 362-364, 397-398, 408, 411-412, 423-424
Greene — *Revol. See* index p.474
Kraus — *U.S. (1)* p.176-180
Morris — *American* p.191-195
Morris — *Ency.* p.121-130

NATIONALITIES
See also **Immigrants and immigration;** names of nationalities
Cable — *American* p.40, 42
Handlin — *This* p.5-103

NATURAL HISTORY
See also **Botany and botanists; Zoology;** etc.
Morris — *Ency.* p.528

NATURAL PHILOSOPHY
Miller — *Origins* p.170-173, 187, 215-216
Wilson — *American* p.14-15
Wright — *Cultural* p.234-236

NATURALISTS
Wright — *Cultural* p.229-231

NATURE
Colbourn — *Colonial* p.292-297
Kraus — *U.S. (1)* p.163-164

NAVAL ARCHITECTURE
Amer. Her. — *Rev.* p.274-275, 279

NAVAL STORES ACT
Morris — *Ency.* p.484

NAVIGATION, INLAND
See also **River traffic**
Morris — *Ency.* p.418

NAVIGATION ACTS
Adams — *Provincial* p.47-49
Colbourn — *Colonial* p.253-268
Miller — *Origins. See* index p.514

NAVIGATION SCIENCE
Wilson — *American* p.44-45

NAVY
See also **Revolutionary War — Navy**
Adams — *Album* p.400
Forbes — *Paul* p.332, 340, 342, 367, 378, 409
Greene — *Revol.* p.246-247
Morison — *Oxford (1)* p.309-311, 317-319, 343-348
Stember — *Middle* p.122, 132, 135, 139-140
Stember — *North* p.49-52, 57, 119, 123-125, 261
- Birth
Amer. Her. — *Rev.* p.288-289
, British
Stember — *Middle* p.75, 79, 132, 135-137, 139
Stember — *North. See* index p.384
- Commodore and senior officers
Schemmer — *Almanac* p.233
, French
Stember — *North* p.325-326
- Secretaries (1798-1799)
Schemmer — *Almanac* p.230
, State
Amer. Her. — *Rev.* p.290-291

NEEDLEWORK
See also types of needlework
Adams — *Album* p.292
Earle — *Colonial* p.230-233
Earle — *Customs* p.29-30
Glubok — *Home* p.218-227
Speare — *Life* p.81-82
Train — *Story* p.235
, by children
Earle — *Child* p.321-341
- Stitches
Earle — *Child* p.337-338
Earle — *Home* p.264-265

NEGROES
See also **Music, Negro; Slaves and slavery**
Alden — *Pioneer* p.33, 48-49, 82, 96
Bridenbaugh — *Revolt. See* index p.xiii
Crèvecoeur — *Sketches* p.44, 46, 110, 111, 121, 143-144, 148, 160, 168
Greene — *Revol. See* index p.474-475
Handlin — *This* p.30-32
Hofstadter — *Amer.* p.viii-ix
Sanderlin — *1776* p.223-224, 242-243
Scott — *Trumpet. See* index p.301
- Charlestown
Bridenbaugh — *Wild. See* index p.495
, in colonies
Adams — *Provincial* p.103-107
- Plots and insurrections
Morris — *Ency.* p.513
- Religious life
Handlin — *This* p.89-90

- Revolutionary War
Amer. Her. — *Rev.* p.248, 265
Brodie — *Jefferson* p.167-169
Ingraham — *Album* p.71
Morris — *Amer.* p.349-350
- South
Spruill — *Women's. See* index p.415
- Virginia
Axtell — *18th* p.41-43

NEIGHBORS
See also **Hospitality**
Glubok — *Home* p.312-323
Speare — *Life* p.41-51

NELSON, THOMAS
Bakeless — *Signers* p.92-96
Malone — *Story* p.218-219
- Biography
Lossing — *Biog.* p.188-193

NETTING
Earle — *Home* p.263-264
, of Washington, Martha
Earle — *Home* p.264

NEW BRUNSWICK, NEW JERSEY
Wheeler — *Voices* p.195-197, 217-218, 221

NEW ENGLAND
See also **Colonies and colonists;** names of colonies and states
Adams — *Album* p.259-260
Glubok — *Home. See* index p.353-354
Greene — *Revol. See* index p.475
Hofstadter — *Amer.* p.ix
Miller — *Origins* p.514-515
Morison — *Oxford (1). See* index p.416
Sirkis — *Reflect.* p.22-80
Stember — *North* p.257-371
Train — *Story* p.151-178
- Hills
Pettengill — *Yankee* p.131-133
- Life
Belote — *Compleat* p.32-35
Holliday — *Woman's* p.192-193
Train — *Story* p.174-178
- Women
Benson — *Women 18th* p.104-127, 134, 145-155, 279-283, 294, 298-302, 305-306

NEW ENGLAND PRIMER
Glubok — *Home* p.142-145
Speare — *Life* p.106

NEW FRANCE
- Fall
Kraus — *U.S. (1)* p.153-159

NEW HAMPSHIRE
Greene — *Revol.* p.43, 56, 67, 155, 157, 165, 210, 231, 323, 338-339, 344, 348, 364, 395
Morison — *Oxford (1)* p.186, 246-247, 365, 385, 405-406
Stember — *North* p.4, 84, 278-279
, and Declaration of Independence
Bakeless — *Signers* p.221-230
Malone — *Story* p.97-103

NEW HAVEN, CONNECTICUT
Greene — *Revol.* p.42, 120, 130, 307, 383, 390
Handlin — *This* p.80

NEW HAVEN CONVENTION (1778)
Morris — *American* p.251-254

NEW JERSEY
Greene — *Revol. See* index p.475
Hofstadter — *Amer.* p.11, 14-15, 90, 125, 156, 185, 187, 198, 200, 204
Life — *Making* p.30-31, 48-49, 56-57, 68-69, 78-79, 111, 134
Morison — *Oxford (1). See* index p.417
Scott — *Trumpet. See* index p.305
200 Years p.87-104, 169-170
, and Declaration of Independence
Bakeless — *Signers* p.159-177
Malone — *Story* p.145-148

NEW JERSEY (continued)
- *Revolutionary War*
Amer. Her. — *Rev.* p.188-192, 202-207, 222-224, 229
Ingraham — *Album* p.57-58
Morison — *Oxford (1)* p.319-323
Morris — *Voices* p.108-110
Stember — *Middle. See* index p.170

"NEW LIGHTS"
Bridenbaugh — *Wild.* p.422
Kraus — *U.S. (1)* p.137-138
Wertenbaker — *Golden* p.23-24, 73, 79

NEW LONDON, CONNECTICUT
Stember — *North* p.362-371

NEW ORLEANS, LOUISIANA
Amer. Reader p.48-49
Davie — *Profile* p.46-48
National — *History.* p.322-329

"NEW PENN. FIREPLACE"
See also **Franklin stove**
Earle — *Home* p.70

NEW REFORMED CHURCH (Phila.)
Axtell — *18th* p.180

NEW WINDSOR, NEW YORK
Stember — *Bicen. See* index p.385

NEW YEAR'S DAY
Earle — *Customs* p.228-229

NEW YORK (state and city)
Adams — *Album* p.254-257
Axtell — *18th* p.69-73, 115-126
Bridenbaugh — *Revolt* p.3, 16, 25, 42, 219, 232, 358
Crèvecoeur — *Sketches. See* index p.338
Evans — *Weather.* p.285-286, 300-301
Glubok — *Home. See* index p.284
Greene — *Revol. See* index p.475-476
Hofstadter — *Amer. See* index p.ix
Life — *Making. See* index p.158
McDowell — *Rev.* p.34, 54, 79, 86-87, 92-93, 114, 138
Miller — *Origins. See* index p.515
Morison — *Oxford (1). See* index p.417
Scott — *Trumpet. See* index p.305
Stember — *North. See* index p.385
200 Years p.20, 82-83, 87, 143-144, 164
Wertenbaker — *Golden. See* index p.167
Wheeler — *Voices. See* index p.477
Woodward — *War* p.104-132

, and Declaration of Independence
Bakeless — *Signers* p.170-192
Malone — *Story* p.135-144
, as capitol
Speare — *Life* p.62-63
, Battle of
Lawlor — *Bicen.* p.53-80
National — *History.* p.198-201
- *British occupation*
200 Years p.18, 52-53, 77, 80, 82-85, 109, 137, 170, 176, 189, 234
- *Commerce*
Handlin — *This* p.23-24
Wright — *Cultural* p.40-42
- *Culture*
Wertenbaker — *Golden* p.42-43
, Dutch in
Axtell — *18th* p.122-124
Wertenbaker — *Golden* p.16, 40-41
- *Early settlements*
Morris — *Voices* p.150-152
- *Evacuation, American*
Amer. Her. — *Rev.* p.183, 186
- *Evacuation, British*
Amer. Her. — *Rev.* p.364-365
McDowell — *Rev.* p.185, 192
- *Federal Hall*
Landmarks Liberty p.18-19
- *Fires*
Amer. Her. — *Rev.* p.185, 199

McDowell — *Rev.* p.90-91, 97
Tunis — *Young* p.113
, French fleet at
Amer. Her. — *Rev.* p.264, 280-281
- Frontier
See also **New York — Early settlements**
Main — *Social* p.9, 15-16
, Germans in
Axtell — *18th* p.123
- Government
Axtell — *18th* p.72, 118-122
Bridenbaugh — *Revolt* p.8, 12-13, 218, 223
- Manhattan Island
Wheeler — *Voices* p.151, 167-176, 185
- Mayor
Adams — *Album* p.268
- Mosquitoes
Axtell — *18th* p.122
- Rent riots
Morris — *American* p.32-33
- Revolutionary War
See also **New York, Battle of;** related subjects
Amer. Her. — *Rev.* p.178-188, 193-201, 203
Morison — *Oxford (1)* p.317-319
- Society
Earle — *Colonial* p.218-219
- Streets
Handlin — *This* p.92
- Trade
See also **New York — Commerce**
Adams — *Provincial* p.35-36
, Victory procession in
McDowell — *Rev.* p.184-185
- Views of Alexander Hamilton
Miller — *Colonial* p.409-413
- Women
Benson — *Women 18th* p.134-135, 282-283, 294, 300-301, 306

NEW YORK CHAMBER OF COMMERCE
Greene — *Revol.* p.38, 40-42, 50, 217, 260

NEW YORK PUBLIC LIBRARY
, Founding of
Wright — *Cultural* p.147

NEW YORK SOCIETY LIBRARY
Wright — *Cultural* p.150

NEW YORK STOCK EXCHANGE
Locke — *Birth* p.133-148
Morris — *Ency.* p.504

NEWBERY, JOHN
Glubok — *Home* p.172-173, 175-176, 178, 191-192

NEWBOLD, CHARLES
Dolan — *Yankee* p.188

NEWPORT, RHODE ISLAND
Bridenbaugh — *Revolt* p.17, 166, 227, 232, 257, 359, 368-370, 416-417
Dulles — *History* p.64-65
Evans — *Weather.* p.245-250, 267-269
Stearns — *Story* p.73
Stember — *North* p.4, 324-326, 329, 332-338, 341
- Politics and government
Bridenbaugh — *Revolt* p.13, 222-223

NEWSPAPERS
Adams — *Provincial* p.267-268
Amer. Her. — *Rev.* p.51, 53, 57-58, 63
Bridenbaugh — *Revolt. See* index p.xiv
Bridenbaugh — *Wild.* p.292-294, 452-453, 456, 460-461
Dannett — *Yankee* p.227-228
Greene — *Revol. See* index p.476
Langdon — *Every.* p.299-304
Miller — *Origins* p.64, 288-293
Morris — *Ency.* p.550-582
Speare — *Life* p.130-131
Train — *Story* p.176
Wertenbaker — *Golden* p.51, 55, 72-73, 93-94, 103, 109-110, 136-137, 141-143, 146-147
Wright — *Cultural* p.242-246
- Boston
Wright — *Cultural* p.244

NEWSPAPERS (continued)
, Colonial
Life — *New* p.100-101, 126-127
, Conservative
Boorstin — *Americans* p.330-335
- Federalist and Republican
Morris — *Ency.* p.581-582
, First
Dexter — *Colonial* p.6-7, 19-20
Earle — *Colonial* p.137-138
Langdon — *Every.* p.299, 302-304
- Foreign languages
Morris — *Ency.* p.580
- New York
Wright — *Cultural* p.245
- Pennsylvania — First
Earle — *Colonial* p.67-68
- Philadelphia
Burt — *Phila.* p.241
Wright — *Cultural* p.244
- Politics and circulation
Morris — *Ency.* p.581
- Revolutionary period
McDowell — *Rev.* p.14, 16, 18-19, 22, 60, 74, 87, 102, 148
, Rise of
Boorstin — *American* p.324-329

NEWTOWN, NEW YORK
, Battle of
Stember — *Middle* p.156-161

NICHOLSON, FRANCIS
Wertenbaker — *Golden* p.85-86, 110

"NIDDY-NODDY"
Earle — *Home* p.200-201, 320

NIGHT SCHOOLS
Bridenbaugh — *Revolt* p.176, 377

NIGHTGOWNS
, Forbidden at Harvard
Earle — *Home* p.294

NILES, NATHANIEL
Dannett — *Yankee* p.274-275

NINETY-SIX, SOUTH CAROLINA
Stember — *South. See* index p.214

"NO-GOODERS" (beggars)
Wilson — *Early* p.175-178

"NOMINI HALL"
Spruill — *Women's* p.32, 64-66, 71n-72, 88-90, 102, 132-133, 194-195

NONIMPORTATION AGREEMENTS
Beach — *Samuel* p.142-143, 173, 188-191, 222, 227
Miller — *Origins. See* index p.575
Morison — *Oxford (1)* p.266-270
Morris — *American* p.100-104
Morris — *Ency.* p.75-76, 78

NORFOLK, VIRGINIA
Handlin — *This* p.88-92

NORRIS, DEBORAH
Brooks — *Colonial* p.245-284
- Views on reading Declaration of Independence
Burt — *Phila.* p.281

NORRIS, ISAAC
Burt — *Phila.* p.161-162

NORTH, FREDERICK
Beach — *Samuel* p.128, 132, 174, 215-216, 249
Carman — *History* p.158-159, 175, 177, 181, 185-187
Miller — *Origins. See* index p.515
200 Years p.13, 25-26, 121, 158

NORTH
- Characteristics, acc. to Thomas Jefferson
Sanderlin — *1776* p.xxiv
- Commercialization
Adams — *Provincial* p.222-257
- Conciliatory Resolution (1775)
Alden — *Pioneer* p.78-79, 83
- Economic class structure
Main — *Social* p.7-43

- *Frontier*
Main — *Social* p.7-17, 39-40
- *Illiterates*
Adams — *Provincial* p.256-257

NORTH AMERICA
Tunis — *Frontier* p.14

NORTH CAROLINA
Greene — *Revol. See* index p.476
Hofstadter — *Amer.* p.13, 21, 59, 89, 124, 167-169, 178, 185, 187, 202-203, 208, 265
Life — *Growing* p.7, 56
Life — *Making* p.13, 81, 83-85, 110-111, 136
Life — *New* p.104, 120, 125, 162
Miller — *Origins* p.381
Morison — *Oxford (1). See* index p.417
National — *History.* p.165-166
Stember — *South* p.100-150
200 Years p.70-72, 176
Wright — *Frontier* p.41-45
, and Declaration of Independence
Bakeless — *Signers* p.263-272
Malone — *Story* p.221-237
- *Anson County*
, Loyalism in
Morris — *American* p.213-216
- *Boundaries (with Virginia)*
Burner — *America* p.46-52
Miller — *Colonial* p.291-349
, British in
Wheeler — *Voices* p.409, 418-420
- *Life*
Morris — *Voices* p.62-63
Spruill — *Women's* p.97-101
- *Protest and rebellion*
Colbourn — *Colonial* p.186-198
- *Regulators (1769)*
Morris — *American* p.34-37
- *Revolutionary War*
Amer. Her. — *Rev.* p.52, 325, 331-332, 337, 342
Morison — *Oxford (1)* p.338-343
- *Trade*
Adams — *Provincial* p.207-208
- *Whigs and Tories*
Stember — *South* p.118-124

NORTHEAST
See also **Colonies and colonists; New England**
- *Bicentennial*
Lawlor — *Bicen.* p.107-137

NORTHWEST
See also **Frontier**
Amer. Her. — *Rev.* p.313
National — *History.* p.347-348
Tunis — *Frontier* p.69-70

NORTHWEST ORDINANCE (1781)
Angle — *By* p.87-94
Bartlett — *New* p.66, 80-82
Carman — *History* p.239-241
Morris — *Ency.* p.117, 419
Sweet — *Story* p.206
200 Years p.181

NORTHWEST TERRITORY
Morris — *Voices* p.150, 152-153
National — *History.* p.284-291
Sweet — *Story* p.206
- *Appalachians*
Tunis — *Feature* p.42-43

NORWALK, CONNECTICUT
Stember — *North* p.357-359

NOVELISTS
See also **Fiction**
Morris — *Ency.* p.565

NOVELS. *See* Fiction

NURSES AND NURSING
Dexter — *Colonial* p.61-68
- *South*
Spruill — *Women's* p.55-57, 270-272

O

OATHS. ***See*** **Profanity**

OBSTETRICS
See also **Midwives**
Bridenbaugh — *Wild.* p.243, 245, 405

OCCUPATIONS
See also **Professions;** names of occupations
Miller — *First* p.163-172
, Children's
Glubok — *Home* p.198-217

OGLETHORPE, JAMES EDWARD
Boorstin — *Americans* p.75-79, 86
Life — *New* p.60-61, 66-67
Morris — *Ency.* p.64
- Peace with Indians
Collins — *Story* p.70
- Settlements in Georgia
Spruill — *Women's* p.15-16, 18n

OHIO
Adams — *Album* p.349
Greene — *Revol.* p.398-399, 400, 403
Morris — *Voices* p.149, 152-155
Tunis — *Frontier* p.69-70
, Routes to
National — *History.* p.273-283
- Settlements (1786-1788)
Morris — *Ency.* p.419

OHIO COMPANY
Greene — *Revol.* p.56-57, 400, 404, 406
Tunis — *Young* p.48

OHIO VALLEY
Greene — *Revol.* p.56-57, 175
Morris — *Ency.* p.65-66
, French-English struggle for
Life — *New* p.146-147

OLD AGE. ***See*** **Longevity**

OLD GERMAN REFORMED CHURCH (Phila.)
Axtell — *18th* p.180

"OLD HOUSE" (John Adams's home)
Life — *Growing* p.34

OLD IRONSIDES (Constitution)
Burt — *Phila.* p.112

OLD NORTH MEETING HOUSE (Boston)
Forbes — *Paul* p.164, 295, 370, 460

OLD NORTHWEST. ***See*** **Northwest; Northwest Territory**

OLIVE BRANCH PETITION
Amer. Her. — *Rev.* p.138
Beach — *Samuel* p.290-292
Life — *Making* p.34
Morison — *Oxford (1)* p.290-291
Morris — *American* p.163-166
Morris — *Ency.* p.88

OLIVER, ANDREW
Beach — *Samuel* p.30, 52-53, 80-84, 96-97, 113, 169, 225, 247, 249, 256

OLIVER, PETER
Beach — *Samuel* p.37, 100, 113, 245, 254-256

OPERAS
Morris — *Ency.* p.613-614

ORDINANCE FOR RELIGIOUS FREEDOM. ***See*** **Virginia Statute for Religious Freedom**

ORDINANCE OF 1784
Bartlett — *New* p.80

ORDINANCE OF 1785
Bartlett — *New* p.61, 66, 71, 79-82

ORDINANCE OF 1787. ***See*** **Northwest Ordinance (1787)**

ORDINARIES. ***See*** **Taverns**

ORGANS
Morris — *Ency.* p.611-612
Speare — *Life* p.166

, First
Adams — *Provincial* p.146
Howard — *Our* p.17-20
Train — *Story* p.175
Wright — *Cultural* p.193

ORISKANY, NEW YORK
, Battle of
Stember — *North* p.4, 59, 61, 66-70, 73

ORNAMENTS
Dreppard — *Pioneer* p.57-65, 67, 73, 77

ORPHANAGES
See also names of orphanages
Sweet — *Story* p.169-171

ORPHANS
- Apprentices
Spruill — *Women's* p.57-59

OSBORN, SARAH
Benson — *Women* p.119, 260-262

OTIS, JAMES
Beach — *Samuel. See* index p.328
Forbes — *Paul. See* index p.494
Life — *New* p.126, 148-149, 151-152, 159, 166
Miller — *Origins. See* index p.515
Whitney — *Abigail* p.14-15, 30, 36-37, 42, 47, 50, 55-56, 60, 71
, against Writs of Assistance
Morris — *American* p.2-5
, Denounces tyranny
Angle — *By* p.30-37

OVENS
See also **Dutch ovens**
Gould — *Early* p.52-56, 58
, Brick
Gould — *Early* p.74
Speare — *Life* p.72-73
, Farm
Dow — *Early* p.93
, Smoke
Gould — *Early* p.55-56, 58
, Tin
Gould — *Early* p.75, 98
, Tin roasting ("tin kitchen")
Gould — *Early* p.72

OXEN
Crèvecoeur — *Sketches* p.43, 47, 49, 71, 140, 142, 208-209
Tunis — *Living* p.106-107

OXYGEN
- Joseph Priestley's discoveries
Wilson — *American* p.34-35

OYSTERS
Handlin — *This* p.27-28, 97

P

PACA, WILLIAM
Bakeless — *Signers* p.242-244
Malone — *Story* p.194-195
- Biography
Lossing — *Biog.* p.154-156

PACHELBEL, KARL THEODORE
Morris — *Ency.* p.612

PACIFISM
See also **Dunkers; Mennonites; Moravians; Quakers**
Boorstin — *Americans* p.50-54
Greene — *Revol.* p.103-105, 130, 164, 223, 228
Sweet — *Religion* p.40-45

PACK TRAINS
Langdon — *Every.* p.122-124
Tunis — *Frontier* p.35-37

PACKET BOATS
Bridenbaugh — *Revolt* p.55, 289-290
Train — *Story* p.167-168

PAGE, JOHN
Wertenbaker — *Golden* p.122-123

PAINE, ROBERT TREAT
Bakeless — *Signers* p.64-67
Malone — *Story* p.116-117
- Biography
Lossing — *Biog.* p.37-39

PAINE, THOMAS, AND *COMMON SENSE*
Baldwin — *Ideas* p.183-186
Brodie — *Jefferson. See* index p.806
Burt — *Phila.* p.269-272
Carman — *History* p.188-189
Collins — *Story* p.129
Davis — *Heroes* p.56-63
Kraus — *U.S. (1)* p.216-217
Miers — *American* p.77-79
Miller — *Origins* p.66-67, 171, 467-474, 476, 492, 504-505
Morison — *Oxford (1)* p.292, 323, 333, 363, 383, 404
Morris — *American* p.175-186
Morris — *Voices* p.94-97, 108-110
Sanderlin — *1776* p.202-206
200 Years p.68-71, 87-88, 92, 94, 291
- Biography
Morris — *Ency.* p.701-702

PAINTERS AND PAINTINGS
See also **Limners**
Adams — *Provincial* p.309
Bridenbaugh — *Revolt* p.196-199, 403-408
Bridenbaugh — *Wild.* p.454-455, 458, 460, 463
Greene — *Revol.* p.148-149, 299, 396, 425, 446-447
Morris — *Ency.* p.596-597, 599
Tunis — *Young* p.124-126
Wertenbaker — *Golden* p.33-34, 82-83, 96-98, 117, 155-156
, Historical
Morris — *Ency.* p.600
- New England
Morris — *Ency.* p.596-597
- Philadelphia
Burt — *Phila.* p.234-238
- South
Spruill — *Women's* p.203-204
, Unknown
Dreppard — *Pioneer* p.137-141, 143, 145-146

PAINTS
See also **Dyes**
Gould — *Early* p.113

PALATINATES
See also **Germans; Pennsylvania Dutch (Germans)**
Adams — *Provincial* p.179, 189
Morris — *Ency.* p.444

PALEONTOLOGY
Morris — *Ency.* p.530

"PALINURUS PEEPER" (pseud.)
Burt — *Phila.* p.241-243

PALLBEARERS. ***See*** **Funerals**

PANSIES
- Folk names
Earle — *Home* p.425-426

PANTRIES
Gould — *Early* p.35-36

PAOLI MASSACRE (Pa.)
Burt — *Phila.* p.273
Stember — *Middle* p.110-115

PAPER CUTTING
Earle — *Colonial* p.233-234
Earle — *Home* p.277-280
Glubok — *Home* p.205-206

PAPER HANGINGS. ***See*** **Wall decoration and wallpaper**

PAPER INDUSTRY
Tunis — *Colonial* p.132-136
Tunis — *Living* p.116-118

"PAPYROTAMIA." ***See*** **Paper cutting**

PARIS
- Treaties of Peace
Alden — *Pioneer* p.45-47, 63, 94-105, 109, 112
Life — *New* p.109, 147
Morris — *Voices* p.111, 124-129

PARLIAMENTARY ACT OF 1709
Morris — *Ency.* p.444

PARLORS
Sirkis — *Reflect.* p.26

PAROCHIAL SCHOOLS
, First (1782)
Morris — *Ency.* p.550

PARSONAGES
Smith — *Colonial* p.222-232, 234-246

PATENT OFFICE
, Creation of (1790)
Dolan — *Yankee* p.49

PATERSON, WILLIAM
Morris — *Voices* p.162-163

PATRIOTIC SOCIETIES
See also names of societies
Earle — *Colonial* p.240-257

PATRIOTISM
Sloane — *Spirits* p.13-17
- Definition
Sloane — *Spirits* p.14-17
- Women
Evans — *Weather.* p.13-15
Holliday — *Woman's* p.303-306
- Women, Southern
Earle — *Colonial* p.251-255

PATRIOTS
Ingraham — *Album* p.45
Malone — *Story* p.33-54
, versus Loyalists
Kraus — *U.S. (1)* p.219-221

PATTISON FAMILY
Dolan — *Yankee* p.143-146

PAVEMENTS
Bridenbaugh — *Revolt* p.29-30, 58, 238-239
Bridenbaugh — *Wild.* p.156, 316-317

PAXTON (PAXTANG) BOYS
Burt — *Phila.* p.172, 175-177
Morris — *Ency.* p.72

PEACE OF UTRECHT
- Effect
Adams — *Provincial* p.42-43, 222

PEALE, CHARLES WILSON
Burt — *Phila.* p.236-237
Life — *Growing* p.26-27
Morris — *American* p.256-257
Morris — *Ency.* p.599-600
Wertenbaker — *Golden* p.96-98, 155

PEALE FAMILY
Burt — *Phila.* p.237-238

PEARSON, RICHARD
Morris — *Ency.* p.102
Morris — *Voices* p.117-118

PEDAGOGUES. See Teachers

PEDDLERS
See also **Antiques;** names of occupations, products
Bridenbaugh — *Revolt* p.79-80, 264-265
Bridenbaugh — *Wild.* p.180-182, 291, 336
Dolan — *Yankee* p.10-11
Gould — *Early* p.125-126
Speare — *Life* p.144-145
Wilson — *Early* p.39-47
- Books
Dolan — *Yankee* p.211-212
- Character
Dolan — *Yankee* p.229
- Life
Dolan — *Yankee* p.66-67

PELISSIER, VICTOR
Howard — *Our* p.94-96

PENCILS
Glubok — *Home* p.120-121

PENMANSHIP
Earle — *Child* p.151-155
Earle — *Customs* p.31-32, 282-283
Glubok — *Home* p.156-158, 160-161
Langdon — *Every.* p.78-81

PENN, JOHN
Bakeless — *Signers* p.270-272
Malone — *Story* p.224
Rublowsky — *Music* p.41
- Biography
Lossing — *Biog.* p.208-210

PENN, WILLIAM
Hofstadter — *Amer.* p.7, 18-19, 33, 187, 194-200
Morison — *Oxford (1)* p.179-180, 182-185, 194, 198
Wertenbaker — *Golden* p.7, 61-62, 81-82
, and Indians
Burt — *Phila.* p.46-47
Tunis — *Tavern* p.23, 32-33
, as Quaker
Burt — *Phila.* p.47-48, 67-68
- Character
Burt — *Phila.* p.97-99
- Homes
See also **"Pennsbury"**
Langdon — *Every.* p.54

"PENNSBURY"
Burt — *Phila.* p.66-67, 90-91

PENNSYLVANIA
Adams — *Album* p.261
Axtell — *18th* p.54-69
Crèvecoeur — *Sketches. See* index p.339
Glubok — *Home.* See index p.354
Greene — *Revol. See* index p.477
Hofstadter — *Amer.* p.x
Life — *Growing* p.16-17, 38, 131, 146
Life — *Making* p.57-58, 75-77, 108, 110-111, 130, 134
Life — *New. See* index p.175
Main — *Social* p.10, 16, 25, 33-34, 80, 104, 106-107, 109, 128n, 221-223, 238
Miller — *Origins. See* index p.515-516
Morison — *Oxford (1). See* index p.417
Stember — *Middle. See* index p.170
Tunis — *Living* p.99-104
Wheeler — *Voices* p.79, 82-83, 159, 211, 215, 243-251, 261-262
, and Declaration of Independence
Bakeless — *Signers* p.105-157
Malone — *Story* p.159-180
- Charter of Privileges
Davie — *Profile* p.90-91
- Chester County
Main — *Social* p.29, 33-34, 38, 41, 73, 91, 180-183, 186, 194
- Crossing
Miller — *Colonial* p.83-98
- Decorative symbols
Train — *Story* p.188-189
- Early settlers
Axtell — *18th* p.60-65
- Frontier
Main — *Social* p.16
Morris — *American* p.27-31
, Germans in
See also **Palatinates; Pennsylvania Dutch**
Axtell — *18th* p.54-59
- Lancaster County
Train — *Story* p.195
- Lands
Axtell — *18th* p.66-68
, Migrants from
Axtell — *18th* p.65-66
- Shipbuilding
Kraus — *U.S. (1)* p.118-119
- Traders
Morris — *Ency.* p.413

PENNSYLVANIA DUTCH (Germans)
Cable — *American* p.70-71
Kraus — *U.S. (1)* p.108
National — *History.* p.108-111
- Farms
Langdon — *Every.* p.63-73

PENNSYLVANIA HOSPITAL
Bridenbaugh — *Revolt* p.21, 36, 103, 126, 131-132, 330, 380, 383

PENNSYLVANIA JOURNAL
McDowell — *Rev.* p.14, 102

PENNSYLVANIA, UNIVERSITY OF
Wertenbaker — *Golden* p.66-67, 90

PENOBSCOT CAMPAIGN
Forbes — *Paul* p.339-345
Stember — *North* p.237, 239, 260

PENOLOGY
See also **Prisons**
Greene — *Revol.* p.319-321

PEOPLE
Tunis — *Living* p.103-104
- *Basic mix and traits*
Bartlett — *New* p.117-142, 143-149
- *Meaning*
Kraus — *U.S. (1)* p.175-176

PEPPER
Dolan — *Yankee* p.260

PEPPERELL, WILLIAM
Stearns — *Story* p.64-65

PERFUME
Belote — *Compleat* p.149-151
Earle — *Customs* p.312-313

PERIODICALS. *See* Magazines; Newspapers

PERIPATETICS
Wilson — *Early* p.38-39

PERKINS, NATHAN
, on pioneer life
Pettengill — *Yankee* p.68-72

PERRY, OLIVER HAZARD
- *Biography*
Morris — *Ency.* p.704

PERSONALITIES
See also names of individuals
Dreppard — *Pioneer* p.107-112, 114-115

PERUKERS. *See* Wigs and wigmakers

PETER, JOHN FREDERICK
Howard — *Our* p.29-30
Rublowsky — *Music* p.26

PETS
See also **Cats; Dogs;** etc.
Speare — *Life* p.103-104

PETTY, WILLIAM (Lord Shelburne)
Life — *Making* p.34, 87-88, 105, 107
Morris — *Ency.* p.71
- *on Preliminary Articles of Peace (1783)*
Morris — *American* p.279-284

PEWS. *See* Churches — Pews

PEWTER AND PEWTERERS
Earle — *Customs* p.139-140
Langdon — *Every.* p.175
Speare — *Life* p.123-124
Tunis — *Colonial* p.72-76
Wright — *Cultural* p.214
- *Utensils*
Gould — *Early* p.25, 86-87

PHI BETA KAPPA
- *Founding (1776)*
Dolan — *Yankee* p.88
Train — *Story* p.205

PHILADELPHIA, PENNSYLVANIA
See also under special subjects
Adams — *Album* p.256
Axtell — *18th* p.88-115, 196-199
Bridenbaugh — *Revolt* p.13-15, 210, 217n
Evans — *Weather.* p.107-108, 188-189
Glubok — *Home* p.226, 243-244
Greene — *Revol. See* index p.477-478
Handlin — *This* p.20-23
Howard — *Our. See* index p.812
Life — *Growing* p.20-31
Life — *New* p.95, 108-109, 120-121, 123, 125-126, 132-133, 140-141
Main — *Social. See* index p.322
Miller — *Origins* p.54-55, 136-137, 273, 340-341, 364-366, 416
Morison — *Oxford (1). See* index p.418
Morris — *Voices* p.65-70, 104, 114, 140-142, 158
National — *History.* p.207-219
Ross — *Taste* p.7
Scott — *Trumpet. See* index p.305
Speare — *Life* p.65-67
Stember — *Middle* p.119-136
Train — *Story* p.258-259
Tunis — *Living* p.99-100
Tunis — *Tavern. See* index p.108
Tunis — *Young* p.49-51
Wertenbaker — *Golden. See* index p.168
Wheeler — *Voices. See* index p.478

PHILADELPHIA, PA. (*continued*)
Whitney — *Abigail* p.87, 133, 246-258, 261-283, 287, 299
Wright — *New* p.109-117
, American troops in
Evans — *Weather.* p.171-173
- Architecture
Gowans — *Images* p.188-199
, as port
Burt — *Phila.* p.109-110, 118-119
Tunis — *Young* p.52, 85
- Bicentennial
Lawler — *Bicen.* p.29-52
, British occupation of
Amer. Her. — *Rev.* p.213-214, 228
Evans — *Weather.* p.158-172
- Buildings
Axtell — *18th* p.91-93
Life — *Growing* p.28-29
, Oldest
Axtell — *18th* p.100
- Celebrities
Burt — *Phila.* p.230-231
- Climate
Burt — *Phila.* p.73-74, 324-325
- Commerce and trade
Axtell — *18th* p.93-97
Scott — *Settlers* p.170-172
Wright — *Cultural* p.42-43
- Countryside
Scott — *Settlers* p.173
- Crime and punishment
Burt — *Phila.* p.79-82
- Culture
Wertenbaker — *Golden* p.65-66, 83-84
- Dynasties
Wright — *Cultural* p.42
- Early settlers, origin of
Wertenbaker — *Golden* p.6-7
- Evacuation, by British
Amer. Her. — *Rev.* p.221, 230, 280
- "Firsts"
Burt — *Phila.* p.226-227
- Freedom
Axtell — *18th* p.99
- Fuel
Axtell — *18th* p.100-101
- Girls
Earle — *Colonial* p.191
- Government
Bridenbaugh — *Revolt* p.2-9, 218
- Growth
Axtell — *18th* p.99-100
- Hospitals
Burt — *Phila.* p.322
, Howe's campaign in
Stember — *Middle* p.85-142
- Incorporation as city
Burt — *Phila.* p.80
- Independence Square
Tunis — *Young* p.52
- Industry
See also **Philadelphia — Commerce and trade**
Wright — *New* p.114-115
- Inns
Tunis — *Young* p.53
- Legends and superstitions
Burt — *Phila.* p.325-326
- Life
Axtell — *18th* p.100
Belote — *Compleat* p.30-31
- Local enterprises
Tunis — *Young* p.55-56
- Nicknames
Burt — *Phila.* p.328
- Parties
Burt — *Phila.* p.289-293, 295
- Politics
See also **Philadelphia — Government**
Bridenbaugh — *Revolt* p.12
- Population
Axtell — *18th* p.98-99, 105
- Prosperity
Axtell — *18th* p.113-114
- Revolutionary War
See also related subjects
Amer. Her. — *Rev.* p.211-217, 230
McDowell — *Rev.* p.31, 34, 47, 74, 80-81, 85-86, 98, 113-114, 123, 135-136
- 1708
Sirkis — *Reflect.* p.87-88
- 1710
Burt — *Phila.* p.72-73
- 1750
Scott — *Settlers* p.168-171, 173

- *1776*
Wilson — *American* p.2-3
Woodward — *Way* p.133-159
- *1798*
Cable — *American* p.91
- *Society*
Earle — *Colonial* p.199-202
Holliday — *Woman's* p.226-234
- *Streets*
Burt — *Phila.* p.159
Life — *Growing* p.28-29
Scott — *Settlers* p.168-169
Tunis — *Young* p.49-52
Wright — *New* p.110
, *Lighting of*
Tunis — *Young* p.50-51
- *Swedes*
Axtell — *18th* p.109
- *"Thinkers"*
Tunis — *Young* p.56
- *Travel*
Tunis — *Young* p.57
- *Trees*
Burt — *Phila.* p.15
- *Trials and dangers*
Wright — *New* p.113-114
, *Tuberculosis in*
Burt — *Phila.* p.324
- *Views of Hamilton*
Miller — *Colonial* p.398-405
- *Washington Square*
Burt — *Phila.* p.276
- *Wealth*
Burt — *Phila.* p.334
- *Women*
Benson — *Women 18th* p.133-135, 282-283, 295
Burt — *Phila.* p.71, 74, 160, 243, 302-303, 320
, *Beauty of*
Holliday — *Woman's* p.229-231
, *Education of*
Benson — *Women 18th* p.133-134, 137-144
- *Writers and writing*
Wright — *Cultural* p.172-173
- *Yellow fever epidemic (1793)*
Burt — *Phila.* p.322-326

PHILE, PHILIP
Howard — *Our* p.107

PHILIPSE, MARY
Ellet — *Eminent* p.136-141

PHILLIPS, CATHERINE
Benson — *Women* p.266-267

PHILLIPS, JOHN ("Portugee")
- *Famous ride*
Burt — *Phila.* p.280

PHOEBE LAMPS
Earle — *Home* p.44
Glubok — *Home* p.23-24

PHYSICIANS
Bridenbaugh — *Revolt* p.192, 199, 201, 330, 380, 409
Earle — *Customs* p.333-336
Forbes — *Paul* p.36, 76-77, 443-445
Main — *Social* p.310-311
Morris — *Ency.* p.541
Smith — *Colonial* p.330-346
Wright — *Cultural* p.235-236
, *Itinerant*
Dolan — *Yankee* p.197
- *Massachusetts*
Dow — *Every* p.175-178
- *Philadelphia*
Burt — *Phila.* p.224-225

PHYSICS
Morris — *Ency.* p.528

PIANOS
Earle — *Colonial* p.224-230
Glubok — *Home* p.128

PIAZZAS
Gould — *Early* p.41-42

PICKERING, TIMOTHY
Morris — *Voices* p.177, 183, 185-186

PICKLING
Glubok — *Home* p.84-85

PIEDMONT PLATEAU
Tunis — *Frontier* p.15-16

PIES
Gould — *Early* p.94-95

PIETISM
Hofstadter — *Amer.* p.217, 221, 232, 260, 275, 285-286, 288, 290
Sweet — *Story* p.138-139
Wright — *Cultural* p.194

PIGEONS
Earle — *Home* p.110
Pettengill — *Yankee* p.121-123
- *Shooting*
Glubok — *Home* p.59-60

"PILING BEES"
Glubok — *Home* p.319-320

PINCKNEY, CHARLES C.
Morris — *Voices* p.183-185

PINCKNEY, ELIZA LUCAS
Benson — *Women 18th* p.21n, 45, 288n-289, 309, 311-312
Brooks — *Dames* p.103-131
Earle — *Colonial* p.76-83
Dexter — *Colonial* p.119-124
Spruill — *Women's. See* index p.413 (Lucas), 417 (Pinckney)
Train — *Story* p.215-217

PINCKNEY'S TREATY. ***See*** **Treaty of San Lorenzo**

PINE-NEEDLE TOYS
Earle — *Child* p.394-395

PIONEERS
See also **Frontier;** names of localities, etc.
Dreppard — *Pioneers* p.1-11
Tunis — *Young* p.45-46
Wilson — *Early* p.13-21
- *Food*
Tunis — *Young* p.46
- *Spirit*
Sloane — *Spirits* p.38-39
- *Tools*
Tunis — *Young* p.46

PIPES
Tunis — *Living* p.152

PIRACY
See also **Barbary Pirates**
Adams — *Provincial* p.53-54
Kraus — *U.S. (1)* p.117-118
Wilson — *Early* p.168-174
, Punishment for, Massachusetts
Dow — *Every* p.220-221

PITCAIRN, JOHN
Forbes — *Paul. See* index p.494
Stember — *North* p.296, 300-301, 305-309, 311, 316

"PITCHER, MOLLY" (Mary Ludwig McCauley)
Adelman — *Famous* p.88
Cook — *What* p.231-233
Evans — *Weather.* p.10-12
McDowell — *Rev.* p.12, 136-137
Somerville — *Women* p.6-11
Stember — *Middle* p.70-71
200 Years p.128

PITT, WILLIAM
McDowell — *Rev.* p.16-17, 78
Miller — *Origins. See* index p.516
, on Stamp Act repeal
Morris — *American* p.78-80

PITTSBURGH, PENNSYLVANIA
Greene — *Revol.* p.176, 226, 345, 412, 414-415

PITTSFIELD, MASSACHUSETTS
- *Petition (1775)*
Morris — *American* p.290-293

"PLACEMEN"
Bridenbaugh — *Revolt* p.79, 281-282, 306, 335-336

PLAINS OF ABRAHAM (Quebec)
Sanderlin — *1776* p.1-24
Wheeler — *Voices* p.85-108, 133

PLANTAIN
Earle — *Home* p.435-436

PLANTATIONS AND PLANTERS
Carman — *History* p.54-55, 114, 116
Life — *New* p.62, 64, 66, 68, 71-73, 98-99, 101-102, 115
Sirkis — *Reflect.* p.144-146
Tunis — *Living* p.111-112

- *Economy*
Kraus — *U.S. (1)* p.119-122
- *Life*
Benson — *Women 18th* p.284-286, 288-290
Miller — *First* p.94-106
Speare — *Life* p.13-23
Wright — *Cultural* p.3-19
- *Maryland*
Wright — *Cultural* p.13-16
- *Society*
Gowans — *Images* p.178-188
- *South Carolina*
Wright — *Cultural* p.16-19
- *Virginia*
Boorstin — *Americans* p.301-306
National — *History.* p.138-146
Woodward — *Way* p.70-103
Wright — *Cultural* p.4-13
- *Women*
Spruill — *Women* p.306-312

PLATE WARMERS
Gould — *Early* p.78

PLAYHOUSES. *See* Theater

PLAYS. *See* Drama

PLAYWRIGHTS. *See* Dramatists

PLEASURES. *See* Amusements; Sports and games; other types of pleasure

PLOWS
Crèvecoeur — *Sketches* p.25-27, 31, 48, 71, 81, 93, 117, 139-140, 148, 163, 178, 204, 230, 241
Dolan — *Yankee* p.188

PLUMBERS
Tunis — *Colonial* p.70-72

POETS AND POETRY
See also **Almanacs — Poetry**
Adams — *Provincial* p.127
Boorstin — *Americans* p.314-316
Bridenbaugh — *Revolt* p.190-191, 395, 397
Greene — *Revol.* p.126, 129, 132-133, 135, 141, 295-299, 391-394
Morris — *Ency.* p.564
Wright — *Cultural* p.171-172
- *Annapolis*
Wertenbaker — *Golden* p.92-95
- *Broadsides*
Nye — *Unembar.* p.89-92
- *Newspapers*
Nye — *Unembar.* p.93
- *Virginia*
Wertenbaker — *Golden* p.112

POLICEMEN
Wilson — *Early* p.32-34

POLITICS
See also **Government;** names of localities, political parties
Carman — *History* p.128-131
Crèvecoeur — *Sketches. See* index p.339
Wright — *New* p.21-31
, and enlightenment
Baldwin — *Ideas* p.156-164
- *Boston*
Bridenbaugh — *Revolt* p.12, 221-222
- *Creative period (1785-1788)*
Morison — *Oxford (1)* p.385-408
, Drama of
Burner — *America* p.52-59
- *Family dynasties*
Kraus — *U.S. (1)* p.130
- *Leaders*
Wertenbaker — *Golden* p.111-112
- *Literature*
Morris — *Ency.* p.562-564
- *Strife*
Butterfield — *Amer.* p.12
- *Women*
Benson — *Women 18th* p.172-174, 224, 244-250, 255-258

PONTIAC (Ottawa Indian chief)
Collins — *Story* p.95
Greene — *Revol.* p.53, 169-171
Morris — *Ency.* p.71-72
Wright — *Frontier* p.49

POOR RELIEF
See also **Almshouses;** etc.
Bridenbaugh — *Wild. See* index p.496
Main — *Social. See* index p.322
- *Boston*
Bridenbaugh — *Revolt* p.123-127, 319
- *Charlestown*
Bridenbaugh — *Revolt* p.123-126, 322-323
- *New York*
Bridenbaugh — *Revolt* p.122-124, 126-127, 324-325
- *Newport, R.I.*
Bridenbaugh — *Revolt* p.124-126, 323-324
- *Philadelphia*
Bridenbaugh — *Revolt* p.126, 218, 321-322

POOR RICHARD'S ALMANAC
Burner — *America* p.66-72
Burt — *Phila.* p.157-173
Cable — *American* p.76-77

"POPE'S NIGHT" (November 5)
- *Massachusetts*
Dow — *Every* p.116

POPULATION
See also **Birth rate**
Bridenbaugh — *Revolt* p.4-5, 51, 134, 216-217, 261, 285, 333
Bridenbaugh — *Wild.* p.143-144, 249-251, 303
Greene — *Revol. See* index p.478
Life — *New* p.95-96; *See also* index
Miller — *Origins* p.53-54, 434-435
Morris — *Ency.* p.442
Scott — *Settlers* p.184-185
- *Regional distribution (1710-1790)*
Morris — *Ency.* p.442-443
-1700
Morison — *Oxford (1)* p.186, 196, 203, 207-208, 236-237
- *1750*
Hofstadter — *Amer.* p.3, 32
- *1780*
McDowell — *Rev.* p.196
- *1790*
Carman — *History* p.780-781
Morris — *Ency.* p.513-514
- *Western movement*
Sweet — *Story* p.205-206

PORK
Tunis — *Living* p.108-109

PORRIDGE
Gould — *Early* p.88-89, 93

PORT ROYAL ISLAND, SOUTH CAROLINA
, Battle of
Stember — *South* p.56-58

PORTRAITS AND PORTRAIT PAINTING
See also names of artists
Adams — *Album* p.268, 304-307
Adams — *Provincial* p.148-149, 274-275
Dolan — *Yankee* p.133-136
Morris — *Ency.* p.599
Ross — *Taste* p.168-169
Stearns — *Story* p.73
Wright — *Cultural* p.208-210
- *Boys*
Earle — *Child* p.51-52
- *Children*
Earle — *Child* p.44-61
- *Philadelphia*
Burt — *Phila.* p.235-240

PORTSMOUTH, NEW HAMPSHIRE
Main — *Social* p.35, 37-38, 74, 146-147, 157, 254

POSTAL SERVICE
Adams — *Provincial* p.130, 302
Bridenbaugh — *Revolt* p.96-97, 290-291
Bridenbaugh — *Wild.* p.204-205, 361-362
Earle — *Home* p.333-335, 344
Forbes — *Paul* p.197-198
Glubok — *Home* p.335-336
Greene — *Revol.* p.2-3, 36-37, 342, 344-345, 407-408
Langdon — *Every.* p.264-272
Morris — *Ency.* p.411-414, 419
Tunis — *Living* p.122
Wright — *Cultural* p.241-242

POSTRIDERS
Speare — *Life* p.144
Tunis — *Living* p.122
Tunis — *Tavern* p.36-38

POTASH
Pettengill — *Yankee* p.100-104

POTATOES
Earle — *Home* p.144-145
Glubok — *Home* p.79-80
Gould — *Early* p.92-93
- *Massachusetts*
Earle — *Home* p.144

POTHOOKS
Gould — *Early* p.68-69

POTS AND PANS. *See* Kitchen utensils

POTTERY AND POTTERS
See also **Chinaware and porcelain**
Bridenbaugh — *Revolt* p.269-271
Dreppard — *Pioneers* p.165-169; 174-176
Tunis — *Colonial* p.119-122
Tunis — *Young* p.30-31
Wright — *Cultural* p.213
- *First, in South Carolina*
Dolan — *Yankee* p.180

POULTRY
See also names of types of poultry
Gould — *Early* p.103

***POWER OF SYMPATHY* (novel)**
Benson — *Women 18th* p.189-192

POWNALL, MARY ANN
Howard — *Our* p.108-109

PRAYER
Sloane — *Spirits* p.33-34

PRESBYTERIANS
Bridenbaugh — *Revolt* p.152, 356-357
Bridenbaugh — *Wild.* p.260-267, 421, 423
Greene — *Revol. See* index p.498
Hofstadter — *Amer. See* index p.x
Miller — *Origins* p.53, 188-189, 192-194
Morris — *Ency.* p.549
Sweet — *Religion* p.3-13, 59-62
Sweet — *Story. See* index p.487
- *Log College*
Adams — *Album* p.275
- *Philadelphia*
Axtell — *18th* p.179-180

PRESERVING AND PICKLING
Gould — *Early* p.138

PRESIDENTIAL SUCCESSION ACT
Morris — *Ency.* p.124

PRESIDENTS
See also names of presidents
Cable — *American* p.82
- *Dignity*
Holliday — *Woman's* p.222-225
Wright — *New* p.61
- *Elections*
- *First (1789)*
Morris — *Ency.* p.121, 128

PRESS. *See* Newspapers

PRESTON, THOMAS
Morris — *Voices* p.74-76

PRICES
See also individual products and subjects
Morris — *Ency.* p.508
Tunis — *Colonial* p.17
- *Controls*
Morris — *Ency.* p.517

PRIESTLEY, JOSEPH
Wilson — *American* p.32-35

PRIMERS
Adams — *Album* p.286
Earle — *Child* p.128-132
Glubok — *Home* p.142

PRINCE, THOMAS
Wright — *Cultural* p.145, 162

***PRINCE OF PARTHIA* (play)**
Benson — *Women 18th* p.203

PRINCETON, NEW JERSEY
, Battle of
Amer. Her. — *Rev.* p.189, 191-192, 207
Collins — *Story* p.113
Ingraham — *Album* p.59-60
Life — *Making* p.55-57, 66, 68-69
Morris — *American* p.238-240
Stember — *Middle* p.33-39
Tunis — *Tavern* p.80, 82, 86, 97-99
200 Years p.91, 102-104
Wheeler — *Voices* p.196, 210-219, 439

PRINCETON UNIVERSITY
Greene — *Revol.* p.82, 100, 105, 123-127, 141, 291-292, 379
Wertenbaker — *Golden* p.14-16, 70

PRINTERS AND PRINTING
See also **Publishers**
Adams — *Album* p.343
Adams — *Provincial* p.128
Boorstin — *Americans* p.335-340
Bridenbaugh — *Revolt* p.385-386, 390-393, 396-397; *See also* index p.xv
Bridenbaugh — *Wild.* p.291-295, 457, 459, 461
Speare — *Life* p.126-130
Tunis — *Living* p.118
Wright — *Cultural* p.173-174
- Block
Tunis — *Colonial* p.122-125
- First
Earle — *Customs* p.270-271
- Letterpress
Tunis — *Colonial* p.125-131
- Philadelphia
Burt — *Phila.* p.232
- Road
Dolan — *Yankee* p.131-132
- Women
Dexter — *Colonial* p.168-179
Forbes — *Paul* p.40-41

PRISON SHIPS
- "Jersey"
Amer. Reader p.124-127
Scott — *Trumpet* p.170-177

PRISONERS OF WAR
Burner — *America* p.113-117
Scott — *Trumpet* p.160-177

PRISONS AND PRISONERS
Bridenbaugh — *Revolt* p.22, 118-119, 229, 303-305
Bridenbaugh — *Wild.* p.224-226, 384-386
Greene — *Revol.* p.257, 320-321
Tunis — *Living* p.154-155
- Camps
Amer. Her. — *Rev.* p.163
- Philadelphia
Burt — *Phila.* p.276
- Women
Benson — *Women 18th* p.230-232

PRIVATE SCHOOLS
Bridenbaugh — *Revolt* p.175-177, 374-375, 377

PRIVATEERS
See also **Piracy**
Adams — *Provincial* p.293-294, 296
Amer. Her. — *Rev.* p.271, 388, 291-293
Bridenbaugh — *Revolt* p.23, 26, 43, 59, 61-64
Cook — *What* p.303-335
Kraus — *U.S. (1)* p.117-118
Train — *Story* p.172-173

PROBATE RECORDS
Main — *Social. See* index p.323

PROCLAMATION OF 1763
Kraus — *U.S. (1)* p.196-198
Miller — *Origins* p.74-77, 103, 210, 374, 473
Morris — *American* p.17-20
Morris — *Ency.* p.71

PROFANITY
Bridenbaugh — *Wild.* p.228-229

PROFESSIONS
See also names of professions
Boorstin — *Americans* p.191-195
Kraus — *U.S. (1)* p.171
Main — *Social* p.17, 22, 28, 31, 34, 38-39, 64, 112-113, 200-207, 219, 257, 275

Morris — *Ency.* p.555-556
Wilson — *Early* p.103-112

PROGRESS
- *200 years*
Sloane — *Spirits* p.7-11

PROHIBITION
- *Georgia (first law)*
Adams — *Provincial* p.203
Downey — *Our* p.57-66

PROPAGANDA
Bridenbaugh — *Revolt* p.364, 392, 399
Greene — *Revol. See* index p.479

PROPERTY
See also **Land;** and related subjects
Main — *Social. See* index p.323-324
, and income
Main — *Social* p.68-114
- *Distribution*
Main — *Social* p.324
- *Women, rights of*
Benson — *Women 18th* p.234-235, 244

PROSPERITY
, Dream of
Wright — *New* p.97-98

PROSTITUTION
Bridenbaugh — *Revolt* p.121-122, 160, 316-318
Holliday — *Woman's* p.286-287

"PROTESTANT EPISCOPAL"
See also **Episcopalians**
Morris — *Ency.* p.551
- *Origin of name*
Burt — *Phila.* p.172

PROTESTANTS
See also names of denominations
Carman — *History* p.149-150
Life — *New* p.122-124
Morison — *Oxford (1). See* index p.418

PROVIDENCE, RHODE ISLAND
Stember — *North* p.321-342

PROVINCIAL GOVERNMENT
See also **Politics;** names of localities
Bridenbaugh — *Revolt* p.11-12, 219, 221, 252
, Breaking down of
Wertenbaker — *Golden* p.59-61

PSALM SINGING
See also **Bay Psalm Book; Hymns**
Howard — *Our* p.11-17
- *by note*
Howard — *Our* p.12
- *Confusion and controversy*
Howard — *Our* p.11-12
- *Improvement*
Wright — *Cultural* p.192-193

PUBLIC HEALTH
Adams — *Album* p.331
Bridenbaugh — *Revolt* p.128-132, 325-330
Bridenbaugh — *Wild.* p.238-242, 398-401
Greene — *Revol.* p.28, 68-69, 252-253, 293

PUBLIC OPINION
See also **Colonies and colonists**
Bridenbaugh — *Revolt* p.14, 116-117, 187, 390-393

PUBLIC SERVANTS
Wilson — *Early* p.22-36

PUBLISHERS
- *Women*
Earle — *Colonial* p.57-69

PUDDINGS
Gould — *Early* p.82, 88-89, 103, 187
Tunis — *Living* p.148

PUMPKINS
Earle — *Home* p.143, 309
Gould — *Early* p.92
- *Bread*
Earle — *Home* p.143

PUNCHES
Dolan — *Yankee* p.107

PUNISHMENT
See also types of punishment
Adams — *Provincial* p.162-163

PURITANS AND PURITANISM
Greene — *Revol.* p.65, 195-196, 326-327
Hofstadter — *Amer.* p.x
, and Anglicans
Adams — *Album* p.279
- Faces
Adams — *Album* p.268
, Human quality of
Rublowsky — *Music* p.13
- 1760
Amer. Reader p.59-61

PUTNAM, ISRAEL
Amer. Her. — *Rev.* p.105, 107, 110-112, 179-180, 183-184, 196
Stember — *North* p.119-121, 123, 128, 133-134, 213-214, 227, 235-236, 299, 309, 347-348, 360-362
Wheeler — *Voices* p.55, 58, 60, 67, 71, 77-78, 152, 165, 171-172

PUTNAM, RUFUS
Tunis — *Young* p.48

Q

QUACKS
, and cures
Dreppard — *Pioneer* p.226

QUADRANT
Burt — *Phila.* p.123
Morris — *Ency.* p.534

QUAKERS
See also **"Fighting Quakers"**
Axtell — *18th* p.193-209
Belote — *Compleat* p.29-30
Benson — *Women 18th* p.119, 248, 263-267, 270-271
Bridenbaugh — *Wild.* p.261-262; *See also* index p.492
Evans — *Weather. See* index p.371
Greene — *Revol. See* index p.479
Hofstadter — *Amer.* p.18, 21, 28, 156, 168, 184-186, 188, 200-201, 208-209
Kraus — *U.S. (1)* p.174
Langdon — *Every.* p.52-62
Life — *New* p.84-85, 90, 99, 120, 123, 133
Miller — *Colonial* p.437-478
Miller — *First* p.81-83
Miller — *Origins* p.61-64, 193, 260, 379
Morison — *Oxford (1). See* index p.418
Speare — *Life* p.65-67
Sweet — *Religion* p.40-41
Sweet — *Story* p.99-101, 185-187, 201-202; *See also* index p.487-488
Tunis — *Tavern. See* index p.108
Wertenbaker — *Golden. See* index p.169
Wright — *New* p.206

, and Indians
Boorstin — *Americans* p.54-58
- Churches
Axtell — *18th* p.180
- Clothing and dress
Benson — *Women 18th* p.296, 300
Life — *Growing* p.25
- Women
Tunis — *Young* p.54
- Education
Benson — *Women 18th* p.134
Wertenbaker — *Golden* p.61-63
, Insularity of
Boorstin — *Americans* p.66-69
- Life
Benson — *Women 18th* p.295-296
- Marriage
Benson — *Women 18th* p.264
- Philadelphia
Downey — *Our* p.79-89
- Pennsylvania
Boorstin — *Americans* p.33-69
- Persecution
Burner — *America* p.30-32

- *Philadelphia*
Axtell — *18th* p.112, 114
- *Rhode Island*
Earle — *Colonial* p.173-188
- *Secrecy*
Wright — *Cultural* p.43
- *Simplicity*
Sirkis — *Reflect.* p.88-89
- *Wealth*
Burt — *Phila.* p.65
- *Westward movement*
Sweet — *Religion* p.126-127
- *Women*
Benson — *Women 18th* p.263-267, 295-296
, *as preachers*
Benson — *Women 18th* p.263-267
Spruill — *Women's* p.251-254

QUARANTINE
Bridenbaugh — *Wild.* p.241-242, 400-401

QUARTERING ACTS
Morris — *Ency.* p.73, 76, 83

QUEBEC, CANADA
, *Revolutionary War in*
Amer. Her. — *Rev.* p.16, 25, 50, 73, 123-125, 129-131
Greene — *Revol.* p.181, 195-196, 200-201
Morison — *Oxford (1). See* index p.418
Morris — *Ency.* p.88-89
Sanderlin — *1776* p.10-20
Stember — *North* p.34-36; *See also* index p.387
200 Years p.54, 56-61
Wheeler — *Voices* p.85, 94-95, 97-98

QUEBEC ACT
Carman — *History* p.180
Kraus — *U.S. (1)* p.206-207
Miller — *Origins* p.191, 369, 373-376, 457, 462, 473
Morison — *Oxford (1)* p.275, 280, 282-283
Morris — *American* p.23-25
Morris — *Ency.* p.82

QUEEN ANNE'S WAR
Kraus — *U.S. (1)* p.151
Morison — *Oxford (1)* p.191-195, 213, 217
Morris — *Ency.* p.63

QUIETISTS
Miller — *Origins* p.479-480

QUILTS AND QUILTING BEES
Earle — *Home* p.270-276
Glubok — *Home* p.202-205
Gould — *Early* p.141
Speare — *Life* p.82, 155-156
- *Names of patterns*
Earle — *Home* p.272-273

QUINCY, ELIZA MORTON
- *Views (1782)*
Glubok — *Home* p.135-136

QUINCY, JOSEPH
Glubok — *Home* p.102, 146, 341-342

QUITRENT SYSTEM
Greene — *Revol.* p.15, 25, 29, 56, 333, 336

QUOCK WALKER CASE (1783)
Baldwin — *Ideas* p.186-187

R

RADICALS
See also **Whigs**
Miller — *Origins. See* index p.516
, *Revolutionary*
Alden — *Pioneer* p.101-102, 112-113, 122

RAG CARPETS
Earle — *Home* p.239-240

RAIL SPLITTING
Wright — *Frontier* p.66-67

RAISING, HOUSE. *See* House raising

RALEIGH TAVERN (Williamsburg, Va.)
Dolan — *Yankee* p.87-88

RAMSAY, DAVID
Benson — *Women 18th* p.86n, 178, 183-184, 186, 309
- *Views on Revolutionary War*
Morris — *American* p.355-361

RANDOLPH, EDMUND
Butterfield — *Amer.* p.17
Life — *Growing* p.13

RAPE
, during Revolutionary War
Evans — *Weather.* p.24-27

RATHBUN, JOHN PECK
Cook — *What* p.247-271

RATIONALISM
See also **Age of Reason**
Morris — *Ency.* p.550
Tunis — *Young* p.33-34

RATTLESNAKES
Pettengill — *Yankee* p.124-125

RAWDON, FRANCIS
Wheeler — *Voices* p.67-68, 71, 425-426, 431-432

READ, GEORGE
Bakeless — *Signers* p.259-261
Malone — *Story* p.184-185
- *Biography*
Lossing — *Biog.* p.137-140

READ, JACOB
Morris — *Voices* p.145-146

READING BOARDS
Earle — *Child* p.125-126
Glubok — *Home* p.141-142

REAL ESTATE
See also **Land**
- *Agents*
Dexter — *Colonial* p.109-110
- *Values*
Bridenbaugh — *Revolt* p.14, 16, 225-228, 231

RECREATION. *See* **Amusements; Sports and games**

REDWOOD, ABRAHAM
Wright — *Cultural* p.149

REDWOOD LIBRARY (Newport, R.I.)
Wright — *Cultural* p.149-150

REED, ESTHER DE BERDT
Ellet — *Eminent* p.32-40
Somerville — *Women* p.46-47

REED, JOHN
Adams — *Provincial* p.63-64

REFORMED DUTCH CHURCH (New York)
Bridenbaugh — *Revolt* p.153-154, 156, 174, 378
Sweet — *Religion* p.81

REGULATORS
Adams — *Album* p.364
Miller — *Origins* p.56, 320-321, 351, 479

REICHEL, JOHN FREDERICK
Handlin — *This* p.59-67

REINAGLE, ALEXANDER
Howard — *Our* p.75-81

RELIGION
See also names of religions and denominations; related subjects
Axtell — *18th* p.190-193
Bridenbaugh — *Revolt* p.150-156, 352-358
Carman — *History* p.85-100, 117, 123, 149-150, 222-224
Evans — *Weather.* p.6-10, 15-16
Glubok — *Home* p.292-311
Greene — *Revol. See* index p.479
Hofstadter — *Amer. See* index p.x-xi
Kraus — *U.S. (1)* p.135-139
Life — *New* p.61, 122-125
Miller — *First* p.268-276
Morison — *Oxford (1). See* index p.418
Morris — *Ency.* p.549-551
Scott — *Trumpet* p.9-12, 18, 49-51, 137, 229-230
Treasury Amer. p.120-121
Tunis — *Young* p.31-33

, and Continental Congress
Sweet — *Religion* p.50-52
, and cultural foundations
Sweet — *Religion* p.160-162
, and reform
Morison — *Oxford (1)* p.380-384
, and Westward movement
Sweet — *Religion* p.96-99
- Census (1775)
Morris — *Ency.* p.550
- Charlestown
Bridenbaugh — *Wild.* p.262-263
- Cities
Bridenbaugh — *Revolt* p.152, 156, 354
- Constitution
Sweet — *Religion* p.85-90
- Denominations
See also names of denominations
Axtell — *18th* p.177-209
- Dissenters
Miller — *Origins* p.193-196
- Diversity
Wright — *Cultural* p.87-97
- Doctrinal controversy
Sweet — *Story* p.135-137
- History-making factor
Sweet — *Religion* p.161-162
- Journalism
Sweet — *Religion* p.184
- Kentucky frontier
Wright — *Frontier* p.72-74
, Lack of
Sweet — *Religion* p.92-96
- Massachusetts
Axtell — *18th* p.79
- New York
Axtell — *18th* p.72
- Newport, R.I.
Bridenbaugh — *Wild.* p.263-264
, Post-Revolutionary
Sweet — *Religion* p.91-96
, Pre-Revolutionary
Greene — *Revol.* p.99-154
Sweet — *Story* p.173
- Revolutionary War
Sweet — *Religion* p.1-53
, Spirit of
Sloane — *Spirits* p.40-43
- Tolerance
See also **Religious freedom**
Hofstadter — *Amer.* p.xi
Life — *Making* p.40, 105, 109, 137
- Towns
Bridenbaugh — *Wild. See* index p.496-497
- Virginia
Wertenbaker — *Golden* p.124-125
- Women
Benson — *Women 18th* p.120-121
Holliday — *Woman's* p.48, 65-69
- Leaders
Benson — *Women 18th* p.258-273
Dexter — *Colonial* p.147-153

RELIGIOUS COMMUNITIES
See also names of communities
Miller — *First* p.81

RELIGIOUS FREEDOM
Alden — *Pioneer* p.105-106
Crèvecoeur — *Sketches* p.152-171
Morison — *Oxford (1)* p.187, 244, 246, 282-283, 357, 361, 380-382
Sanderlin — *1776* p.88-90
Sweet — *Story* p.189-193
- Virginia
See also **Virginia Statute for Religious Freedom**
Angle — *By* p.78-82

RELIGIOUS SCHOOLS
See also **Parochial schools**
Morris — *Ency.* p.551

RELIGIOUS SOCIETIES
See also names of societies
, Number of
Sweet — *Story* p.172-173
- Women
Benson — *Women 18th* p.259-261

RELIGIOUS WRITERS
Morris — *Ency.* p.561-562

REMEDIES
See also **Babies — Sickness, remedies for; Medicine;** etc.
Belote — *Compleat* p.133-137
Earle — *Customs* p.333-362
Pettengill — *Yankee* p.152-155
Speare — *Life* p.77-78
- *Massachusetts*
Dow — *Every* p.99
- *Peddlers*
Dolan — *Yankee* p.197
- *South*
Spruill — *Women's* p.268-269

REPRESENTATION
See also **Taxation**
Kraus — *U.S. (1)* p.192-195

REPUBLIC
, Building of
Morris — *American* p.289-337
- *Society*
Greene — *Revol.* p.306-329
Train — *Story* p.256-259
, Young
Kraus — *U.S. (1)* p.265-267
Train — *Story* p.225-259
200 Years p.120-176

RESPECT
, Spirit of
Sloane — *Spirits* p.12-17

RESTORATIVES. *See* Remedies

RETAIL TRADE
See also **Shops and shopkeepers;** etc.
Bridenbaugh — *Revolt* p.76-78, 274-276
Bridenbaugh — *Wild.* p.188-190, 341-345
- *Clerks*
Wilson — *Early* p.79-87

REVERE, PAUL
Amer. Her. — *Rev.* p.67-68, 72, 78-79, 88, 100-101
Beach — *Samuel* p.28, 152, 160, 199, 250-251, 269, 274-276
Bridenbaugh — *Revolt* p.17, 327, 362, 367, 387, 401, 408
Burt — *Phila.* p.265, 278
Davis — *Heroes* p.3-17
Forbes — *Paul. See* index p.495-496
McDowell — *Rev.* p.10, 18-19, 34-39
Morison — *Oxford (1)* p.261, 270, 278, 284
National — *History.* p.185-188
Sanderlin — *1776* p.69-70, 115, 120, 146-151, 251
Stearns — *Story* p.75, 77-78, 80-82, 84, 89, 91, 97
Stember — *North* p.18, 261, 279, 284, 291-294, 296-297, 301, 305, 307-310, 315, 317
Wertenbaker — *Golden* p.4, 13, 29, 32-33, 37-38
Wheeler — *Voices* p.15-19
, as dentist
Train — *Story* p.177
- *Ride*
Collins — *Story* p.101
Hale — *Through* p.102-107
Ingraham — *Album* p.33
Morris — *Voices* p.81-85
- *Washington's funeral urn*
Forbes — *Paul* p.395

REVERE, RACHEL WALKER
Forbes — *Paul. See* index p.475-476, 496

REVERE FAMILY
Forbes — *Paul. See* index p.473-478

REVIVALISM
See also **"Great Awakening"**
Bridenbaugh — *Revolt* p.353
Carman — *History* p.98-101
Morris — *Ency.* p.551
Sweet — *Religion* p.146-149

REVOLUTIONARY WAR
See also related subjects
Adams — *Album* p.358-407
Alden — *Pioneer* p.66-78, 80-101, 291
Amer. Reader p.104-129
Carman — *History* p.194-227
Colbourn — *Colonial* p.325-386

Forbes — *Paul. See* index p.496
Greene — *Revol. See* index p.480
Kraus — *U.S. (1)* p.221-237
Life — *Making. See* index p.158
Miller — *Origins. See* index p.512-513 (Independence, War of)
Morison — *Oxford (1). See* index (War of Independence)
Morris — *Ency.* p.71-120
National — *History.* p.177-265
Scott — *Trumpet* p.86-114
- *Allies, quest for*
  See also **Revolutionary War — Foreign aid;** names of countries
  Amer. Her. — *Rev.* p.257-272
- *Army. See* **Continental army; Revolutionary War — Logistics; Revolutionary War — Soldiers, Recruiting and training**
- *Atrocities*
  See also **Massacres**
  200 Years. See index p.345
- *Battles and campaigns*
  See also **Revolutionary War — Navy;** names of battles, campaigns, names of localities
  Amer. Her. — *Rev.* p.121-152
  Carman — *History* p.202-214
  Life — *Making. See* index p.158-159
  Morris — *Voices* p.105-129
- *Beginnings*
  See also **Revolutionary War — Causes**
  Amer. Her. — *Rev.* p.49-95, 97-119
  Baldwin — *Ideas* p.165-167, 169-175, 181
- *Casualties*
  See also **Revolutionary War —Sick and wounded**
  200 Years p.345-346
- *Causes*
  Alden — *Pioneer* p.66-78
  Baldwin — *Ideas* p.156
  Colbourn — *Colonial* p.305-323
  Davie — *Profile* p.267-269
- *Cavalrymen*
  Cook — *What* p.19-81
- *Commander in chief*
  See also **Washington, George**
  Butterfield — *Amer.* p.6-7
  Morison — *Oxford (1)* p.314-315
- *Crisis*
  Amer. Her. — *Rev.* p.177-207
- *Democratic spirit*
  Carman — *History* p.219-226
- *Difficulties*
  Adams — *Album* p.382-384
- *East and South*
  Ingraham — *Album* p.80-81
- *Economic conditions*
  Baldwin — *Ideas* p.178-181
- *Effects. See* **Revolutionary War — Results**
- *Ending*
  See also **Revolutionary War — Peace**
  Amer. Her. — *Rev.* p.345-376
  Kraus — *U.S. (1)* p.238-264
- *Finance*
  See also names of financiers
  Carman — *History* p.200-202
  Morison — *Oxford (1)* p.305-306
- *Foreign aid*
  Adams — *Album* p.398-399
  Carman — *History* p.208-209, 212-215
  Ingraham — *Album* p.69
- *French fleet and army*
  Ingraham — *Album* p.85
- *Frontiers*
  Amer. Her. — *Rev.* p.299-319
  Tunis — *Frontier* p.44
- *Generals*
  See also names of generals
  McDowell — *Rev.* p.57-58
- *Guerillas*
  Scott — *Trumpet* p.82-84, 158-159, 185, 260-261
  , Whaleboat
    Cook — *What* p.273-302
- *Heroism*
  Cook — *What* p.177-214
- *Infantrymen*
  Amer. Her. — *Rev.* p.164-167
- *Inflation*
  Carman — *History* p.200-201

REVOLUTIONARY WAR (*continued*)
- *International influences*
  Greene — *Revol. See* index p.469
- *Issues*
  Baldwin — *Ideas* p.155-189
- *Logistics*
  Morison — *Oxford (1)* p.303-307
- *Map*
  Kraus — *U.S. (1)* p.221-225
- *Meaning*
  Scott — *Trumpet* p.278-283
- *Navy*
  Amer. Her. — *Rev.* p.273-295
  Cook — *What* p.245-271
  Ingraham — *Album* p.74-75
  Life — *Making* p.12-13, 62, 81, 85-87, 90, 98-99
  200 Years. See index p.349
- *New England*
  Wheeler — *Voices* p.39, 51, 78-79, 219, 226
- *New Jersey*
  Scott — *Trumpet* p.130-159
- *New York*
  Adams — *Album* p.385
  Scott — *Trumpet* p.130-159
- *North*
  Stember — *North. See* index p.375-391
- *Organizations*
  Morris — *American* p.114-122
- *Patriots*
  Carman — *History* p.196-202
- *Peace*
  Ingraham — *Album* p.86
  Morris — *Voices* p.124-129
- *Philadelphia*
  Adams — *Album* p.392
- *Philosophy*
  Colbourn — *Colonial* p.292-305
- *Post-Revolutionary life*
  Morris — *Voices* p.133-142
- *Profiteers, war on*
  Morris — *American* p.258-261
- *Quotations*
  Baldwin — *Ideas* p.164-165
- *Reasons. See* **Revolutionary War — Causes**
- *Results*
  Alden — *Pioneer* p.62-63, 95-110
  Carman — *History* p.216-226
  Greene — *Revol.* p.259-281
  Ingraham — *Album* p.90
  Morris — *Ency.* p.111
- *Rhode Island*
  Wheeler — *Voices* p.196, 310-311, 313-314, 323, 380, 437
- *Riflemen*
  Cook — *What* p.83-85, 87-139
- *Sick and wounded*
  See also **Revolutionary War — Atrocities; Revolutionary War — Casualties**
  Ingraham — *Album* p.73
- *Social conditions*
  Carman — *History* p.216-226
- *Social movement*
  Colbourn — *Colonial* p.372-386
- *Soldiers, recruiting and training*
  Amer. Her. — *Rev.* p. 153-175, 209-231
  Amer. Reader p.104-106
  Colbourn — *Colonial* p.359-372
  Pettengill — *Yankee* p.51-62
  Treasury Amer. p.112-117
  200 Years. See index p.345
- *South*
  Adams — *Album* p.388-389
  Amer. Her. — *Rev.* p.321-343
  Scott — *Trumpet* p.257-277
- *Stalemate (1778-1780)*
  Scott — *Trumpet* p.234-256
- *Success, influences towards*
  Earle — *Home* p.166-167, 189
- *Suffering*
  Adams — *Album* p.403
- *Summary*
  Ingraham — *Album* p.9-13, 91-95
  Morris — *American* p.xi-xix
- *Turning point*
  Amer. Her. — *Rev.* p.233-255
- *Virginia*
  Morris — *Voices* p.121-123
- *West*
  Ingraham — *Album* p.74-77

- *Women*
Benson — *Women 18th* p.249-253
Earle — *Colonial* p.240-257
Ellet — *Eminent. See* index under Women, names of women
Greene — *Revol.* p.249
- *as coat makers*
Earle — *Home* p.247-248
, Southern
Spruill — *Women's* p.244-245
- *Writers*
Benson — *Women 18th* p.170

REYNOLDS, MARY (Mari)
Burt — *Phila.* p.311-315

RHODE ISLAND
Axtell — *18th* p.73-77
Greene — *Revol. See* index p.480
Hofstadter — *Amer.* p.72-74, 89-90, 105-106, 111, 145, 149, 173, 185, 187, 190, 198-199
Main — *Social* p.41, 103-105, 154, 225
Morison — *Oxford (1). See* Index p.419
Scott — *Trumpet. See* index p.306
Stember — *North* p.4-5, 114, 212, 321-342
, and Declaration of Independence
Bakeless — *Signers* p.211-219
Malone — *Story* p.121-124
- *Battle*
Evans — *Weather.* p.251-265
- *Government*
Axtell — *18th* p.74-75

RICE
Colbourn — *Colonial* p.258-260
Morris — *Ency.* p.478
- *South*
Adams — *Provincial* p.205
Carman — *History* p.63, 67
- *South Carolina*
Tunis — *Living* p.104-105

RICHES. *See* Wealth

RICHARDSON, DORCAS
Ellet — *Eminent* p.193-203

RICHARDSON, SAMUEL
Nye — *Unembar.* p.17

RICHMOND, VIRGINIA
Greene — *Revol.* p.237, 297, 389, 398
Morison — *Oxford (1)* p.199, 286, 343

RIDDLE, REBECCA
Ellet — *Eminent* p.450-453

RIDES, HISTORICAL. *See* Dawes, William; Phillips, John ("Portugee"); Revere, Paul; Rodney, Caesar

RIDGEFIELD, CONNECTICUT
, Battle of
Stember — *North* p.351-355

"RIDING CHAIRS"
Train — *Story* p.166-167

RIEDESEL, FREDERICA VON
Ellet — *Eminent* p.71-92
McDowell — *Rev.* p.123
Morris — *Voices* p.111-114
Scott — *Trumpet* p.194-197, 200-201
Wheeler — *Voices* p.286-269, 273-279

RIEDESEL, FRIEDRIC ADOLPH VON
McDowell — *Rev.* p.109-110, 119-121, 123
Stember — *North* p.14, 83, 93-95, 98, 111, 281
Wheeler — *Voices* p.229, 257, 269

RIFLES. *See* Guns

RIGHTS OF MAN
Adams — *Provincial* p.86-112
Angle — *By* p.43-51
Colbourn — *Colonial* p.292, 300-305
Cook — *What* p.11-18
Miers — *American* p.99-101
Sanderlin — *1776* p.105-106, 108-109

RIND, CLEMENTINA
Spruill — *Women's* p.265-266

RIOTS
See also **Mobs; Stamp Act;** names of riots
Burner — *America* p.73-84
Miller — *Origins* p.130, 154
Sanderlin — *1776* p.44-49
- Boston
Forbes — *Paul* p.22-23, 90-94, 97-103, 131, 320, 326-327

RITTENHOUSE, DAVID
Wertenbaker — *Golden* p.69-70
Wright — *Cultural* p.233-234

RIVER TRAFFIC
Bartlett — *New* p.306-311
Dolan — *Yankee* p.35-38
Speare — *Life* p.120-121
Tunis — *Living* p.123-124
Tunis — *Young* p.77-78

RIVINGTON, JAMES
Greene — *Revol. See* index p.480

RIVOIRE, APOLLOS
Forbes — *Paul. See* index p.496

ROAD SHOWS (spectacles)
Nye — *Unembar.* p.182-183

ROADS
See also **Highways;** names of roads
Adams — *Album* p.409
Adams — *Provincial* p.259
Bartlett — *New* p.275-278
Burt — *Phila.* p.106-107
Dolan — *Yankee* p.30-31, 40-46
Earle — *Customs* p.204-207
Langdon — *Every.* p.247-254
Life — *Making* p.110-111, 117, 126-127
Morris — *Ency.* p.420
Scott — *Settlers* p.174
Tunis — *Living* p.119-120
Tunis — *Young* p.37-38, 75-76
Wright — *Cultural* p.248-250
Wright — *New* p.76-78
, Map, First
Dolan — *Yankee* p.43
- New England
Train — *Story* p.165
- South
Spruill — *Women's* p.88-90
- Winter, "Breaking out"
Earle — *Home* p.412-415

ROASTERS
Gould — *Early* p.72-74
, Apple
Gould — *Early* p.73
, Rabbit
Gould — *Early* p.74

"ROASTING-KITCHEN." ***See*** **Dutch ovens**

"ROBIN HOODS." ***See*** **Doan brothers**

ROCHAMBEAU, JEAN BAPTISTE DE
Stember — *North* p.52, 134, 149, 321, 332, 349-351, 363, 371
Wheeler — *Voices* p.378, 380, 407, 436-438, 447, 455-456

"ROCKINGHAM"
Stember — *Middle* p.40-43

RODNEY, CAESAR
Bakeless — *Signers* p.251-254
Malone — *Story* p.182-183
- Biography
Lossing — *Biog.* p.133-136
- Ride, famous
Burt — *Phila.* p.280

ROGERS, ROBERT
Stearns — *Story* p.68-69
- Rangers
Adams — *Album* p.352

ROMAN CATHOLIC EPISCOPATE
Morris — *Ency.* p.551

ROMAN CATHOLICISM. ***See*** **Catholicism**

ROMANTICISM
Tunis — *Young* p.34

ROOFS
Gould — *Early* p.38-40
Tunis — *Frontier* p.21-23

ROOMS
See also names of rooms
Tunis — *Living* p.128-129

ROPE
Tunis — *Living* p.124-125

ROSE-HIPS
, as playthings
Earle — *Child* p.386, 397, 400

ROSS, BETSY
Adelman — *Famous* p.88
Burt — *Phila.* p.285
Collins — *Story* p.132
Hale — *Through* p.113-114

ROSS, GEORGE
Bakeless — *Signers* p.155-157
Malone — *Story* p.173-174
- Biography
Lossing — *Biog.* p.130-132

ROTH, PHILIP
Howard — *Our* p.107-108

ROWE, JOHN
Forbes — *Paul. See* index p.496-497

ROWSON, SUSANNA HASWELL
Benson — *Women 18th* p.184-185, 189-191
- Novels
Nye — *Unembar.* p.18-19

RUM
See also **Flip**
Carman — *History* p.77, 79
Earle — *Home* p.163-164
Gould — *Early* p.107

RUMFORD, COUNT. ***See*** **Thompson, Benjamin (Count Rumford)**

RURAL LIFE. ***See*** **Country life**

RUSH, BENJAMIN
Bakeless — *Signers* p.136-141
Benson — *Women 18th. See* index p.341
Bridenbaugh — *Revolt* p.268, 285-286, 316, 330, 333, 352-354, 368, 394, 409-410
Brodie — *Jefferson. See* index p.808
Burt — *Phila.* p.323-325
Greene — *Revol. See* index p.481
Malone — *Story* p.56, 95, 159-160, 177-179
Tunis — *Young* p.56
- Biography
Lossing — *Biog.* p.99-103

RUSSIA
- Neutrality in Revolution
Morris — *Ency.* p.102-103

RUSSIAN ORTHODOX CHURCH
Morris — *Ency.* p.102-103

RUTLEDGE, EDWARD
Bakeless — *Signers* p.280-282
Malone — *Story* p.234-235
- Biography
Lossing — *Biog.* p.211-214

RUTLEDGE, JOHN
Greene — *Revol.* p.213, 248-249, 311

S

S.P.G. ***See*** **Society for the Propagation of the Gospel in Foreign Parts**

SABBATH
Greene — *Revol.* p.112-113, 165, 370-371, 384-385
- Laws
Bridenbaugh — *Wild.* p.229-230
- Virginia
Earle — *Home* p.380-382
Speare — *Life* p.22

SAILORS
See also **Navy**
Adams — *Album* p.401-402
Main — *Social* p.38-39, 74, 191, 255-257
Scott — *Trumpet* p.5, 16-18, 29, 66-75
Wilson — *Early* p.139

ST. CECILIA SOCIETY
Greene — *Revol.* p.151
Howard — *Our* p.30
Rublowsky — *Music* p.38-39
Spruill — *Women's* p.100-101
Wertenbaker — *Golden* p.148-149
Wright — *Cultural* p.194

ST. CLAIR, ARTHUR
Life — *Growing* p.15
Stember — *North* p.47, 56, 58, 84, 172, 184, 281
Wheeler — *Voices* p.226-227, 229-230

ST. LAWRENCE RIVER
Wheeler — *Voices* p.94-95, 100, 134-136, 177

ST. LEGER, BARRY
Stember — *North* p.58-59, 61, 63-65, 68-69, 84

ST. TAMMANY, SONS OF. ***See*** **Sons of St. Tammany**

SALEM, MASSACHUSETTS
Greene — *Revol.* p.42, 44, 46, 136, 231, 267-268, 324, 349
Life — *Growing* p.44
Main — *Social* p.35, 37-38, 144
Stember — *North* p.284-289

SALMON
Earle — *Home* p.123-125

SALOMON, HAYM
Burt — *Phila.* p.260
Greene — *Rev.* p.274
McDowell — *Rev.* p.98, 148, 174, 193

SALOONS. See Taverns

SALT
Dolan — *Yankee* p.259-260
Gould — *Early* p.86
Pettengill — *Yankee* p.97-99

"SALTS" (silver)
Tunis — *Living* p.135

SALZBURGERS (sect)
Spruill — *Women's* p.15, 17-18

SAMPLERS
Earle — *Child* p.327-329
Earle — *Colonial* p.230-232
Glubok — *Home* p.221-224
- *Coat of arms*
Earle — *Home* p.267
, *Mourning*
Earle — *Home* p.268-269

SAMPSON, DEBORAH (Mrs. Gannett)
Cook — *What* p.217-228
Ellet — *Eminent* p.365-378
Evans — *Weather.* p.303-334
Forbes — *Paul* p.415-417
Somerville — *Women* p.28-35

SANITATION
Bridenbaugh — *Wild.* p.238-239

SARATOGA, NEW YORK
, *Battle of*
Amer. Her. — *Rev.* p.247-248, 253-254
Collins — *Story* p.114-115
Ingraham — *Album* p.62
Landmarks Liberty p.66-69
Life — *Making* p.55, 59, 66, 70-71, 81, 118
Life — *100 Events* p.5
McDowell — *Rev.* p.116-122
Morison — *Oxford (1)* p.323-328
Morris — *American* p.241-246
Morris — *Voices* p.93, 111-114
National — *History.* p.226-229
Scott — *Trumpet* p.195-200
Stember — *North* p.90-114
Wheeler — *Voices* p.232, 236, 252, 267-281, 458

SASSAFRAS
Crèvecoeur — *Sketches* p.123, 135-136

SAUSAGE AND SAUSAGE MAKERS
Glubok — *Home* p.85-86
Gould — *Early* p.78, 101-103

SAVANNAH, GEORGIA
Amer. Her. — *Rev.* p.266, 322-323, 336-337, 364, 375
Morris — *Voices* p.99-100
Stember — *South* p.8-21
Wheeler — *Voices* p.324-325, 353-361

SAWYERS
Tunis — *Colonial* p.26

"SCALD HEAD"
Dexter — *Colonial* p.69-70

SCALPING
Burt — *Phila.* p.171

SCANDINAVIANS
Kraus — *U.S. (1)* p.108

SCHETKY, GEORGE
Howard — *Our* p.108

SCHMIDT, JOHN HENRY
Howard — *Our* p.109

SCHOHARIE, NEW YORK
- Valley
Cook — *What* p.141-176

SCHOOL BOOKS. *See* Textbooks

SCHOOLHOUSES
Speare — *Life* p.110-112

SCHOOLS
See also types of schools, e.g. **Religious schools**
Colbourn — *Colonial* p.86-90
Earle — *Child* p.78-89
Glubok — *Home. See* index p.355
Greene — *Revol.* p.117-122
Speare — *Life* p.97-113
Tunis — *Living* p.156
Tunis — *Young* p.34-35
- Boston
Benson — *Women 18th* p.137, 147-150, 184, 218
Bridenbaugh — *Revolt* p.173, 376
Bridenbaugh — *Wild.* p.281-283
Wertenbaker — *Golden* p.21-23, 136-139
- Charleston
Wertenbaker — *Golden* p.136-139
- Charlestown
Bridenbaugh — *Revolt* p.174, 374-375
, Elementary
Morris — *Ency.* p.555
, Evening
Bridenbaugh — *Wild.* p.288-289, 444, 449-450
- Frontier
Main — *Social* p.244-245n
, Grammar
Speare — *Life* p.106-109
- Kentucky
Tunis — *Frontier* p.57-58
- Maryland
Wertenbaker — *Golden* p.88-90
- Massachusetts
Langdon — *Every.* p.317-318
- New York
Bridenbaugh — *Revolt* p.174, 375-376
Wertenbaker — *Golden* p.43-44
, Dutch in
Wertenbaker — *Golden* p.43-44
- Newport, R.I.
Bridenbaugh — *Revolt* p.173, 376
- Philadelphia
Benson — *Women 18th* p.134, 137-141, 143-144
Bridenbaugh — *Revolt* p.135, 173-174, 375
Wertenbaker — *Golden* p.66-68
- South
Spruill — *Women's* p.190-193
, Girls'
Spruill — *Women's* p.188-207
, Home
Spruill — *Women's* p.194-195

SCHUYLER, CATHARINE
Ellet — *Eminent* p.41-45

SCHUYLER, MARGARETTA
Benson — *Women 18th* p.281, 305

SCHUYLER, PHILIP
Amer. Her. — *Rev.* p.110, 112, 122, 142-143, 239, 248
McDowell — *Rev.* p.57, 59, 193
Stember — *North* p.20, 26-27, 29, 40, 58, 64-66, 85, 92, 96, 98, 110-111, 148

SCHUYLER HOUSE
Landmarks Liberty p.69

SCHUYLKILL. *See* **"Fish House"**

SCHWENKFELDERS
Morris — *Ency.* p.549
Sweet — *Story* p.104-105

SCIENCE AND SCIENTISTS
See also **Inventions and inventors**
Adams — *Provincial* p.122-123
Bridenbaugh — *Revolt* p.199-201, 409-416
Colbourn — *Colonial* p.146-157
Greene — *Revol. See* index p.481
Kraus — *U.S. (1)* p.168-169
Langdon — *Every.* p.321-322
Morris — *Ency.* p.528-530
Wright — *Cultural* p.224-237
, and religion
Adams — *Provincial* p.269-270
Wertenbaker — *Golden* p.144-146
- Colleges and universities
Wright — *Cultural* p.224-226
- Limits
Boorstin — *Americans* p.241-265
- Shows
Wright — *Cultural* p.187
- Virginia
Wertenbaker — *Golden* p.122-125

SCIENTIFIC SOCIETIES
Morris — *Ency.* p.529

SCOTCH-IRISH
See also **Irish**; special subjects
Alden — *Pioneer* p.39, 49, 57-58
Bridenbaugh — *Revolt* p.51, 134-136, 261-262, 323, 334
Bridenbaugh — *Wild.* **p.231, 231n,** 250, 309-410, 422-423
Greene — *Revol.* p.157-158, 160, 164, 224
Hofstadter — *Amer.* p.11-12, 17-18, 24-32, 168, 175-176, 181, 215-216, 266
Life — *New* p.120-122
Miller — *Origins* p.53, 61-62, 480, 504
, and Indians
Langdon — *Every.* p.112-113
Morris — *Ency.* p.444
, in mountains
Langdon — *Every.* p.110-124
, on frontier
Carman — *History* p.56-57
Kraus — *U.S. (1)* p.142-143
- Pennsylvania
Tunis — *Living* p.101

SCOTS
See also **Scotch-Irish**
Adams — *Provincial* p.191-192
Alden — *Pioneer* p.39, 45, 49, 58, 82, 84
Bridenbaugh — *Revolt* p.199
Greene — *Revol.* p.19, 23, 42, 130, 158, 161, 166, 218, 222, 224, 246
Kraus — *U.S. (1)* p.106-108
Life — *New* p.120-122
Morison — *Oxford (1)* p.187, 196-198, 214, 214n, 231, 239, 241, 258, 282
- Revolutionary War
Morison — *Oxford (1)* p.292-293, 313

SCRIBES
See also **Writing**
Wilson — *Early* p.104-107

SCRUBBING AND SCOURING
Speare — *Life* p.77-78

SCULPTURE
Morris — *Ency.* p.597-601

SEA
See also **Sailors; Navy**
- Crafts
Wilson — *American* p.12-13
- Life
Speare — *Life* p.119-120
, Lure of
Wright — *New* p.159-164

SEAL OF THE UNITED STATES
Adams — *Album* p.405
Tunis — *Young* p.99

SEAPORTS
See also names of seaports
- *North*
Adams — *Provincial* p.223-224

SECTIONALISM
Greene — *Revol.* p.183-187, 202, 299-300

SEDAN CHAIRS
Earle — *Home* p.356

SEDITION ACTS. *See* Alien and Sedition Acts

SEEDS
, *Selling of*
Dexter — *Colonial* p.26-27

SEISMOLOGY
Morris — *Ency.* p.528

"SEMPSTRESSES." *See* Dressmaking

SENATE
Morris — *Ency.* p.121

SENTER, ISAAC
Wheeler — *Voices* p.87-88, 90-93, 100, 106, 131, 134-137, 141

***SERAPIS* (British warship)**
Amer. Reader p.119-124
Morris — *Voices* p.116-118

SERLE, AMBROSE
Morris — *Voices* p.106-108

SERMONS
See also **Funerals — Sermons**
- *Charity*
Benson — *Women 18th* p.179, 332-333

SERVANTS
See also **Slaves and slavery**
Axtell — *18th* p.152-159
Wilson — *Early* p.89-102
- *Bond and bound. See* **Servants — Indentured**
- *Convicts*
Bridenbaugh — *Revolt* p.44, 50, 135
- *Cost*
Main — *Social* p.120, 122
- *Culture*
Main — *Social* p.264
- *Free*
Axtell — 18th p.152-154
-*Household*
Earle — *Customs* p.85-106
Wilson — *Early* p.94-97
- *Indentured*
Adams — *Provincial* p.98-100, 107-108
Alden — *Pioneer* p.38-39, 49, 51
Axtell — *18th* p.153-154
Belote — *Compleat* p.17
Benson — *Women 18th* p.225-227, 266
Bridenbaugh — *Revolt* p.44, 50, 87, 135-136
Burt — *Phila.* p.120
Dolan — *Yankee* p.114-115
Earle — *Customs* p.96-97, 99-100
Greene — *Revol.* p.76-78
Hofstadter — *Amer. See* index p.vii
Life — *New* p.96-97
Main — *Social. See* index p.326
Scott — *Trumpet* p.9, 17, 101-102
- *Types*
Morris — *Ency.* p.518
- *Women*
Benson — *Women 18th* p.225, 227, 266
- *Revolutionary War*
Earle — *Colonial* p.263-275
, *Runaway*
Earle — *Customs* p.84-86, 93-94
- *Types*
Hanlin — *This* p.29-32
- *White*
Hofstadter — *Amer.* p.33-65
- *"Wights"*
Earle — *Customs* p.104-106
- *Women*
, *Clothing of Southern*
Spruill — *Women's* p.133-134

SETTLERS. ***See*** **Colonies and colonists; Frontier; Frontiersmen; Immigrants and immigration;** names of nationalities and localities

SEVEN YEARS' WAR. ***See*** **French and Indian War**

1700's
See also **Chronology (dates)**
- *1761*
  Morris — *American* p.1-10
- *1776*
  Linton — *Bicentennial* p.18-21
  - *Drama*
    Early Amer. Life — *Yrbk. 1970* p.28-29
  , *"Spirits of"*
    Sloane — *Spirits* p.61-64
    200 Years p.10-118
  - *Superstition*
    McDowell — *Rev.* p.109
- *1777*
  Linton — *Bicentennial* p.22-23
- *1778*
  Linton — *Bicentennial* p.24-25
- *1779*
  Linton — *Bicentennial* p.26-27
- *1780*
  Linton — *Bicentennial* p.28-29
- *1781*
  Linton — *Bicentennial* p.30-31
- *1782*
  Linton — *Bicentennial* p.32-33
- *1783*
  Linton — *Bicentennial* p.34
- *1784*
  Linton — *Bicentennial* p.35
- *1785*
  Linton — *Bicentennial* p.36
- *1786*
  Linton — *Bicentennial* p.38-39
- *1787*
  Linton — *Bicentennial* p.40-41
- *1788*
  Linton — *Bicentennial* p.42-43
- *1789*
  Linton — *Bicentennial* p.44-45
- *1790*
  Linton — *Bicentennial* p.46-47
- *1791*
  Linton — *Bicentennial* p.47
- *1792*
  Linton — *Bicentennial* p.48
- *1793*
  Linton — *Bicentennial* p.49
- *1794*
  Linton — *Bicentennial* p.50
- *1795*
  Linton — *Bicentennial* p.51
- *1796*
  Linton — *Bicentennial* p.52-53
- *1797*
  Linton — *Bicentennial* p.54
- *1798*
  Linton — *Bicentennial* p.55
- *1799*
  Linton — *Bicentennial* p.56

SEVENTH DAY BAPTISTS
Wright — *Cultural* p.194

SEWALL, SAMUEL
Bridenbaugh — *Wild. See* index p.407
Holliday — *Woman's. See* index p.318
- *"Courtship"*
  Holliday — *Woman's* p.251-255
  Miller — *Colonial* p.132-140
- *Diary*
  Earle — *Home* p.418
  Wright — *Cultural* p.163-164
- *Dinner*
  Gould — *Early* p.93-94
, *on women*
  Benson — *Women 18th* p.15, 33, 105-106, 108, 113, 115, 120-123, 125, 228, 262

SEWERS
Bridenbaugh — *Wild.* p.150-160, 318-319

EWING BEES
Gould — *Early* p.141

EXES
, *Comparison of*
Benson — *Women 18th* p.342
, *Freedom of*
Adams — *Provincial* p.159-160
Cable — *American* p.36

HAD (fish)
Earle — *Home* p.123-125
Glubok — *Home* p.68-69

HAKERS
Benson — *Women 18th* p.270, 272-273
Evans — *Weather.* p.7-9
Gould — *Early* p.136-138
Sweet — *Religion* p.295-298
- *"Millennial Church" (1774)*
Morris — *Ency.* p.550
- *Women*
Dexter — *Colonial* p.150-153

'SHARPENER MEN"
Wilson — *Early* p.87-88

HAWMUT PENINSULA
Scott — *Trumpet* p.37-62

HAYS, DANIEL
See also **Shays' Rebellion**
Morison — *Oxford (1)* p.264, 376
Morris — *Ency.* p.116
Stearns — *Story* p.92

HAYS' REBELLION
Butterfield — *Amer.* p.10-11
Forbes — *Paul* p.365-366
Greene — *Revol.* p.168, 318, 338-340, 395
Life — *Making* p.111-113
Morison — *Oxford (1)* p.390-395
Morris — *Ency.* p.115-116
Morris — *Voices* p.146-149
Wright — *New* p.13
, *and nationalism*
Kraus — *U.S. (1)* p.249-253

SHEEP
See also **Wool**
Earle — *Customs* p.232-233
Gould — *Early* p.127-128

SHELBURNE, LORD. See Petty, William (Lord Shelburne)

SHENANDOAH VALLEY (Virginia)
Main — *Social* p.46, 51, 87, 92, 111, 243, 255

SHERIFFS. See Constables and sheriffs

SHERMAN, ROGER
Bakeless — *Signers* p.195-202
Malone — *Story* p.126-127
- *Biography*
Lossing — *Biog.* p.50-52

SHERWOOD, GRACE
Earle — *Colonial* p.101-103
- *Witchcraft trial*
Spruill — *Women's* p.328-330

SHIPBUILDING
Adams — *Provincial* p.41-42
Bridenbaugh — *Wild.* p.184-185, 337
Greene — *Revol.* p.42-43, 59, 276-277, 344, 358-359
Kraus — *U.S. (1)* p.112-114, 118-119
Langdon — *Every.* p.215-228
Train — *Story* p.138-139, 168-171
Wilson — *Early* p.139-141
- *Boston*
Bridenbaugh — *Revolt* p.73, 269
- *Charlestown*
Bridenbaugh — *Revolt* p.73, 88, 272
- *New York*
Bridenbaugh — *Revolt* p.73, 271
- *Newport, R.I.*
Bridenbaugh — *Revolt* p.62, 72-73, 270
- *Philadelphia*
Axtell — *18th* p.101-102
Bridenbaugh — *Revolt* p.24, 72, 269
Burt — *Phila.* p.122-123
Langdon — *Every.* p.233-240

SHIPBUILDING (*continued*)
- *Shipwrights*
Tunis — *Colonial* p.111-116

SHIPPEN, MARGARET. *See* **Arnold, Margaret Shippen**

SHIPS AND SHIPPING
See also **Shipbuilding;** names of ships
Adams — *Album* p.283-288, 297-302
Bridenbaugh — *Revolt* p.40, 46, 59, 69, 253, 257
Carman — *History* p.77-79
Life — *New* p.102-103
Morison — *Oxford (1)* p.198, 239-242, 271, 369-371, 400
Train — *Story* p.151, 171, 199, 201, 217, 249-250
Tunis — *Living* p.124
Tunis — *Young* p.85
- *Bark*
Train — *Story* p.170
- *Boston*
Dow — *Every* p.154-155
- *Brigantine*
Train — *Story* p.170, 173, 214, 250
- *Captains*
Main — *Social* p.39, 74, 89, 256
- *Corvette*
Train — *Story* p.250
- *Frigate*
Train — *Story* p.119, 250
- *Immigration*
Adams — *Provincial* p.175-177
- *New England*
Train — *Story* p.169-171
- *Passengers (Mass.)*
Dow — *Every* p.157-165
- *Sailing*
Train — *Story* p.249
- *Salem*
Dow — *Every* p.156-157
- *Schooner*
Train — *Story* p.170-172, 250
- *Sloop*
Train — *Story* p.170, 179, 190, 217
- *Yankee clipper*
Train — *Story* p.171

SHOEMAKERS
Dolan — *Yankee* p.117-120
Main — *Social* p.17, 19, 22, 29, 57, 80, 191, 274-275
Speare — *Life* p.46-47
Train — *Story* p.255
Tunis — *Colonial* p.36-37, 105-106
Tunis — *Young* p.29-30, 61-62
- *Labor union, first*
Tunis — *Young* p.62

SHOES
Adams — *Album* p.310
- *Cost*
Main — *Social* p.116, 123
, Men's
Tunis — *Living* p.142
- *Shoestrings*
Dolan — *Yankee* p.171
- *South*
Spruill — *Women's* p.123-124
, Women's
Tunis — *Living* p.146-147

SHOPLIFTING
Bridenbaugh — *Wild. See* index p.409

SHOPS AND SHOPKEEPERS
See also **Artisans; Merchants;** etc.
Main — *Social. See* index p.326
Tunis — *Colonial* p.39-56
- *South*
Spruill — *Women's* p.276-292

SHOVELS
Gould — *Early* p.75

SICKNESS
See also **Babies — Sickness, remedies for; Diseases; Epidemics; Remedies;** etc.
Langdon — *Every.* p.322-330
Tunis — *Living* p.155

SIDEWALKS
Bridenbaugh — *Revolt* p.33, 229, 238-239, 244
- *Philadelphia*
Bridenbaugh — *Wild.* p.158, 324

SIGNBOARDS
Dreppard — *Pioneer* p.156-162
Earle — *Home* p.358-360
Glubok — *Home* p.345-346

SILHOUETTES
Dolan — *Yankee* p.132

SILK
Adams — *Album* p.308
Earle — *Child* p.310-311
Earle — *Colonial* p.83-84
Glubok — *Home* p.207-208
Morris — *Ency.* p.478
Train — *Story* p.217

SILVER
See also **Silverware;** etc.
Earle — *Home* p.88-92
Forbes — *Paul. See* index p.497
Sirkis — *Reflect.* p.22-23
- Uses
Glubok — *Home* p.46-51

SILVERSMITHS
See also **Revere, Paul**
Adams — *Album* p.290-293
Adams — *Provincial* p.145-146
Forbes — *Paul* p.22, 34, 68, 363
Hale — *Through* p.76-84
Langdon — *Every.* p.176-191
Tunis — *Colonial* p.80-85
Wertenbaker — *Golden* p.36-38, 43, 57-58, 77-79, 102, 119
Wright — *Cultural* p.213-214

SILVERWARE
Adams — *Album* p.319-320
Langdon — *Every.* p.190-191
Tunis — *Living* p.126
Wertenbaker — *Golden* p.36-38, 57-58
- New York
Wertenbaker — *Golden* p.57-58

SIN AND SINNERS
Adams — *Album* p.274
Adams — *Provincial* p.160-161
Miller — *Colonial* p.207-211

SINGING
See also **Songs**
Speare — *Life* p.165-166

SINGING SCHOOLS
Downey — *Our* p.135
Gould — *Early* p.142
Nye — *Unembar.* p.306-307
- First, in Boston
Howard — *Our* p.16

SIX NATIONS
Amer. Her. — *Rev.* p.306-310, 316, 319

SKEWERS
Gould — *Early* p.72

SKILLETS
Gould — *Early* p.76

SLATER, SAMUEL
Dolan — *Yankee* p.50
Morris — *Ency.* p.535
Tunis — *Young* p.61
Wilson — *American* p.84-85
- Biography
Morris — *Ency.* p.714-715

SLATES
Glubok — *Home* p.121-122

SLAVE ENLISTMENT ACT (R.I., 1778)
Morris — *American* p.352-354

SLAVES AND SLAVERY
Alden — *Pioneer* p.51, 87, 103, 106-107, 109
Amer. Reader p.57-59
Axtell — *18th* p.154-162, 166-176
Bridenbaugh — *Revolt* p.74, 88, 253, 255, 353-355, 394
Brodie — *Jefferson. See* index p.801-803
Greene — *Revol.* p.16-17, 24-26, 32, 76-78, 112, 324, 333-334
Hofstadter — *Amer.* p.89-130
Kraus — *U.S. (1)* p.110-112
Life — *New* p.97-99, 102
Main — *Social. See* index p.326-327
Miller — *Origins* p.9, 12, 17-18, 478-479
Morison — *Oxford (1)* p.419
Morris — *Ency.* p.512-514
Morris — *Voices* p.242-246

SLAVES AND SLAVERY (continued)
Scott — *Trumpet* p.13-15, 106, 123-124, 126, 176, 281; *See also* index p.306
Speare — *Life* p.18-19
Tunis — *Living* p.155
Wilson — *Early* p.90-92
Wright — *New* p.143-144
, and law
Baldwin — *Ideas* p.186-187
, and Revolutionary War
Morris — *Amer.* p.349-350
- Connecticut
Earle — *Customs* p.91
- Excerpts, personal
200 Years p.308-309
- Houses
Main — *Social* p.124
- Maryland
Kraus — *U.S. (1)* p.110
- New England
Earle — *Home* p.163-164
- Opposition
See also **Antislavery movement**
Carman — *History* p.224-225
Morris — *American* p.351-352
- Runaways
Adams — *Album* p.333-334
- Schools, Southern
Train — *Story* p.218-219
- Ships
Hofstadter — *Amer.* p.74, 80-88, 120-121
- Slaveholders
Wilson — *Early* p.92-93
- South
Adams — *Provincial* p.196-198
- South Carolina
Kraus — *U.S. (1)* p.111
- Trade
Alden — *Pioneer* p.40-41, 107-108
Greene — *Revol.* p.46, 48, 52, 103, 288, 308, 322-323, 328, 333
Hofstadter — *Amer.* p.66-88
Life — *New* p.98-99, 103
Sanderlin — *1776* p.xvi, xxii-xxiii, p.220-221, 223-234, 242
Scott — *Settlers* p.115-118
Train — *Story* p.171-172
- Virginia
Axtell — *18th* p.41-43
Cable — *American* p.44
Kraus — *U.S. (1)* p.110-112

SLEIGHS AND SLEIGHING
Bridenbaugh — *Revolt* p.34-35, 366
Earle — *Colonial* p.218-221
Earle — *Customs* p.209-210
Earle — *Home* p.355
Glubok — *Home* p.343-344
Speare — *Life* p.139-140
Train — *Story* p.166

SLOCUMB, MARY
Ellet — *Eminent* p.234-260

SMALLPOX
See also **Inoculation, Smallpox**
Bridenbaugh — *Revolt* p.126, 129-130, 326-330
Bridenbaugh — *Wild.* p.240-241, 399-400
Forbes — *Paul* p.71-77

SMIBERT, JOHN
Wright — *Cultural* p.211

SMITH, FRANCIS
Forbes — *Paul* p.232-234, 241, 249, 257-262, 274

SMITH, GEORGE
Malone — *Story* p.172

SMITH, JAMES
Bakeless — *Signers* p.146-148
- Biography
Lossing — *Biog.* p.119-122

"-SMITHS" (artisans)
Wilson — *Early* p.67-71

"SMOCK-MARRIAGES"
Earle — *Customs* p.77-79

SMOKING
See also **Tobacco**
Handlin — *This* p.97

"SMOOTHING." *See* **Ironing**

SMUGGLING
See also **Gaspee (affair)**
Bridenbaugh — *Revolt* p.53, 66-67, 258-259, 266, 271

Ingraham — *Album* p.20-21
Kraus — *U.S. (1)* p.116-118
Miller — *Origins* p.8, 11-12, 45-46, 83-86, 180, 266-267, 280, 338, 340-341, 351-352
Scott — *Trumpet* p.64-65

SNOW WARDENS
Wilson — *Early* p.36

SNOWSTORMS
- *Blizzard (1779)*
Smith — *Colonial* p.300-313
- *Effect on farmers*
Crèvecoeur — *Sketches* p.39-50
- *New England*
Earle — *Home* p.410-413
Glubok — *Home* p.321-322

SNUFF
Tunis — *Living* p.152

SOAP AND SOAP MAKING
Earle — *Customs* p.311-312
Earle — *Home* p.253-255
Glubok — *Home* p.200-201
Gould — *Early* p.113-114
- *Massachusetts*
Dow — *Every* p.97
- *Women*
Dexter — *Colonial* p.52

SOCIAL CLASSES. *See* **Classes**

SOCIAL EVENTS **(magazine)**
Bridenbaugh — *Wild.* p.251, 256-257

SOCIETY
See also **Aristocracy; Cities — Society; Classes; Upper classes**
Benson — *Women 18th* p.292-298, 303
Miller — *First* p.110-112, 117-120
- *British influences*
Holliday — *Woman's* p.217-222
, *Democratic*
Wright — *New* p.59-61
- *Dutch*
Holliday — *Woman's* p.209-217
- *Economic basis*
Adams — *Provincial* p.35-55
- *Importance*
Glubok — *Home* p.108-109
- *Intellectual outlook (1700-1713)*
Adams — *Provincial* p.113-138
, *Mixed*
Kraus — *U.S. (1)* p.121-122
- *New York*
Holliday — *Woman's* p.218-222
- *Problems, of growing*
Bridenbaugh — *Wild.* p.206-248
- *Relations*
Greene — *Revol.* p.67-98
- *Social and regional conflict*
Morris — *American* p.26-49
- *Social contract*
Sanderlin — *1776* p.107-113

SOCIETY FOR THE PROPAGATION OF THE GOSPEL IN FOREIGN PARTS (S.P.G.)
Sweet — *Story* p.165-167, 174-176

SOCIETY OF TAMMANY
See also **Sons of St. Tammany; Tammany Hall**
Life — *100 Events* p.46

SOCIETY OF THE CINCINNATI
Adams — *Album* p.405
Cable — *American* p.81

SOIL
- *Wearing out*
Adams — *Provincial* p.227-238

SOLDIERS
See also **Continental army;** names of wars
, *and civilians*
Greene — *Revol.* p.231-258
- *Excerpts from letters*
200 Years p.294-295
, *Unprofessional*
Boorstin — *Americans* p.363-372

"SOLITUDE" (Penn's estate)
Burt — *Phila.* p.164

SONGS
See also **Singing;** types of songs, etc.
Scott — *Settlers* p.187-208
- *"Battle of the kegs"*
Scott — *Trumpet* p.223-228, 286
- *Books*
Morris — *Ency.* p.613
, *Colonial*
Dannett — *Yankee* p.264-292
- *"The Deserter"*
Scott — *Trumpet* p.53-55, 284
- *"The Dying redcoat"*
Scott — *Trumpet* p.143-147, 285
- *"Foc'sle" (Scotch-Irish sailor songs)*
Rublowsky — *Music* p.76-77
- *"General Burgoyne's surrender"*
Scott — *Trumpet* p.213-215, 285
- *"How stands the glass around"*
Scott — *Trumpet* p.213-215, 285-286
- *Indian*
Howard — *Our* p.620-622
- *"Junto song"*
Scott — *Trumpet* p.94-96, 284
- *"The Liberty song" (song of American freedom)*
Miers — *American* p.74
- *"Lord Cornwallis' surrender"*
Scott — *Trumpet* p.271-275, 286
- *Mother Goose (c1715)*
Morris — *Ency.* p.612
, *Popular*
Morris — *Ency.* p.613
, *Religious*
- *Frontier*
Sweet — *Religion* p.154-159
, *Revolutionary, patriotic*
Burner — *America* p.98-103
- *"The Rich Lady over the sea"*
Scott — *Trumpet* p.67-70, 284
, *Secular (1759-1788)*
Morris — *Ency.* p.613
- *"Sir Peter Parker"*
Scott — *Trumpet* p.111-114, 285
- *War*
Dannett — *Yankee* p.265-287
- *"Young ladies in town"*
Scott — *Trumpet* p.46-48, 284

SONS OF LIBERTY
Amer. Her. — *Rev.* p.59, 62-64, 66-67, 91, 98
Bridenbaugh — *Revolt* p.284, 290, 358, 362
Burt — *Phila.* p.48
Carman — *History* p.165
Forbes — *Paul. See* index p.497
Greene — *Revol.* p.190-191
Miller — *Origins. See* index p.517
Morris — *Ency.* p.74
Sanderlin — *1776* p.41-44, 74, 119, 147
Scott — *Trumpet* p.31-32, 36, 140
Stearns — *Story* p.77-79
Tunis — *Tavern* p.72, 74
Whitney — *Abigail* p.41-42, 46, 50, 54, 59n, 68
- *New London agreement (1765)*
Morris — *American* p.114-116

SONS OF ST. TAMMANY
See also **Society of Tammany**
Burt — *Phila.* p.48-49

SOUPS
Belote — *Compleat* p.57-63

SOUTH
See also names of Southern states and cities
Glubok — *Home. See* index p.356
Greene — *Revol. See* index p.482
Hofstadter — *Amer. See* index p.xii
Life — *Making* p.12-13, 39-40, 81-87, 103
Life — *New* p.61-62
Miller — *Colonial* p.291-349
National — *History.* p.158-169, 402-407
- *Bicentennial*
Lawlor — *Bicen.* p.139-166
- *British relations*
Adams — *Provincial* p.210-211, 221

, *Changing (1713-1745)*
Adams — *Provincial* p.194-221
- *Characteristics*
Sanderlin — *1776 p.xxiv*
, *Colonial*
Alden — *Pioneer* p.48-51, 59
- *Description*
Sanderlin — *1776* p.xxiv-xxv
- *Economy*
Amer. Her. — *Rev.* p.80-81
Main — *Social* p.44-67
- *Frontier*
Main — *Social* p.45-49, 60-61
Morris — *Ency.* p.409-410
- *Land grants*
Adams — *Provincial* p.194-196, 203
- *Leaders*
Train — *Story* p.203-224
- *Life*
Belote — *Compleat* p.22-25
Benson — *Women 18th* p.296-298
Holliday — *Woman's* p.175-176, 178-179
Train — *Story* p.218-221
- *Revolutionary War*
National — *History.* p.230-231
Stember — *South. See* index, under localities and special subjects
, *Understanding of*
Burner — *America* p.59-61
- *Valleys*
Tunis — *Frontier* p.39-40
- *Women*
Benson — *Women 18th* p.103-104, 284-290, 296-298

SOUTH CAROLINA
Greene — *Revol. See* index p.482
Hofstadter — *Amer. See* index p.xii
Life — *Making* p.13, 35-36, 81-85, 94-95, 108, 110
Main — *Social. See* index p.327
Miller — *Origins* p.55, 134, 361-362, 380-381
Morison — *Oxford (1). See* index p.419
Scott — *Trumpet. See* index p.306
Stember — *South* p.39-108
200 Years p.70, 73-75, 77, 80, 176
, *and Declaration of Independence*
Bakeless — *Signers* p.273-284
Malone — *Story* p.227-238
- *Regulators (1767)*
Morris — *American* p.37-48
- *Revolutionary War*
Amer. Her. — *Rev.* p.52, 311-312, 323-325, 332-337, 339-340, 342
Wheeler — *Voices* p.111, 142-146, 325-326, 362-372

SOUTHGATE, ELIZA. *See* Bowne, Eliza Southgate

SPAIN AND SPANIARDS
Greene — *Revol.* p.46, 169, 173, 250, 264, 284, 304, 348, 398-399, 410-411
Miller — *Origins* p.69, 73, 205, 446, 483
Morison — *Oxford (1). See* index p.420
, *and the Americas*
Alden — *Pioneer. See* index p.ix

"SPARTANUS" (pseud.)
, *on unicameral legislature (1776)*
Morris — *American* p.294-297

SPAS
Bridenbaugh — *Revolt* p.166, 326, 367-368
Bridenbaugh — *Wild.* p.276, 338-340

SPECULATION
See also **Land — Speculation**
Adams — *Provincial* p.296-301
Main — *Social* p.9-10, 12, 16, 45-46, 51, 225

SPEECH
Bridenbaugh — *Revolt* p.149-150, 333, 377, 397
Greene — *Revol.* p.183-184, 386-387, 417

SPELLING
Boorstin — *Americans* p.284-290
Earle — *Home* p.180-181; *See*
Glubok — *Home* p.147-148
Wright — *Frontier* p.74
- *"Bees"*
Gould — *Early* p.142

"SPENDERS" (wastrels)
Wilson — *Early* p.178-180

SPICES
Earle — *Home* p.153, 158
Glubok — *Home* p.84, 87-88

SPINETS. *See* Pianos

SPINNING
Earle — *Home* p.180-181; *See also* index p.466
Glubok — *Home* p.235-239
Gould — *Early* p.128
Speare — *Life* p.80-81
- *Irish immigrants*
Earle — *Home* p.180
- *Machines*
Tunis — *Young* p.61
- *Massachusetts*
Dow — *Every* p.95
- *"Matches"*
Earle — *Colonial* p.242
- *Wheels*
Speare — *Life* p.78-79
- *Lettering*
Earle — *Home* p.320
- *New Hampshire*
Glubok — *Home* p.235-236
- *Wool*
Glubok — *Home* p.247-251
- *Yarn*
Glubok — *Home* p.247-248

SPINSTERS
- *Origin of word*
Glubok — *Home* p.240
- *South*
Spruill — *Women's* p.137-140

SPOONS
Earle — *Home* p.87-91
Glubok — *Home* p.46-48

SPORTS AND GAMES
See also **Amusements;** names of sports and games; special subjects
Dulles — *History* p.42-43
Earle — *Customs* p.238-256
Glubok — *Home* p.190-197
Miller — *First* p.86-92
Speare — *Life* p.103, 154, 156
- *Boston*
Bridenbaugh — *Wild.* p.276
- *Charlestown*
Bridenbaugh — *Wild.* p.279
- *Massachusetts*
Dow — *Every* p.112-119
- *New York*
Bridenbaugh — *Wild.* p.274-275
- *Newport, R.I.*
Bridenbaugh — *Wild.* p.279-280
- *Philadelphia*
Bridenbaugh — *Wild.* p.278
- *Prizes*
Dulles — *History* p.30

SPOTSWOOD, ALEXANDER
Morris — *Voices* p.64-65
- *Exploration, Va.*
Wright — *Frontier* p.39-41

SPRINGFIELD, NEW JERSEY
- *Raid*
Stember — *Middle* p.52-58

SPRINGHOUSES
Tunis — *Living* p.136

SQUIRRELS
Earle — *Home* p.110
- *Pennsylvania*
Earle — *Home* p.210

STABLES
Tunis — *Tavern* p.44-45

STAGECOACHES AND STAGE LINES
Bridenbaugh — *Revolt* p.56-57
Earle — *Home* p.345-349
Glubok — *Home* p.341-343
Speare — *Life* p.141-144
Train — *Story* p.244-245
Tunis — *Tavern* p.40-44
Tunis — *Young* p.57

- *Drivers*
Earle — *Customs* p.197-198
Gould — *Early* p.62

STAGE-WAGONS
Tunis — *Tavern* p.40-44

STAIRWAYS
Gould — *Early* p.22-24
, *Georgian*
Langdon — *Every.* p.142-146

STAMFORD, CONNECTICUT
Stember — *North* p.359-360

STAMP ACT
Adams — *Album* p.357
Alden — *Pioneer* p.67, 72-75, 81
Amer. Her. — *Rev.* p.22-23, 47, 56-57, 59, 88
Amer. Reader p.80-83
Beach — *Samuel. See* index p.329
Bridenbaugh — *Revolt* p.186-187, 307, 310, 312, 391
Collins — *Story* p.96
Forbes — *Paul* p.96-99, 110-112
Greene — *Revol.* p.54-55, 131, 136, 140, 190-192
Kraus — *U.S. (1)* p.187-192
Life — *New* p.133, 148, 150-152, 159-160
Lossing — *Biog.* p.371-382
McDowell — *Rev.* p.12, 14, 16, 18-20, 22
Malone — *Story* p.11-16
Miller — *Origins. See* index p.517
Morison — *Oxford (1)* p.190, 246, 251-254
Morris — *American* p.64-71
Morris — *Ency.* p.73-75
Sanderlin — *1776* p.25-57
Scott — *Trumpet* p.23-24, 26-27, 30-36
200 Years p.17-18, 20-23
- *Collapse of authority*
Morris — *American* p.87-94
- *Congress*
Amer. Her. — *Rev.* p.58, 111
Colbourn — *Colonial* p.332-333
Miller — *Origins* p.137-139, 226, 366
Morison — *Oxford (1)* p.253-254, 264
Morris — *Ency.* p.74
Sanderlin — *1776* p.49-50, 71, 250
- *Resolutions (1765)*
Angle — *By* p.40-42
Baldwin — *Ideas* p.167-168
Morris — *American* p.75-77
- *Repeal*
Morison — *Oxford (1)* p.254-257, 267-268, 284
Morris — *American* p.78-94
Morris — *Ency.* p.75
- *Riot*
Morris — *American* p.73-75

"STAMP MASTERS"
Miller — *Origins* p.131-137, 144

STANDARD OF LIVING
Bridenbaugh — *Wild.* p.148, 150, 413
Main — *Social* p.115-163; *See also* index p.327

"STARS AND STRIPES." ***See* Flags — "Stars and Stripes"**

STATE HOUSE. ***See* Independence Hall**

"STATE IN SCHUYLKILL." ***See* "Fish House"**

STATES
See also names of states
Angle — *By* p.52-61
Greene — *Revol. See* index p.482-483
- *Admission to Union (chronology)*
Carman — *History* p.782
- *Constitutions*
Greene — *Revol.* p.210, 248, 288-290, 294, 310-315, 319, 361-364
Morris — *Ency.* p.111-112

STATUE OF LIBERTY
National — *History.* p.530

STAYS
Earle — *Child* p.56-58

STEAM ENGINES
Morris — *Ency.* p.535
Tunis — *Young* p.63
Wilson — *American* p.50-51

STEAM POWER
Greene — *Revol.* p.65-66

STEAMBOATS
Life — *Growing* p.160
Morris — *Ency.* p.535
Tunis — *Young* p.142
, First
Wilson — *American* p.52-53
- Philadelphia
Burt — *Phila.* p.113-114

"STEBBINS HOUSE"
Gould — *Early* p.48-49

STEDMAN, CHARLES
Wheeler — *Voices. See* index p.479

STEEL, KATHARINE
Ellet — *Eminent* p.554-587

STEEL. *See* **Iron industry, and steel**

STEELE, ELIZABETH
Ellet — *Eminent* p.227-230

STEUBEN, FRIEDRICH VON
Davis — *Heroes* p.79-88

STEVENS, JOHN
Wilson — *American* p.59-63

STEVENS FAMILY
Wilson — *American* p.59

STIEGEL, HEINRICH WILHELM
Burt — *Phila.* p.231-232
Langdon — *Every.* p.203-210

STILES, EZRA
- Views on women
Benson — *Women 18th* p.88, 95, 150, 153-154, 252, 254, 261-263, 267, 270-272

STOCK EXCHANGES
See also **New York Stock Exchange**
, First (Philadelphia)
Morris — *Ency.* p.504

STOCKINGS (hosiery)
Earle — *Home* p.190, 261-262

STOCKS AND PILLORY
Bridenbaugh — *Wild.* p.224-225

STOCKTON, ANNIS
Ellet — *Eminent* p.503-507

STOCKTON, RICHARD
Bakeless — *Signers* p.166-169
Malone — *Story* p.152-153
- Biography
Lossing — *Biog.* p.77-80

STODDARD, SOLOMON
Hofstadter — *Amer.* p.211-212, 225, 236-237, 242, 282

STONE, CHARLES
Malone — *Story* p.199-200

STONE, THOMAS
Bakeless — *Signers* p.240-242
- Biography
Lossing — *Biog.* p.151-153

STONE BEES
Earle — *Home* p.407

"STONE BOATS"
- New England
Train — *Story* p.166

STONECUTTING
Adams — *Album* p.344

STONY POINT, NEW YORK
, Battle of
Morris — *Ency.* p.101
Stember — *North* p.181-198; *See also* index p.389

STOVES
See also **Franklin stove; Heating**
Dreppard — *Pioneer* p.232-234, 240
Earle — *Home* p.69-71, 385
Glubok — *Home* p.37-38
Tunis — *Living* p.133-134
- Pennsylvania Germans
Earle — *Home* p.69-70

STREET CLEANING
Bridenbaugh — *Revolt* p.30-32, 239-241

STREET LAMPS AND LIGHTING
- *Boston*
  Train — *Story* p.177
- *First*
  Tunis — *Young* p.50

STREET VENDORS
Wilson — *Early* p.52-54

STREETS
Bridenbaugh — *Revolt* p.28-36, 231-232, 235-245
Bridenbaugh — *Wild. See* index p.498

STUART, GILBERT
Morris — *Ency.* p.599, 719-720

SUBMARINES
- *Philadelphia*
  Burt — *Phila.* p.114

SUGAR
See also **Maple sugar**
Gould — *Early* p.86
Miller — *Origins* p.14, 70, 96-97
- *Imports*
  Morison — *Oxford (1)* p.192-200
- *Substitutes*
  Earle — *Home* p.110-111, 147, 157

SUGAR ACT
Alden — *Pioneer* p.71-72, 75
Beach — *Samuel* p.6, 44, 54, 63-64, 66-68, 75-76
Greene — *Revol.* p.4, 45, 190-191
McDowell — *Rev.* p.18
Miller — *Origins* p.100-106, 149, 181
Morison — *Oxford (1)* p.249
Morris — *American* p.58-63
Morris — *Ency.* p.485

SUGAR BOWLS
Gould — *Early* p.86-87

SULLIVAN, JOHN
Amer. Her. — *Rev. See* index p.384
McDowell — *Rev.* p.77, 93, 105, 114, 138-139
Stember — *North* p.47, 75, 199, 221, 224, 227, 230, 279, 324-325, 327-328, 330
Wheeler — *Voices* p.136, 160, 164, 205, 248, 262, 310-312, 341-342
- *Expedition against Iroquois*
  Stember — *Middle* p.142-161
  Stember — *North* p.20, 28, 31, 60-61, 64, 67, 71

SUMNER, MARY OSGOOD
Glubok — *Home* p.164-166

SUMTER, THOMAS
Ellet — *Eminent* p.757-763

SUNBURY, GEORGIA
Stember — *South* p.22-25

SUNDAY. *See* Sabbath

SUPPERS. *See* Dinners

SUPREME COURT OF THE UNITED STATES
Alden — *Pioneer* p.121, 128-129
- *Chief justices*
  Morris — *Ency.* p.461
- *Decisions*
  Morris — *Ency.* p.462-463
- *Justices*
  Morris — *Ency.* p.461

SURGERY
Morris — *Ency.* p.541

SURNAMES. *See* Names

SUSQUEHANNA RIVER VALLEY (Pa.)
McDowell — *Rev.* p.138-139

SWANWICK, JOHN
- *Views on women*
  Benson — *Women 18th* p.141-142, 162-163, 166, 218

SWEARING. *See* Profanity

SWEDISH
Sirkis — *Reflect.* p.86-87

SWEEPING
Belote — *Compleat* p.18

SWEETS
Glubok — *Home* p.86-88

SWIMMING
Ross — *Taste* p.185

SWITZERLAND
, Emigration from
Adams — *Provincial* p.173

SYMMES, THOMAS
Howard — *Our* p.13-14

SYMPHONY ORCHESTRAS
, First
Langdon — *Every.* p.96

SYMS, WIDOW SARAH
Earle — *Colonial* p.36-37

T

TABLECLOTHS
Earle — *Customs* p.133

TABLES
Gould — *Early* p.84-85
Tunis — *Living* p.130-131
- Furnishings
Earle — *Customs* p.138

TABLEWARE
See also **Pewter and pewterers; Silverware**
Earle — *Customs* p.137
Gould — *Early* p.85-88
Tunis — *Living* p.136
- Advertisements
Earle — *Home* p.106-107
- Inventory, Southern
Spruill — *Women's* p.37

TAG (games)
Earle — *Child* p.344-345
Glubok — *Home* p.184-185

TAILORS AND TAILORING
Adams — *Album* p.310
Tunis — *Colonial* p.37

TALKERS
, Irresponsible
Wilson — *Early* p.180-182

TALLEYRAND, CHARLES M., DE
Morris — *Voices* p.183-187

TAMBOUR WORK (embroidery)
Earle — *Home* p.269-270

TAMMANY HALL
, Founding of (1789)
Life — *100 Events* p.46

TANEY, ROGER BROOKE
- Biography
Morris — *Ency.* p.721-722

TANNERS AND TANNING
See also **Leather**
Tunis — *Colonial* p.32-34
Tunis — *Living* p.114-115

TARIFFS
See also **Taxation**
Colbourn — *Colonial* p.265
Morris — *Ency.* p.491

TARRING AND FEATHERING
Sanderlin — *1776* p.79-84

TAVERNS
See also **Inns and innkeepers**
Adams — *Album* p.272
Belote — *Compleat* p.123-124
Bridenbaugh — *Revolt* p.156-162, 358-361
Bridenbaugh — *Wild.* See index p.498-499
Burner — *America* p.96-97
Dolan — *Yankee* p.86-88
Earle — *Customs* p.196-199
Earle — *Home* p.358-360
Glubok — *Home* p.345-347
Gould — *Early* p.32, 48-49, 61-62, 93
Greene — *Revol.* p.28, 95, 163, 342
Langdon — *Every.* p.253-254

Ross — *Taste* p.67-68
Speare — *Life* p.48-49
Train — *Story* p.176
Wilson — *Early* p.59
Wright — *Cultural* p.248

, as "stage-line" stations
Tunis — *Tavern* p.56
- Backwoods, Southern
Spruill — *Women's* p.301
- Contests and games
Tunis — *Tavern* p.53-54
- Conversation
Tunis — *Tavern* p.59-64
- Food
Tunis — *Tavern* p.57
- Hostesses, Southern
Spruill — *Women's* p.295-302
- Names
Tunis — *Tavern* p.54
- New York (city)
Downey — *Our* p.91-102
- on Mohawk turnpike
Dolan — *Yankee* p.90
- "Ordinaries"
Bridenbaugh — *Wild. See* index p.498-499
Speare — *Life* p.150
- Philadelphia
Burt — *Phila.* p.107-108, 116-117
- "Queen's Head"
Tunis — *Tavern* p.55-56
- "Raleigh Tavern"
Tunis — *Tavern* p.51-52
- Sports
Dulles — *History* p.36-37
- "Sun Inn"
Tunis — *Tavern* p.50-51
- "Tun Tavern"
Burt — *Phila.* p.116-117
- Women as keepers
Dexter — *Colonial* p.1-17

TAXATION
See also **Boston Tea Party; Stamp Act; Sugar Act; Townshend Acts;** etc.
Adams — *Provincial* p.318-319
Amer. Her. — *Rev.* p.22, 44, 46, 55-57, 59-61, 64
Bridenbaugh — *Revolt* p.7, 11-12, 28, 219-221
Greene — *Revol.* p.4, 28-29, 99, 101, 191, 198-200, 337-338, 364, 401
Ingraham — *Album* p.17-19
Kraus — *U.S. (1)* p.176
Life — *Growing* p.11, 16, 38
Life — *Making* p.38, 64, 110-113, 132
Life — *New* p.144-145, 150-152, 154-156, 160, 163-165
McDowell — *Rev. See* index
Miller — *Origins. See* index p.518
Morison — *Oxford (1). See* index p.420
Sanderlin — *1776* p.xxvii, 8, 32-41, 51, 54, 116-118
Scott — *Trumpet* p.23, 27, 30-31, 36, 55, 63-64, 67-70

- Assessment lists
Main — *Social* p.13-14, 20-21, 26, 31, 36, 38-39
- Collection
Beach — *Samuel* p.58-62
- Colonial resistance
Angle — *By* p.38-42

TAYLOR, GEORGE
Bakeless — *Signers* p.148-149
Malone — *Story* p.171
- Biography
Lossing — *Biog.* p.123-125

TAYLOR, JOHN
Sweet — *Story* p.215-216, 225

TAYLOR, RAYNOR
Howard — *Our* p.90-94

TEA
See also **Boston Tea Party**
Amer. Her. — *Rev.* p.23-24, 60, 64, 67-68
Earle — *Home* p.164-165
Forbes — *Paul. See* index p.498
Glubok — *Home* p.92-93
Gould — *Early* p.107
Miller — *Origins* p.518
Speare — *Life* p.74-75

- Drinking
Belote — *Compleat* p.125-126
Handlin — *This* p.15-16

TEA *(continued)*
- Self-denial
Earle — *Colonial* p.247-257
- East Indian
Sanderlin — *1776* p.59-92
- Etiquette
Belote — *Compleat* p.165
- Parties
Earle — *Colonial* p.251-255
- Scarcity
Earle — *Colonial* p.249-251
- Substitutes
Earle — *Colonial* p.255-257
Earle — *Home* p.158-159, 165

TEA ACT
Beach — *Samuel* p.174, 189, 216, 228, 249-251
Miller — *Origins* p.267, 339-343, 345-346, 405

TEACHERS
See also **Tutors**
Glubok — *Home* p.125
Wilson — *Early* p.103
- Chester Co., Pa.
Main — *Social* p.182
- Competence
Main — *Social* p.142
- Economic status
Main — *Social* p.113, 141-142
- General position
Main — *Social* p.275
- Income
Main — *Social* p.91, 95, 141
- Lunenburg Co., Va.
Main — *Social* p.46
- Prestige
Main — *Social* p.219
- Property
Main — *Social* p.95-96
- Standard of living
Main — *Social* p.142-144
- Women
Dexter — *Colonial* p.78-97
Earle — *Child* p.91-116
, Southern
Spruill — *Women's* p.255-259

TEAKETTLES
- First, iron
Gould — *Early* p.67

TECHNOLOGY
, and organization
Morris — *Ency.* p.493-494

"TEDYUSCUNG" (Delaware Indians)
Burt — *Phila.* p.130, 169, 172, 177

TEETH
See also **Dentistry**
Earle — *Customs* p.303-306
Handlin — *This* p.15-16
Scott — *Settlers* p.183

TEMPERATURE
- Discomforts
Earle — *Home* p.70-71

TENNENT, GILBERT
Adams — *Provincial* p.281-282
Hofstadter — *Amer.* p.233, 234, 251, 254-261, 269, 273, 277-278, 289
Sweet — *Story* p.123, 139-140, 142

TENNENT, WILLIAM
Hofstadter — *Amer.* p.231-235, 251, 255-256, 266, 269, 278, 286
Sweet — *Story* p.123, 140, 144-145

TENNESSEE
Greene — *Revol.* p.174-175, 226, 239, 399, 401, 405, 407-409, 412-413, 415
Life — *Making* p.107-109

TERRITORIAL EXPANSION
Morris — *Ency.* p.411-420

TERRY, ELI
Dolan — *Yankee* p.160-162

TEXTBOOKS
Earle — *Child* p.134-139, 147-149
Glubok — *Home* p.138-150, 153-155
Wright — *New* p.189-190

TEXTILES. *See* **Fabrics**

THACHER, JAMES
Morris — *Voices* p.119-123
Wheeler — *Voices. See* index p.479

THANKFULNESS
Sloane — *Spirits* p.31-35

THANKSGIVING DAY
Earle — *Customs* p.220-223
Gould — *Early* p.94-95, 142
Sloane — *Spirits* p.34
Speare — *Life* p.159
- Menu
Belote — *Compleat* p.161
- 1779
Smith — *Colonial* p.290-297

THEATER
Adams — *Album* p.327
Adams — *Provincial* p.308-309
Bridenbaugh — *Revolt* p.168-169, 230, 369-371
Bridenbaugh — *Wild.* p.279, 435-437, 439, 439n, 441, 463
Dannett — *Yankee* p.249-263
Earle — *Customs* p.246-249
Greene — *Revol. See* index p.483
Holliday — *Woman's* p.234-287
Morris — *Ency.* p.589
Nye — *Unembar.* p.140-142
Ross — *Taste* p.82
Speare — *Life* p.167
Train — *Story* p.258
Wertenbaker — *Golden. See* index p.170
Wright — *Cultural* p.180-187
- Boston
Dulles — *History* p.48-49
Wertenbaker — *Golden* p.34-35
- Charleston
Dulles — *History* p.63
Wertenbaker — *Golden* p.146-148
, First (Williamsburg, Va.)
Howard — *Our* p.30-31
Train — *Story* p.222
Wertenbaker — *Golden* p.106, 119-120
Wright — *Cultural* p.180
- New York
Dulles — *History* p.53-57
Wertenbaker — *Golden* p.43, 52-55
- Philadelphia
Burt — *Phila.* p.185-189
Dulles — *History* p.101-102
Wertenbaker — *Golden* p.79-81
- Virginia
Dulles — *History* p.62-63
Wertenbaker — *Golden* p.119-121
- Williamsburg, Va. See **Theater, First (Williamsburg, Va.)**

THEUS, JEREMIAH
Wertenbaker — *Golden* p.135-136
Wright — *Culture* p.210

"THIMELL PIE" (punishment)
Glubok — *Home* p.132-133

THOMAS, ISAIAH
- Biography
Morris — *Ency.* p.723

THOMAS, JANE
Ellet — *Eminent* p.180-190

THOMPSON, BENJAMIN (Count Rumford)
Morris — *Ency.* p.530
Wilson — *American* p.24-31

THOMSON, CHARLES
McDowell — *Rev.* p.54-55, 90

THOMSON, HANNAH
Benson — *Women 18th* p.294

THORNTON, MATTHEW
Bakeless — *Signers* p.227-230
Malone — *Story* p.102-103
- Biography
Lossing — *Biog.* p.20-21

THRESHING
Gould — *Early* p.133-134

THRIFT
Cable — *American* p.39
Sloane — *Spirits* p.25-29

TICONDEROGA, NEW YORK. *See* **Forts — Ticonderoga**

TILGHMAN, MOLLY
Spruill — *Women's* p.50, 90, 94-95, 135, 149

TIMOTHY, ELIZABETH
Spruill — *Women's* p.263-264

TINDER BOXES
Earle — *Home* p.48-50
Gould — *Early* p.66

TINKERS
Tunis — *Colonial* p.38

TINWARE AND TINSMITHS
Dolan — *Yankee* p.142-146
Dreppard — *Pioneer* p.178-180, 182-186
- *Peddlers*
Dolan — *Yankee* p.149

TITHING-MAN
Glubok — *Home* p.302-303

TITLES
, *Fear of*
Wright — *New* p.59-60
- *"Honorable"*
Main — *Social* p.218-219

TOASTERS
Gould — *Early* p.79

TOASTS
, *Drinking of*
Spruill — *Women's* p.73-74

TOBACCO
See also **Smoking**
Alden — *Pioneer* p.41-42, 48
Colbourn — *Colonial* p.255-258
Greene — *Revol.* p.17-19, 51, 189, 272, 279-280, 332, 334
Hofstadter — *Amer.* p.95-96, 157-159, 167
Langdon — *Every.* p.310-313
Life — *New* p.60, 64, 68-69, 98, 101-102, 105, 114-115, 122
Miller — *Origins* p.10, 14-17, 84
Morison — *Oxford (1)* p.161, 166, 189, 239, 269, 334, 343, 369-370
Tunis — *Colonial* p.52-54
- *Maryland*
Wertenbaker — *Golden* p.10-11
- *South*
Adams — *Provincial* p.204-206
Carman — *History* p.65-67, 80-82
Morris — *Ency.* p.477-478
- *Virginia*
Handlin — *This* p.86-87
Wertenbaker — *Golden* p.144

TOLERANCE
Burt — *Phila.* p.58

TOMBSTONES
Cable — *American* p.64-65
Earle — *Customs* p.380-387
- *New England*
Sirkis — *Reflect.* p.23

TOOLS
See also **Farm implements**
Dreppard — *Pioneer* p.56, 308-310
Tunis — *Living* p.132-133
- *Frontier*
Kraus — *U.S. (1)* p.146

TORIES. *See* **Loyalists**

"TOWER" (woman's cap). *See* **Headdress**

TOWN CRIERS
Wilson — *Early* p.23-24

TOWN MEETINGS
Bridenbaugh — *Wild.* p.144-145
- *New England*
Life — *Growing* p.10

TOWNS
See also **Cities**
Carman — *History* p.110-113
Pettengill — *Yankee* p.86-89
Tunis — *Living* p.126
Tunis — *Young* p.30-42

, *Colonial*
Langdon — *Every.* p.299-334
- *Population*
See also names of cities and towns
Bridenbaugh — *Wild.* p.143-144
- *Congestion*
Bridenbaugh — *Wild.* p.147-148, 150-151, 305-308, 310
- *Culture*
Bridenbaugh — *Wild.* p.464-466
- *Expansion*
Bridenbaugh — *Wild.* p.143-174
Kraus — *U.S. (1)* p.101
- *Industries*
Bridenbaugh — *Wild.* p.182-185, 337-338
, *Inland*
Tunis — *Young* p.37-42
- *Life*
Bridenbaugh — *Wild.* p.249-300
National — *History.* p.292-303
Wright — *New* p.109-117
- *North*
Adams — *Provincial* p.247-250
, *Secondary*
Bridenbaugh — *Revolt* p.5, 48, 50, 55-56, 211, 260-261, 263-264, 267
- *South*
Adams — *Provincial* p.202
- *Squares and courtyards*
Tunis — *Young* p.39-41

TOWNSEND-GODDARD (cabinet makers)
Train — *Story* p.156-157

TOWNSHEND, CHARLES
Miller — *Origins. See* index p.518
Morison — *Oxford (1)* p.257-258, 333

TOWNSHEND ACTS
Amer. Her. — *Rev.* p.60-62, 64-65
Beach — *Samuel* p.131-133, 135, 138, 174, 216
Brodie — *Jefferson* p.108-111
Carman — *History* p.166-167, 174-175
Greene — *Revol.* p.4, 55, 191, 198
Life — *New* p.152-153
McDowell — *Rev.* p.22, 27, 29
Miller — *Origins. See* index p.518
Morison — *Oxford (1)* p.256-262
Morris — *American* p.95-98
Morris — *Ency.* p.76
Sanderlin — *1776* p.51, 73, 250
Scott — *Trumpet* p.37-42, 63
Whitney — *Abigail* p.46, 50, 51n, 54

TOYS
See also **Dolls**
Adams — *Album* p.336
Dreppard — *Pioneer* p.116-119
Earle — *Child* p.361-365, 374-376
Glubok — *Home* p.191-197
Speare — *Life* p.102-103

TRADE AND TRADERS
See also **Commerce; Industry; Retail trade;** names of localities
Greene — *Revol. See* index p.484
Life — *New. See* index p.176
Morison — *Oxford (1). See* index p.420
Tunis — *Young* p.41-42
, *and money*
Tunis — *Living* p.125-126
, *Balance of*
Colbourn — *Colonial* p.260-261
Morris — *Ency.* p.487
, *Foreign*
Morris — *Ency.* p.486-488
- *Revolutionary period*
Amer. Her. — *Rev.* p.16, 31-32, 34, 36, 53, 55-57, 76

TRADE UNIONS
Adams — *Album* p.342
- *Origin*
Morris — *Ency.* p.518

TRADES
See also **Occupations;** names of trades
Wilson — *American* p.6-13
- *Comparison with European*
Wilson — *American* p.8-9
- *Dictionary*
Dow — *Every* p.121-142

TRAFFIC
Bridenbaugh — *Revolt* p.30, 34-35, 243-244, 341
Bridenbaugh — *Wild.* p.168-169, 323-324

"TRAINING DAY"
Earle — *Customs* p.223-224

TRAITORS
See also names of traitors
Burt — *Phila.* p.245

TRAMPS
Speare — *Life* p.145

TRANSPORTATION
See also **Travel and travelers;** types of transportation
Bridenbaugh — *Revolt* p.37, 55, 57, 265-266
Dreppard — *Pioneer* p.300-306
Glubok — *Home* p.336-344
Greene — *Revol.* p.31, 36-37, 158, 275, 340-346, 408
Morris — *Voices* p.58-61
Ross — *Taste* p.267
Wright — *Cultural* p.249-250

- Interior, early
Morris — *Ency.* p.411
- Middle Colonies
Train — *Story* p.196-198
- New England
Train — *Story* p.165-168
, People of
Wilson — *Early* p.139-150
- Republic
Train — *Story* p.242-250
- South
Train — *Story* p.215-217

TRAVEL AND TRAVELERS
See also **Transportation;** names of travelers; types of traveling
Adams — *Album* p.271
Adams — *Provincial* p.77-79, 128
Earle — *Customs* p.187-193, 203-204, 206-213
Glubok — *Home* p.335-343
Greene — *Revol. See* index p.484
Miller — *Colonial* p.389-418
Ross — *Taste* p.267-268
, and communication
Bridenbaugh — *Revolt* p.54-58, 166, 289-290, 340-342, 347-348
, and explorers
Morris — *Ency.* p.560, 564
- Excitement and trials
Wright — *New* p.75-78
, Foreign
Axtell — *18th* p.13-239
Wright — *Cultural* p.251
- Girls, Southern
Spruill — *Women's* p.205-206
- Modes
Adams — *Provincial* p.301-302
- Service
Wilson — *Early* p.47-51
- Women
Earle — *Colonial* p.135-159

"TREADMILL DOGS." *See* **"Turnspit dogs"**

TREATIES
See also names of treaties
, with Holland
Life — *Making* p.62

TREATY OF ALLIANCE WITH FRANCE
Ingraham — *Album* p.67
Life — *Making* p.17, 55, 61, 81
Morris — *Amer.* p.269-271

TREATY OF GREENVILLE
Morris — *Ency.* p.420

TREATY OF PARIS
Carman — *History* p.154, 156, 214-216, 241-242
Ingraham — *Album* p.88
Life — *Making* p.89, 105-107
Morison — *Oxford (1)* p.321, 245, 350
Morris — *American* p.285-288
Morris — *Ency.* p.70
Train — *Story* p.256
Wright — *Frontier* p.46
- Preliminary
Morris — *American* p.12-16, 279-284

TREATY OF SAN LORENZO (Pinckney's treaty)
Morris — *Ency.* p.127-128

TREATY OF UTRECHT
Morison — *Oxford (1)* p.191, 193, 195-196, 202

TREES
Wright — *Frontier* p.68-69
- *Saplings, uses of*
Glubok — *Home* p.213-214

TRENCHERS (wooden plates)
Gould — *Early* p.37, 85

TRENTON, NEW JERSEY
, Battle of
Burt — *Phila.* p.273-274
Downey — *Our* p.151-160
Life — *Making* p.54-57, 66, 68
McDowell — *Rev.* p.101, 104-107
Morris — *American* p.236-238
National — *History.* p.202-205
Stember — *Middle* p.26-33
Tunis — *Tavern* p.97-102
200 Years p.91, 95-98, 100, 102-103

TREVETT, JOHN
Cook — *What* p.247-271

TROIS RIVIÈRES, CANADA
Stember — *North* p.46-47

TROLLEYMEN
Wilson — *Early* p.143-147

TRUMBULL, FAITH ROBINSON
Somerville — *Women* p.40-41

TUCKEY, WILLIAM
Howard — *Our* p.34-36

TUDOR, JOHN
Morris — *Voices* p.73-76

TUESDAY CLUB
Wertenbaker — *Golden* p.92-93

TUFTS, JOHN
Howard — *Our* p.12-13

TURKEYS
Gould — *Early* p.139
- *Georgia*
Tunis — *Tavern* p.110
- *"Shoots"*
Tunis — *Tavern* p.53-54

"TURNERS"
Wilson — *Early* p.65-67

TURNPIKES. *See* Highways; Roads

"TURNSPIT DOGS"
Earle — *Home* p.65
Glubok — *Home* p.33-34
Gould — *Early* p.72
Train — *Story* p.194
Tunis — *Living* p.138
Tunis — *Tavern* p.57

"TURTLE FROLICS" (feasts)
Earle — *Colonial* p.221-224
Train — Story p.164-165

TUTORS
- *South*
Spruill — *Women's* p.193-195

"TWO-PENNY ACTS"
Miller — *Origins* p.41-42
- *Virginia*
Sanderlin — *1776* p.28-29

TYRANNY
- *Views of James Otis*
Angle — *By* p.30-32

U

UMBRELLAS
Ross — *Taste* p.222
Train — *Story* p.163

UNIFORMS. *See* Continental army — Uniforms; Military uniforms

"UNION"
- *Formation*
Angle — *By* p.100-118

UNITARIANS
Greene — *Revol.* p.285- 370

UNITED BRETHREN. ***See*** **Moravians**

"UNIVERSAL FRIEND." ***See*** **Wilkinson, Jemima**

UNIVERSALISTS
Greene — *Revol.* p.373
Morris — *Ency.* p.550
Sweet — *Religion* p.196-197

UNIVERSITY OF PENNSYLVANIA
Burt — *Phila.* p.147, 216, 218, 220
Sweet — *Story* p.145-146
Wertenbaker — *Golden* p.66-67, 90

UPPER CLASSES
See also **Aristocracy**
Main — *Social* p.17, 113, 195, 233-234, 256, 258-265, 268, 275-277, 279
- Philadelphia
Gowans — *Images* p.188

URBAN LIFE. ***See*** **Cities**

V

VALCOUR ISLAND, NEW YORK
Stember — *North* p.49-53

VALLEY FORGE, PENNSYLVANIA
Adams — *Album* p.397
Amer. Her. — *Rev.* p.163, 213, 217-220, 228-229
Amer. Reader p.110-112
Collins — *Story* p.118
Greene — *Revol.* p.236, 252-253, 274-275, 277
Ingraham — *Album* p.65
Morison — *Oxford (1)* p.303-304, 328
Morris — *Ency.* p.96, 99-100
Morris — *Voices* p.114-115
National — *History.* p.220-223
Scott — *Trumpet* p.204-233
Stember — *Middle* p.115-118

VAN ALSTINE, NANCY
Ellet — *Eminent* p.726-744

VAN DAM, RIP
Scott — *Settlers* p.128-129

VAN HAGEN, PETER ALBRECHT, SR.
Howard — *Our* p.73-75

VAN HAGEN, PETER, JR.
Howard — *Our* p.75

VAN SCHAACK, PETER
Morris — *American* p.205-208

VARIETY SHOWS
Wright — *Cultural* p.186-187

VEGETABLES
Belote — *Compleat* p.85-90
Gould — *Early* p.92
Tunis — *Young* p.21
- South
Spruill — *Women's* p.67-68

VEHICLES
See also **Transportation;** types of vehicles
Adams — *Album* p.240-341
Tunis — *Living* p.119-120
Tunis — *Young* p.20

VERGENNES, CHARLES GRAVIER DE
Life — *Making* p.60-61, 88-89, 104, 113
Morris — *Voices* p.127-129

VERMONT
Greene — *Revol. See* index p.485
Morison — *Oxford (1)* p.287, 324-328, 358-359, 365, 375
Stearns — *Story* p.102
Stember — *North* p.4, 16-17, 50, 84, 279-283
200 Years p.49-50

VICES. ***See*** **Sin and sinners**

"VIEWERS" (inspectors)
Wilson — *Early* p.28-29

VIGILANCE
Bridenbaugh — *Wild. See* index p.499
Whitney — *Abigail* p.79-80, 82
Wilson — *Early* p.15, 20

VILLAGES
See also **Towns**
Tunis — *Young* p.29-35
- Life
Speare — *Life* p.41-43

VINING, MARY
Burt — *Phila.* p.310-311

VIRGINIA
See also special subjects
Adams — *Album* p.263
Axtell — *18th* p.20-54
Boorstin — *Americans* p.102-143
Crèvecoeur — *Sketches* p.23, 51, 85, 135, 145, 175-177
Earle — *Home. See* index p.468
Glubok — *Home. See* index p.357
Greene — *Revol. See* index p.485
Handlin — *This* p.85-87
Hofstadter — *Amer. See* index p.xiii
Life — *Growing. See* index p.176
Life — *Making. See* index p.159
Life — *New. See* index p.176
Miller — *Colonial* p.159-166, 293-309
Miller — *Origins. See* index p.518
Morison — *Oxford (1). See* index p.421
Morris — *Ency. See* index p.774
Scott — *Trumpet. See* index p.306-307
Stember — *South* p.151-204
200 Years p.17, 20-22, 68, 70, 114-115, 143, 147, 176
, and Declaration of Independence
Bakeless — *Signers* p.69-103
Malone — *Story* p.201-220
- Animals
Axtell — *18th* p.25-28
- Aristocracy
Wertenbaker — *Golden* p.9-10
- Assembly
Sanderlin — *1776* p.36-40, 71, 90-91, 250
- Boundaries
See also **North Carolina — Boundaries**
Miller — *Colonial* p.291-349
- Boys
Hale — *Through* p.92-96
- Commerce
Axtell — *18th* p.50-51
- Culture
Wertenbaker — *Golden* p.113-114
- Homes
Cable — *American* p.43
Holliday — *Woman's* p.179-180
- Landowners
Cable — *American* p.42
- Life
Morris — *Voices* p.61-64
Spruill — *Women's* p.95-97
- Plants and crops
Axtell — *18th* p.20-23
, Ravaging
Stember — *South* p.158-170
- 1759
Amer. Reader p.53-55
- Sports
Earle — *Colonial* p.207-209
- Trees
Axtell — *18th* p.29-30
- Views of Robert Beverley
Miller — *Colonial* p.293-309
- Views of Thomas Jefferson
Brodie — *Jefferson. See* index p.798
- Water
Axtell — *18th* p.23-25
- Women
Axtell — *18th* p.34-35
Earle — *Colonial* p.243-244

VIRGINIA DECLARATION OF RIGHTS
Baldwin — *Ideas* p.182-183
National — *History.* p.147

VIRGINIA GAZETTE
Train — *Story* p.220-221

VIRGINIA RESOLUTIONS
Alden — *Pioneer* p.139-140
Baldwin — *Ideas* p.249-251
Beach — *Samuel* p.79-80, 180
Miller — *Origins* p.125-126, 129, 289, 316
Morris — *American* p.71-72
Morris — *Ency.* p.78
Sanderlin — *1776* p.36-39, 46
200 Years p.20, 65-166, 169-170

VIRGINIA STATUTE FOR RELIGIOUS FREEDOM
Angle — *By* p.81-82
Baldwin — *Ideas* p.187-188
Davie — *Profile* p.91
Morris — *Ency.* p.114

VOCABULARY
Adams — *Provincial* p.288-290

W

"WACHOVIA." *See* **Moravians — "Wachovia"**

WAFER IRONS
Gould — *Early* p.97-98

WAGES
Bridenbaugh — *Revolt* p.48, 87, 298
, and prices
Morris — *American* p.251-254
- Controls
Morris — *Ency.* p.517
- Scales
Morris — *Ency.* p.318

"WAGON DOCTORS"
Wilson — *Early* p.115-117

WAGONS
See also **Conestoga wagons**
Crèvecoeur — *Sketches* p.138-139, 142, 144, 146, 192, 206
Tunis — *Living* p.119-120
Tunis — *Tavern* p.39-40
- Traffic
Bridenbaugh — *Revolt* p.51, 57-58, 261, 265-266

WAINWRIGHTS AND COACH-MAKERS
Tunis — *Colonial* p.93-97

WALKER, ESTHER
Ellet — *Eminent* p.626-644

WALKER, MARTHA I'ANS
Evans — *Weather.* p.52-72

WALKER, THOMAS
Evans — *Weather.* p. 52, 54-59, 70-72

"WALKING PURCHASE"
Burt — *Phila.* p.17, 166-167, 171

WALL DECORATION AND WALL-PAPER
Adams — *Album* p.315
Earle — *Customs* p.121
Tunis — *Living* p.129
- Massachusetts
Dow — *Every* p.46-49

WALLS
, Stone
Sloane — *Spirits* p.112

WALTER, THOMAS
Howard — *Our* p.13
Rublowsky — *Music* p.20-21

WALTON, GEORGE
Bakeless — *Signers* p.296-298
Malone — *Story* p.244-245
- Biography
Lossing — *Biog.* p.233-237

WANDERERS. *See* **Itinerants; Travel and travelers**

WAR
See also names of wars, especially **Revolutionary War**
, Hatred of
Burt — *Phila.* p.149
- Secretaries of war (1789-1799)
Schemmer — *Almanac* p.230

WAR OF INDEPENDENCE. *See* **Revolutionary War**

WAR OF JENKINS' EAR
Morris — *Ency.* p.65

WARDER, ANN HEAD
Benson — *Women 18th* p.295-296

WARREN, JOSEPH
Forbes — *Paul. See* index p.498
Miller — *Origins* p.372, 384, 401, 408-409, 411
, on controlling militia
Morris — *American* p.149-150

WARREN, MERCY OTIS
Adelman — *Famous* p.85
Benson — *Women 18th* p.171, 177, 203, 247, 250, 254-257, 305
Ellet — *Eminent* p.58-65
Evans — *Weather.* p.27-30

WARVILLE, BRISSOT DE
Morris — *Voices* p.134-137

"WASHBALLS"
See also **Soap and soap making**
Earle — *Customs* p.310-311

WASHING (clothes)
Gould — *Early* p.114-117

WASHINGTON, AUGUSTINE
Adams — *Provincial* p.38-39

WASHINGTON, ELIZABETH FOOTE
Evans — *Weather.* p.335-360

WASHINGTON, GEORGE
Adams — *Album* p.372
Alden — *Pioneer. See* index p.x
Amer. Her. — *Rev. See* index p.384
Brodie — *Jefferson. See* index p.810-811
Butterfield — *Amer.* p.4-5
Collins — *Story* p.464
Davis — *Heroes* p.127-145
Evans — *Weather. See* index p.372
Forbes — *Paul. See* index p.498
Glubok — *Home* p.116, 144, 205, 220-221, 271-272, 279, 343
Greene — *Revol. See* index p.485-486
Hale — *Through* p.135-138
Holliday — *Woman's. See* index p.319
Life — *Making. See* index p.159
McDowell — *Rev. See* index p.199
Malone — *Story* p.19, 35, 43, 48, 56, 82, 96, 108, 252
Miller — *Origins. See* index p.519
Morison — *Oxford (1). See* index p.421
Morris — *Voices. See* index p.256
Sanderlin — *1776. See* index p.262
Scott — *Trumpet* p.307
Spruill — *Women's. See* index p.424
Stember — *Middle. See* index p.172
Stember — *North. See* index p.390
Stember — *South. See* index p.217
Tunis — *Tavern. See* index p.108
200 Years. See index p.351
Wheeler — *Voices. See* index p.479-480
Whitney — *Abigail. See* index p.357

- Administration
Life — *Growing* p.7-19
Morris — *Voices* p.170-180

, and cherry-tree story
Dolan — *Yankee* p.213

, and symbols of American life
Burt — *Phila.* p.301

, as commander in chief
Amer. Reader p.99-101
Butterfield — *Amer.* p.6-7
Collins — *Story* p.105, 126
Ingraham — *Album* p.41

, as spy master
Burt — *Phila.* p.274

, as Virginia gentleman
Miers — *American* p.79-83

, at Fort Duquesne
Collins — *Story* p.93

, at New York evacuation
Amer. Reader p.106-107

, at Yorktown
Collins — *Story* p.124
Morris — *American* p.246-249

- Biography
Morris — *Ency.* p.726-727
200 Years p.314-315

- Birthplace
Landmarks Liberty p.30-32

- Cabinet
Carman — *History* p.786

- Clothing and dress
Train — *Story* p.211-212

- Crossing the Delaware
Amer. Reader p.107-109
Collins — *Story* p.112
Tunis — *Tavern* p.94-95

WASHINGTON, GEORGE (*continued*)
- Death
Butterfield — *Amer.* .p.30-31
Life — *Growing* p.39
- Dentures
Dolan — *Yankee* p.206
- Etiquette
Belote — *Compleat* p.171-173
- Farewell address (1796)
Angle — *By* p.135-151
Baldwin — *Ideas* p.245-249
Butterfield — *Amer.* p.23
Davie — *Profile* p.79-80
Kraus — *U.S. (1)* p.286-288
Morris — *Ency.* p.128
Morris — *Voices* p.181-183
- Farewell to soldiers
Kraus — *U.S. (1)* p.237
- Food, favorite
Belote — *Compleat* p.168
- Homes and home life
See also **Mount Vernon**
Burt — *Phila.* p.299
Handlin — *This* p.84-85
- Hospitality
Belote — *Compleat* p.178
- Inauguration
Amer. Reader p.133-135
Butterfield — *Amer.* p.2-3
Collins — *Story* p.136
Morris — *Ency.* p.121
- First inaugural address (1789)
Angle — *By* p.117-131
Baldwin — *Ideas* p.241
- Last illness
See also **Washington, George — Death**
Dolan — *Yankee* p.194-195
- Leadership
Kraus — *U.S. (1)* p.224-225
- Letters
Dannett — *Yankee* p.116-120
- Medical profile
Treasury Amer. p.96-103
, Mourning for
Life — *Growing* p.29
- Neutrality proclamation
Morris — *Ency.* p.125
- on agriculture
Davie — *Profile* p.172-175
- on land speculation (1767)
Morris — *American* p.20-22
- on women
Benson — *Women 18th* p.160
Evans — *Weather.* p.12
- Presidency
See also **Washington, George — Administration**
Angle — *By* p.125-131
Wright — *New* p.16-20
- Dignity
Burt — *Phila.* p.300-301
- Retreat
Morris — *Voices* p.108-114
- Revere's golden funeral urn
Forbes — *Paul* p.395
, Songs of
Burner — *America* p.106-108
- Under attack
Butterfield — *Amer.* p.23
, World of
National — *History.* p.236-254

WASHINGTON, MARTHA CUSTIS
Adelman — *Famous* p.85-86
Amer. Her. — *Rev.* p.111, 210, 220, 356
Brooks — *Dames* p.133-167
Ellet — *Eminent* p.279-297
Glubok — *Home* p.263
Holliday — *Woman's. See* index p.319
Life — *Making* p.11, 88, 142, 145-146, 148
Speare — *Life* p.20
Spruill — *Women's* p.62, 77, 122, 124, 299, 358
Whitney — *Abigail* p.232-233, 235-236, 238, 240-241, 247, 255, 294-296, 303
, as housewife
Belote — *Compleat* p.14
- Thrift
Earle — *Home* p.237-238

WASHINGTON, MARY
Ellet — *Eminent* p.20-31
Spruill — *Women's* p.60-62, 107, 351

WASHINGTON, D.C.
- Bicentennial
Lawlor — *Bicen.* p.81-105

- *Capitol city (1790)*
Life — *100 Events* p.6
Wright — *New* p.19

WASHINGTON MONUMENT
Landmarks Liberty p.82-87

"WASSAIL BOWLS"
Gould — *Early* p.106

WATER AND WATER SUPPLY
Bridenbaugh — *Revolt* p.105-107, 295-296
Bridenbaugh — *Wild.* p.213-215, 373-374
Gould — *Early* p.82-83, 105, 118
- *Waterworks, first (Bethlehem, Pa.)*
Langdon — *Every.* p.108-109

WATERFORD, VIRGINIA
Early Amer. Life — *Yrbk. 1970* p.132-137

WATERS, ABIGAIL DAWES
Benson — *Women 18th* p.259

WAX. *See* **Candles and candlemaking**

WAYNE, ANTHONY ("Mad Anthony")
Amer. Her. — *Rev. See* index p.384
Burt — *Phila.* p.310-311
Life — *Growing* p.15
McDowell — *Rev.* p.122-123, 145, 147-148, 165, 178, 192
200 Years p.127-128, 139, 145, 167

WAYSIDE INN
Gould — *Early* p.32-33, 48, 62

WEALTH
Adams — *Provincial* p.58-59, 82-83, 140, 211, 288, 319, 322
Main — *Social* p.324-325
, *and income*
Bridenbaugh — *Revolt* p.69, 79, 140, 152, 281, 288
, *and social position*
Adams — *Provincial* p.83
- *Cities*
Main — *Social* p.276n
- *Philadelphia*
Wright — *Cultural* p.42-43
, *versus numbers*
Kraus — *U.S. (1)* p.128-131
, *Way to*
Miller — *Colonial* p.377-384

WEAPONS
See also **Guns**
Adams — *Album* p.373-374
Morison — *Oxford (1)* p.307-309
200 Years. See index p.351
, *of infantrymen*
Amer. Her. — *Rev.* p.156-157

WEAVERS AND WEAVING
Adams — *Provincial* p.143-144
Dolan — *Yankee* p.120-122
Glubok — *Home* p.255-256
Gould — *Early* p.132-133, 140-141
Tunis — *Colonial* p.37, 101-105
- *Batten, of loom*
Glubok — *Home* p.258-259
, *Hand*
Earle — *Home* p.221-224
Glubok — *Home* p.254-265
- *Kentucky*
Tunis — *Frontier* p.47-48
- *Machinery*
Tunis — *Young* p.61
- *Massachusetts*
Dow — *Every* p.94-95
- *Shuttles, for looms*
Glubok — *Home* p.256, 258-259
- *Tape looms*
Glubok — *Home* p.259-260
- *Three motions*
Glubok — *Home* p.258-259

WEBSTER, NOAH
Benson — *Women 18th* p.136, 152, 154-155, 158-159, 162, 167, 214
Glubok — *Home* p.121, 148, 151-152
Greene — *Revol.* p.317, 325-326, 369, 374-375, 384, 386-387, 389-390, 392-393, 417
- *Biography*
Morris — *Ency.* p.728
- *"Speller"*
Life — *Growing* p.19

WEDDINGS
Earle — *Colonial* p.201-203
, Colonial
Smith — *Colonial* p.168-181
- Connecticut
Earle — *Customs* p.76-77
- Frontier, Southern
Spruill — *Women* p.110-112
- New England
Holliday — *Woman's* p.247-251
- New Hampshire
Earle — *Customs* p.73-76
- New York
Earle — *Colonial* p.202-203
- Philadelphia
Earle — *Colonial* p.201-202
- South
Spruill — *Women's* p.94-95, 110-112

WEEDS
- Flowers
Earle — *Home* p.435-436, 447-449

WEEMS, MASON LOCKE
Dolan — *Yankee* p.211-212

WEIGHTS AND MEASURES
Bridenbaugh — *Wild.* p.201-203, 356

WELLS
Bridenbaugh — *Wild.* p.213-215, 373-374
Gould — *Early* p.35
- Massachusetts
Dow — *Every* p.99

WENTWORTH, JOHN
Stearns — *Story* p.70-71

WESLEY, JOHN
Greene — *Revol.* p.12, 106-107, 113, 115, 215-216, 283, 366

WESLEY, SUSANNA
Adelman — *Famous* p.69-70

WEST, BENJAMIN
Burt — *Phila.* p.234-236
Locke — *Birth* p.85-99
Morris — *Ency.* p.597
Wertenbaker — *Golden* p.33, 82-83, 97, 135, 155
Wright — *Cultural* p.212

WEST AND WESTWARD MOVEMENT
Angle — *By* p.83-86
Greene — *Revol. See* index p.486
Kraus — *U.S. (1)* p.140-159
Morison — *Oxford (1). See* index p.421
Morris — *Ency.* p.65-66
Morris — *Voices* p.149-155
, and churches
Sweet — *Story* p.205-222
, Bicentennial
Lawlor — *Bicen.* p.205-232
- Influence
Baldwin — *Ideas* p.139-141
- Land controversy
Morris — *Ency.* p.417-418
- Organization
Morris — *Ency.* p.418-419
- Revolutionary War
Morris — *Ency.* p.416-417
, Transappalachian
Morris — *American* p.11-25

WEST INDIES
- Trade
Adams — *Provincial* p.49-52
Bridenbaugh — *Wild.* p.176-177, 331
Carman — *History* p.77-79, 135
Greene — *Revol. See* index p.486
Kraus — *U.S. (1)* p.115-116
Life — *New* p.98, 102-104, 109, 148, 150, 153
Miller — *Origins* p.12-14, 45, 69-70, 73, 95-98, 103-104, 140-142, 386, 391
Morison — *Oxford (1). See* index p.421
Morris — *Ency.* p.487
Stearns — *Story* p.63-65, 73, 94, 96

WEST POINT, NEW YORK
Amer. Her. — *Rev.* p.266-270
Stember — *North* p.132-141; *See also* index p.391
Wheeler — *Voices* p.323, 380-394

WEST VIRGINIA
Greene — *Revol.* p.174-175, 226, 405

"WESTOVER"
Train — *Story* p.206-209

WETHERSFIELD, CONNECTICUT
Handlin — *This* p.80
Stember — *North* p.370-371

WHALE OIL
Tunis — *Living* p.134-135

WHALING
Kraus — *U.S. (1)* p.113
Speare — *Life* p.117-118
Train — *Story* p.156, 173-174, 217
Tunis — *Young* p.87-88
Wilson — *American* p.6-7

WHARVES AND DOCKS
Bridenbaugh — *Revolt* p.38-40, 246-247
Bridenbaugh — *Wild. See* index p.500
- *Construction and regulation*
Greene — *Revol.* p.57-58

WHEAT
Crèvecoeur — *Sketches* p.58, 92, 138, 141, 146, 150, 175, 182, 234

WHEATLEY, PHILLIS
Benson — *Women 18th* p.118, 171, 216
Cable — *American* p.51
Dexter — *Colonial* p.140-142
Evans — *Weather.* p.22-23

WHETTEN, MARGARET
Ellet — *Eminent* p.525-540

WHIGS
Forbes — *Paul* p.84, 104, 114, 137, 179-180, 189, 207, 459
Greene — *Revol. See* index p.486
Miller — *Origins. See* index p.519
Morison — *Oxford (1)* p.254, 256, 265, 272, 276-277, 281, 287, 312
Sirkis — *Reflect.* p.32

WHIPPING
Glubok — *Home* p.134-136

WHIPPLE, WILLIAM
Bakeless — *Signers* p.225-227
Malone — *Story* p.100-101
- *Biography*
Lossing — *Biog.* p.17-19

WHISKY TAX AND INSURRECTION
Alden — *Pioneer* p.134-135
Kraus — *U.S. (1)* p.285-286
Life — *Growing* p.16-17
Morris — *Ency.* p.126
Wright — *New* p.43

WHITE, JOSEPH
Treasury Amer. p.112-117

WHITE HOUSE (Washington, D.C.)
Gowans — *Images* p.167

WHITE PLAINS, NEW YORK
, Battle of
Stember — *North* p.245-253

"WHITE-ELLERY" HOUSE
Earle — *Home* p.19-20

WHITEFIELD, GEORGE
Bridenbaugh — *Wild.* p.386, 419, 422, 424-425, 439, 459
Cable — *American* p.46-47
Carman — *History* p.98-99
Hofstadter — *Amer. See* index p.xiii
Sweet — *Story* p.106-107, 131-133, 141-142, 170
- *Biography*
Morris — *Ency.* p.729-730
- *"Great Awakening"*
Adams — *Provincial* p.268, 280, 282, 284
- *Orphanage*
Sweet — *Story* p.169-171

WHITESMITHS
Tunis — *Colonial* p.65-70

"WHITEWINGS" (street sweepers)
Wilson — *Early* p.34

WHITNEY, ELI
Glubok — *Home* p.252-253
Wilson — *American* p.78-79
, and mass production
Life — *100 Events* p.79
- Biography
Morris — *Ency.* p.730
- Machine tools
Tunis — *Young* p.65-66

WHOLESALE TRADE
Bridenbaugh — *Revolt* p.76-78

WIDOWS
Earle — *Colonial* p.33-41
- Dower rights
Benson — *Women* p.235-238
- Legal rights, Southern
Spruill — *Women's* p.359-361
- New York
Dexter — *Colonial* p.18-19

WIGS AND WIGMAKERS
Earle — *Customs* p.297-302
Earle — *Home* p.297-298
Speare — *Life* p.51
Train — *Story* p.160-161, 191-192, 211
Tunis — *Colonial* p.42-43
Wilson — *Early* p.74-75
, Boys'
Earle — *Child* p.51
Earle — *Home* p.297
, Men's
Ross — *Taste* p.242
Train — *Story* p.191-192
Tunis — *Living* p.142-144
Tunis — *Young* p.100
, Women's
Tunis — *Young* p.55

WILDERNESS
See also **Frontier**; etc.
Adams — *Album* p.257
Tunis — *Young* p.43
, Awareness of
Wilson — *American* p.3-4
- Boundaries
Wilson — *American* p.4-5
- Myth of trackless
Bartlett — *New* p.13-16
- Settlements
Treasury Amer. p.59

WILKINSON, ELIZA
Ellet — *Eminent* p.154-168

WILKINSON, JAMES
Wheeler — *Voices. See* index p.480

WILKINSON, JEMIMA
Benson — *Women 18th* p.270-272
Earle — *Colonial* p.173-188
Evans — *Weather.* p.9-10

WILLETT, MARINUS
Cook — *What* p.143-176

WILLIAM AND MARY COLLEGE
Greene — *Revol. See* index p.486-487

WILLIAMS, HANNAH
Adams — *Provincial* p.123

WILLIAMS, WILLIAM
Bakeless — *Signers* p.204-206
Malone — *Story* p.130-131
- Biography
Lossing — *Biog.* p.56-58

WILLIAMSBURG, VIRGINIA
Adams — *Album* p.253
Greene — *Revol.* p.7, 10, 12, 95, 100, 153, 297, 389, 424-425
Langdon — *Every.* p.304-307, 332-333
McDowell — *Rev.* p.10-11, 14-17, 20, 47, 90, 181
National — *History.* p.121-137
Scott — *Trumpet* p.27-28, 34, 72-73, 120, 268
Sirkis — *Reflect.* p.147
Speare — *Life* p.22-23
Stember — *South* p.186-189
Wertenbaker — *Golden* p.105-106; *See also* index p.171

WILLING, ANN. *See* Bingham, Ann Willing

WILLS
Burner — *America* p.38-40

WILSON, ELEANOR
Ellet — *Eminent* p.745-754

WILSON, JAMES
Bakeless — *Signers* p.150-155
Malone — *Story* p.166-167
- Biography
Lossing — *Biog.* p.126-129

WILSON, MARTHA
Ellet — *Eminent* p.309-321

WINDOWS
Earle — *Home* p.24
Gould — *Early* p.39

WINE
, Making of
Scott — *Settlers* p.180-181
- New York
Earle — *Home* p.159

WINSLOW, ANNA GREEN
Benson — *Women 18th* p.147, 293, 305
Glubok — *Home* p.99, 164, 183

WINTER SPORTS
See also **Sports and games;** names of sports
Speare — *Life* p.158-159
- Rides
Earle — *Customs* p.206-210

WINTHROP, HANNAH
Benson — *Women 18th* p.170, 250, 255

WISTER, SARAH (Sally)
Benson — *Women 18th* p.170, 308
Brooks — *Colonial* p.243-284
Burt — *Phila.* p.281-282
Evans — *Weather.* p.110-151

WITCHCRAFT
Earle — *Colonial* p.101-103
Holliday — *Woman's* p.48
Kraus — *U.S. (1)* p.164-166

WITHERSPOON, JOHN
Bakeless — *Signers* p.161-165
Malone — *Story* p.148-151
Sweet — *Story* p.178-179
- Biography
Lossing — *Biog.* p.81-84
Morris — *Ency.* p.733

- on women
Benson — *Women* p.20, 98, 169-170, 214, 312

WIVES
, as shopkeepers, Southern
Spruill — *Women's* p.289-292
- Boston, sale
Earle — *Colonial* p.28
- Clergymen's. See **Clergymen — Wives of**
- Duties
Benson — *Women 18th* p.123-125, 192
, Imported for colonists
Earle — *Colonial* p.6-8
- Legal status
Spruill — *Women's* p.359
- South
Spruill — *Women's* p.17-19

WOLCOTT, OLIVER
Bakeless — *Signers* p.206-209
Malone — *Story* p.128-129
- Biography
Lossing — *Biog.* p.59-62

WOLFE, JAMES
- Death
Collins — *Story* p.94

WOLVES
Crèvecoeur — *Sketches* p.26, 74, 86, 129-130, 132, 165, 206
Speare — *Life* p.83-84

WOMEN
See also **Daughters; Girls; Housekeepers; Housewives; Midwives; Widows; Wives;** special subjects; names of famous women; Appendix
Belote — *Compleat* p.3
Bridenbaugh — *Revolt* p.149, 163
Cable — *American* p.87
Downey — *Our* p.31-43
Morison — *Oxford (1)* p.204, 358, 361
Tunis — *Young* p.106-107
Wilson — *Early* p.77-78
- Academies. See **Academies — Women and girls**

WOMEN (*continued*)
- *Accessories. See* **Accessories — Women**
- *Accomplishments (virtues)*
  Benson — *Women 18th* p.49, 71, 83, 90, 146, 152, 162-163, 180, 197, 312-313
- *Agriculturists*
  Earle — *Colonial* p.85-87
- *Americanism*
  See also **Patriotism — Women; Patriotism — Women, Southern**
  Benson — *Women 18th* p.103, 136, 143, 165-168, 176, 186-187, 194, 219-220
, and Declaration of Independence. See **Declaration of Independence, Women's place in**
, and home
  Holliday — *Woman's* p.99-105, 115-116, 128-138, 140-151
, and love
  Handlin — *This* p.99-100
, and the initiative
  Holliday — *Woman's* p.294-298, 303-312
- *Appearance*
  See also **Clothing and dress — Women; Clothing and dress — Women, Southern**
  Handlin — *This* p.80,98
- *Apprenticeship*
  See also **Apprentices — Girls, Southern**
  Benson — *Women 18th* p.179, 224-225
- *Art*
  See also **Artists — Women, Southern**
  Adams — *Provincial* p.144
, as adventuresses
  Earle — *Colonial* p.160-172
, at fires
  Bridenbaugh — *Revolt* p.100
- *Authors. See* **Authors — Women**
- *Backwoods, Southern*
  Spruill — *Women's* p.82-83, 242
- *Bible. See* **Bible — on Women**
- *Blacksmiths. See* **Blacksmiths — Women**
- *Books and reading. See* **Books and reading — Women**
- *Bookshops and booksellers. See* **Bookshops and booksellers — Women**
- *Boston, Mass. See* **Boston, Mass. — Women; Women — Riot, in Boston, Mass.**
- *Botany and botanists. See* **Botany and botanists — Women**
- *Business*
  Benson — *Women 18th* p.240-243, 289, 303
  Earle — *Colonial* p.69-71
  Holliday — *Woman's* p.147-148
- *Church. See* **Churches, Women in; Religion — Women**
- *Clothing and dress. See* **Clothing and dress — Women; Clothing and dress — Women, Southern**
- *Colonial life*
  Adams — *Provincial* p.11, 80
- *Crime and criminals. See* **Crime and criminals — Women; Crime and criminals — Women, Southern**
- *Dancing*
  Benson — *Women 18th* p.292-293, 295-297
- *Death duties*
  Wright — *Frontier* p.71-72
- *Divorce*
  Benson — *Women 18th* p.232-234
- *Drama. See* **Drama — Women**
- *Dressmakers. See* **Dressmaking; Revolutionary War — Women, as coat makers**
- *Dutch. See* **Dutch — Women**
- *Editors*
  Earle — *Colonial* p.62-69
  , First (S.C.)
    Dexter — *Colonial* p.173
- *Education. See* **Education — Women**
- *Employment advertisements*
  Earle — *Colonial* p.55-56
- *Ephrata Cloister. See* **Ephrata Cloister — Women**
- *Etiquette. See* **Etiquette — Women**

- *European sources of American opinion*
  Benson — *Women 18th* p.11-33
- *European theory on (1700-1775)*
  Benson — *Women 18th* p.34-78
- *Fecundity — South*
  Spruill — *Women's* p.45-46
- *Ferry keepers. See* **Ferries — Women as keepers, Southern**
- *Fiction. See* **Fiction — Women as characters in; Fiction, Women's**
- *Florists. See* **Florists — Women**
- *Food. See* **Food — Women**
- *French language. See* **French language, Study of — for women**
- *Frontier*
  See also **Women — Backwoods, Southern; Women — Pioneers**
  Crèvecoeur — *Sketches* p.221-227
  Greene — *Revol.* p.177-178
  - *Kentucky*
    See also **Kentucky — Women**
    Wright — *Frontier* p.69-71
- *Funeral sermons. See* **Funerals — Sermons, on women**
- *Germans*
  Benson — *Women 18th* p.302-304
- *Grocers and grocery stores. See* **Grocers and grocery stores — Women, Southern**
- *Guardianships rights*
  Benson — *Women 18th* p.239-240
- *Handiwork*
  See also **Needlework; Spinning; Weavers and weaving;** types of needlework
  Dexter — *Colonial* p.39-57
, Hanging of — South
  Spruill — *Women's* p.335-336
- *Illiteracy*
  Adams — *Provincial* p.133
- *Importers and imports. See* **Importers and imports — Women**
- *Indians*
  Handlin — *This* p.1-14
- *Kentucky. See* **Kentucky — Women; Women — Frontier — Kentucky**
- *Land laws and legislation. See* **Land — Laws and legislation — Women; Women — Legal status**
- *Land ownership. See* **Land — Ownership — Women**
- *Legal status*
  See also related subjects under **Women**
  Benson — *Women 18th* p.93, 173-174, 223-244, 247
  Bridenbaugh — *Wild.* p.387-388
  Forbes — *Paul* p.40, 455
  Holliday — *Woman's* p.297-298
  - *South*
    Spruill — *Women's* p.348-366
- *Liberty, effect on*
  Adams — *Provincial* p.81-82, 89, 125
- *Libraries. See* **Libraries — Women**
- *Literature. See* **Literature — Women**
- *Magazines. See* **Magazines — Women**
- *Marriage*
  Holliday — *Woman's* p.246-255, 264, 278, 286-287
- *Maryland*
  - *Amusements*
    Spruill — *Women's* p.93-95
- *Medicine. See* **Medicine — Women, Southern**
- *Merchants*
  Bridenbaugh — *Wild.* p.340-341
  Dexter — *Colonial* p.18-38
- *Methodists. See* **Methodists — Women leaders**
- *Military activities*
  See also **Revolutionary War — Women;** names of women

WOMEN (*continued*)
Cook — *What* p.217-244
Evans — *Weather.* p.10-12, 14-15
- *Modesty*
Handlin — *This* p.68, 101
- *Moravians. See* **Moravians — Women**
- *Nantucket, Mass. See* **Nantucket, Mass. — Women**
- *New England. See* **New England — Women**
- *New York. See* **New York — Women**
- *Occupations*
Bridenbaugh — *Revolt* p.78, 273-274, 358
- *South*
Spruill — *Women's* p.44-45, 255-275
- *on farms*
See also **Women — Agriculturists**
Adams — *Provincial* p.88
- *Patriotism. See* **Patriotism — Women**
- *Philadelphia, Pa. See* **Philadelphia, Pa. — Girls; Philadelphia, Pa. — Women**
- *Physicians*
See also **Medicine — Women, Southern**
Adams — *Provincial* p.61
- *Pioneers*
See also **Women — Backwoods, Southern; Women — Frontier**
Bartlett — *New* p.149
- *Plantations and planters. See* **Plantations and planters — Women**
- *Poetry about*
Dannett — *Yankee* p.130-133
- *Politics*
Benson — *Women 18th* p.244-258
Bridenbaugh — *Wild.* p.387
, *Post-Revolutionary*
Benson — *Women 18th* p.136-171
- *European influence*
Benson — *Women 18th* p.79-135
- *Pregnancies — South*
Spruill — *Women's* p.49-52
- *Printers and printing. See* **Printers and printing — Women; Publishers — Women; Women — Editors**
- *Prisons and prisoners. See* **Prisons and prisoners — Women; Women — Punishment**
- *Property rights*
See also **Land — Ownership — Women**
Benson — *Women 18th* p.234-235, 238-239, 247
- *Proverbs*
Benson — *Women 18th* p.27, 58, 108, 116, 124, 167, 179
- *Public affairs — South*
Spruill — *Women's* p.242-254
- *Publishers. See* **Publishers — Women**
- *Punishment*
See also **Women — Hanging of — South**
Adams — *Provincial* p.162
- *Quakers. See* **Quakers — Clothing and dress — Women; Quakers — Women; Quakers — Women, as preachers**
- *Refugees, in N.Y. manors*
Smith — *Colonial* p.248-266
- *Relationship to man*
Benson — *18th* p.165-167
- *Religion. See* **Churches — Women; Religion — Women**
- *Religious societies. See* **Religious societies — Women**
- *Revolutionary War. See* **Revolutionary War — Women; Revolutionary War — Women, Southern; Revolutionary War — Women — Writers;** names of famous women
- *Rights. See* **Women — Legal status;** related subjects
- *Riot, in Boston, Mass.*
Forbes — *Paul* p.320
- *Schools — Boston, Mass.*
Benson — *Women 18th* p.280, 292-294, 298-299
- *Servants, indentured. See* **Servants — Indentured — Women**
- *Shakers. See* **Shakers — Women**
- *Shoes. See* **Shoes, Women's**
- *Smoking*
Adams — *Provincial* p.75

- *Soap and soap making. See* **Soap and soap making — Women**
- *Society*
  Benson — *Women 18th* p.292-298, 303
  Greene — *Revol.* p.95, 255
  Holliday — *Woman's* p.175-197, 199-208, 216-237, 241-246
- *Soldiers. See* **Women — Military activities;** names of famous women
- *South. See* **South — Women**
- *Subserviency*
  Benson — *Women 18th* p.126-127
  Greene — *Revol.* p.74-75
- *Suffrage*
  Benson — *Women 18th* p.244-258
  Evans — *Weather.* p.4-5
  Greene — *Revol.* p.9, 29, 79-80, 192-193, 311-313
- *Tavern keepers. See* **Taverns — Women as keepers**
- *Teachers. See* **Teachers — Women; Teachers — Women, Southern**
- *Travel and travelers. See* **Travel and travelers — Women;** names of travelers
- *Tuberculosis*
  Burt — *Phila.* p.324
- *Unfortunate*
  Wilson — *Early* p.183-184
- *Views of Adams, A. See* **Adams, Abigail Smith — Women's rights**
- *Views of Adams, J. See* **Adams, John — on women**
- *Views of Astell, Mary*
  Benson — *Women 18th* p.28-33
- *Views of Belknap. See* **Belknap, Jeremy — on women**
- *Views of Byrd, W. See* **Byrd, William II — on women**
- *Views of clergymen. See* **Clergymen — Views on Women; Clergymen, Wives of**
- *Views of Crèvecoeur*
  Crèvecoeur — *Sketches* p.207-220
- *Views of Dwight. See* **Dwight, Timothy — on women**
- *Views of Edwards. See* **Edwards, Jonathan — on women**
- *Views of Fithian. See* **Fithian, Philip Vickers — on women**
- *Views of Franklin. See* **Franklin, Benjamin — on wives; Franklin, Benjamin — on women**
- *Views of Hitchcock. See* **Hitchcock, Enos — on women**
- *Views of Jefferson. See* **Jefferson, Thomas — on women**
- *Views of Mather. See* **Mather, Cotton — on women**
- *Views of Morse. See* **Morse, Jedidiah — on women**
- *Views of Sewall. See* **Sewall, Samuel — on women**
- *Views of Stiles. See* **Stiles, Ezra — on women**
- *Views of Washington. See* **Washington, George — on women**
- *Views of Witherspoon. See* **Witherspoon, John — on women**
- *Virginia. See* **Virginia — Women**
- *Vocations. See* **Women — Occupations**
- *Wigs. See* **Wigs and wigmakers, Women's**

WOOD
Bridenbaugh — *Revolt* p.26-27, 233-235
Earle — *Home. See* index p.469
Tunis — *Living* p.105-106
- *Prices*
  Main — *Social* p.118-119, 122, 141

WOOD CARVING
Adams — *Provincial* p.142-143
Earle — *Home* p.320

WOODCUTS
Adams — *Album* p.344

WOODENWARE
See also **Dishes and utensils**
Dreppard — *Pioneer* p.269-274
Gould — *Early* p.35-38

WOODMASON, CHARLES
Scott — *Trumpet* p.9-13, 18

WOODSMEN. *See* Frontiersmen

WOOL
See also **Sheep; Weavers and weaving**
Colbourn — *Colonial* p.261-262
Earle — *Home. See* index p.469
Glubok — *Home. See* index p.357
Gould — *Early* p.127-128
Speare — *Life* p.78-79
- Carding
Glubok — *Home* p.246-247, 250-251
- Industry
Carman — *History* p.76
Langdon — *Every.* p.293-295

WOOLMAN, JOHN
Miller — *Colonial* p.437-478

WOOSTER, DAVID
Wheeler — *Voices* p.94-95, 107, 131-132, 136, 220

WORCESTER COUNTY, MASSACHUSETTS
Main — *Social* p.9, 21-22, 31, 40n, 43, 80, 106, 110, 132, 254-257, 262

WORK. *See* Labor

WORKHOUSES. *See* Almshouses

"-WRIGHTS"
Wilson — *Early* p.74

WRITING
See also **Authors;** etc.
Glubok — *Home* p.156-169

WRITS OF ASSISTANCE
Beach — *Samuel* p.55-56
Morris — *American* p.2-5
- Views of Otis, James
Angle — *By* p.32-37

WYANDOT INDIANS
McDowell — *Rev.* p.110, 112, 114-115

WYOMING VALLEY MASSACRE (Pa.)
Crèvecoeur — *Sketches* p.192-206
Life — *Making* p.62-63
Stember — *Middle* p.143, 147, 149-151, 153

WYTHE, GEORGE
Bakeless — *Signers* p.96-100
Greene — *Revol.* p.81-82, 137, 213, 248, 292, 319, 369, 374, 381, 388
Malone — *Story* p.212-213
- Biography
Lossing — *Biog.* p.162-165

X

XYZ AFFAIR
Life — *Growing* p.35
Morris — *Ency.* p.128
Morris — *Voices* p.183-187

Y

YALE UNIVERSITY
Adams — *Album* p.268
Downey — *Our* p.67-77
Greene — *Revol. See* index p.487
Hofstadter — *Amer.* p.212, 228, 236, 255, 287-290
Main — *Social* p.95, 98, 103, 210, 259
Morison — *Oxford (1)* p.186, 208, 210, 251, 337-338
Stearns — *Story* p.71-72
Sweet — *Story* p.223-224, 226
- Library
Wright — *Cultural* p.151-152

YAMASSEE WAR
Morris — *Ency.* p.63-64

YANKEE DOODLE
Adams — *Album* p.390
Dannett — *Yankee* p.299-313
Howard — *Our* p.113-118
McDowell — *Rev.* p.44-45, 170
Morris — *Ency.* p.613

YANKEE-PENNAMITE WARS
Burt — *Phila.* p.177, 179-183, 298

YANKEES
- *Definition*
Howard — *Our* p.114
- *Pioneers*
Pettengill — *Yankee* p.20-21

YEAST
Gould — *Early* p.91

YELLOW FEVER
Bridenbaugh — *Wild.* p.240, 399-401
- *Philadelphia*
Burt — *Phila.* p.322-326
Morris — *Ency.* p.541-542
Morris — *Voices* p.140-142

YORKTOWN, VIRGINIA
, Battle of
Adams — *Album* p.404
Amer. Her. — *Rev.* p.272, 285, 312, 342, 353, 355, 357-361, 371-373
Amer. Reader p.127-129
Burt — *Phila.* p.296-297
Carman — *History* p.213-214
Collins — *Story* p.124-125
Ingraham — *Album* p.83-84
Kraus — *U.S. (1)* p.233-236
Life — *Making* p.62, 81, 86-87, 90, 98-101
McDowell — *Rev.* p.162-163, 174-175, 179, 182-183, 187
Morison — *Oxford (1)* p.306, 308-309, 337, 345-348, 363
Morris — *Amer.* p.246-249
Morris — *Ency.* p.107
Morris — *Voices* p.121-123
National — *History.* p.232-235
Sanderlin — *1776* p.239-241
Scott — *Trumpet* p.262-263, 268-277
Stember — *North* p.66, 79, 141, 171, 176, 204, 321, 329, 345, 348
Stember — *South* p.190-204
Wheeler — *Voices* p.434-458
200 Years p.142-158
- *French fleet*
Amer. Her. — *Rev.* p.282, 285, 369
- *Song*
Burner — *America* p.117-119

YOUTH
Tunis — *Living* p.148

Z

ZANE, ELIZABETH (Betty)
Cook — *What* p.233-235
Ellet — *Eminent* p.476-480

ZENGER, ANNA CATHERINE MAUL
Dexter — *Colonial* p.169-171
Earle — *Colonial* p.68

ZENGER, JOHN PETER
Bridenbaugh — *Wild.* p.426, 461
Carman — *History* p.108
Kraus — *U.S. (1)* p.127-128
Scott — *Settlers* p.129, 132-138, 142, 167
Wertenbaker — *Golden* p.24-25, 41-42
- *Biography*
Morris — *Ency.* p.735

ZINZENDORF, NICHOLAUS LUDWIG VON
Langdon — *Every.* p.69, 71, 87-88, 93-94, 97
Sweet — *Story* p.105-108

ZOOLOGY
Morris — *Ency.* p.528-529

Appendix

Women of The 18th Century

(as found in this index)

A
Adams, Abigail Smith
Adams, Louisa Johnson
Almy, Mary Gould
Anthony, Susanna
Arnett, Hannah White
Arnold, Margaret Shippen
Astell, Mary
Auckland, Harriet

B
Bache, Sarah Franklin
Bailey, "Mad Anne" Hennis
Baker, Rachel Warder
Barker, Penelope Pagett
Beekman, Cornelia
Bingham, Ann Willing
Bleeker, Ann Eliza
Bowne, Eliza Southgate
Bratton, Martha
Brent, Margaret and Mary
Bruyn, Blandina
Buchanan, Sarah
Budd, Rachel
Burr, Esther Edwards
Burr, Theodosia
Burwell, Rebecca
Byrd, Elizabeth Hill Carter

C
Caldwell, Hannah
Caldwell, Rachel
Callender, Hannah
Campbell, Jane
Clifford, Anna Rawle
Colden, Jane
Corbin, Margaret ("Captain Molly")
Cranch, Mary Smith

D
Darragh, Lydia
Deming, Sarah Winslow
Draper, Mary
Drinker, Elizabeth Sandwith
Drinker, Hannah

E
Elliott, Susannah
Eve, Sarah

F
Ferguson, Elizabeth
Ferguson, Isabella
Ferguson, Jane Young
Fitzgerald, Ellenor
Fitzhugh, Anne
Foote, Abigail
Foster, Hannah Webster
Franklin, Ann
Franklin, Deborah Read Rogers
Franklin, Sarah. *See* Bache, Sarah Franklin
Franks, Rebecca

G
Galloway, Grace Growdon
Gannett, Deborah Sampson. *See* Sampson, Deborah
Genlis, Madame de
Gibbes, Sarah Reeve
Goddard, Anna
Goddard, Mary Katharine
Goddard, Sarah
Grant, Anne MacVicar
Green, Anne Catherine
Green, Nancy
Greene, Catharine
Greene, Polly
Griffith, Elizabeth

H
Haddonfield, Elizabeth
Hallam, Sarah
Hamilton, Elizabeth
Hancock, Dorothy
Harrison, Jemima Condict
Hart, Nancy Morgan
Haywood, Eliza
Heck, Barbara Ruckle
Hendee, Hannah Hunter
Hughes, Joan

Hulton, Anne
Hume, Sophia

I
Israel, Hannah Erwin

J
Jefferson, Maria ("Polly")
Jefferson, Martha ("Patsy")
Jefferson, Martha Wayles Skelton
Jemison, Mary
Johnston, Henrietta

K
Knight, Madame Sarah
Knox, Lucy

L
Langston, Dicey
La Toure, Frances Mary Jacqueline
Lee, Ann
Lee, Lucinda
Lucas, Eliza. *See* Pinckney, Eliza Lucas
Ludington, Sybil
Ludwig, Mary. *See* "Pitcher, Molly"

M
McCalla, Sarah
McCauley, Mary. *See* "Pitcher, Molly"
McClure, Mary
McCrae, Jane
McDonald, Flora
Madison, Dolly
Marshall, Mrs. Christopher
More, Hannah
Morris, Margaret Hill
Motte, Rebecca
Murray, Judith Sargent
Murray, Mary

N
Norris, Deborah

O
Osborn, Sarah

P
Philipse, Mary
Phillips, Catherine
Pinckney, Eliza Lucas
"Pitcher, Molly" (Mary Ludwig McCauley)
Pownall, Mary Ann

Q
Quincy, Eliza Morton

R
Reed, Esther de Berdt
Revere, Rachel Walker
Reynolds, Mary (Mari)
Richardson, Dorcas
Riddle, Rebecca
Riedesel, Frederica von
Rind, Clementina
Ross, Betsy
Rowson, Susanna Haswell

S
Sampson, Deborah (Mrs. Gannett)
Schuyler, Catharine
Schuyler, Margaretta
Sherwood, Grace
Shippen, Margaret. *See* Arnold, Margaret Shippen
Slocum, Mary
Southgate, Eliza. *See* Bowne, Eliza Southgate
Steel, Katharine
Steele, Elizabeth
Stockton, Annis
Sumner, Mary Osgood
Syms, Widow Sarah

T
Thomas, Jane
Thomson, Hannah
Tilghman, Molly
Timothy, Elizabeth
Trumbull, Faith Robinson

U

V
Van Alstine, Nancy
Vining, Mary

W
Walker, Esther
Walker, Martha I'ans
Warder, Ann Head
Warren, Mercy Otis
Washington, Elizabeth Foote
Washington, Martha Custis
Washington, Mary
Waters, Abigail Dawes
Wesley, Susanna
Wheatley, Phillis
Whetten, Margaret
Wilkinson, Eliza
Wilkinson, Jemima

Williams, Hannah
Willing, Ann. *See* Bingham, Ann Willing
Wilson, Eleanor
Wilson, Martha
Winslow, Anna Green
Winthrop, Hannah
Wister, Sarah (Sally)

X

Y

Z
Zane, Elizabeth (Betty)
Zenger, Anna Catherine Maul